Mill Valley Days

by
John H. Myers

A collection of stories about growing up in Mill Valley during the 1950s and 60s.

©2018 John H. Myers

Printed by CreateSpace
Available from Amazon.com and other retail outlets

Quotations from the book *Tender Comrades* in chapter 7 are reproduced with the kind permission of Patrick McGilligan and the Watkins/Loomis Agency

Quotations from the book *Elia Kazan: A Life* in chapter 7 are reproduced with the kind permission of Carlton Books.

Cover photo of Jim Myers and Mount Tam taken by the author.

Back cover colour photo of Mount Tam taken by the author and the black & white inset photo is a postcard picture taken by Zan Stark which is reproduced by kind permission of the Anne T. Kent California Room, Marin County Free Library.

Illustrations and front and back cover design by the author.

ISBN 13: 978-1729633199

*For my dear friend, the late Jared Dreyfus,
whose company I miss and whose
lifelong friendship was always
a source of inspiration.*

Contents

Acknowledgements 9
Introduction - The Bearville Massacre 11

1. A Hostage to Nostalgia 33
2. Going to Homestead School 43
3. Of Monsters And Scoundrels 53
4. An Illustrated Access To Classic Literature 63
5. From 3-D To CinemaScope 75
6. A Cultural Link To Manhattan 85
7. A Curious Connection To *On The Waterfront* 95
8. Coonskin Caps At Bennett's Variety Store 105
9. Radio Nights At 10 Seymour Avenue 113
10. Learning To Live With The Fear 123
11. Duckburg At The Bus Depot 131
12. Mr Daddy-O Visits The Sequoia 141
13. An Ice Cream Sandwich On Evergreen 151
14. Escape To The Matinee 161
15. Glen's Top Ten 167
16. Horrors at the Sequoia 175
17. The Discovery of MAD 185
18. Mister Finney's Pods 195
19. Of Bartholomew and Babar 203
20. For The Love of Harryhausen 217
21. So Much More Than a Candy Bar 223
22. Monsters on Market Street 237
23. Kissing: Much Agony and Some Ecstasy 249
24. William Castle Comes to Town 259
25. A Hard Guy Has to Smoke 271
26. Visiting Vertigo Locations 283
27. A Strange Obsession With AIP 293
28. Of Pantsing and Presidents 311
29. Political Films in Marin County 321
30. Days at the Bus Depot 341
31. The Raven at the Fox 351
32. A Shocking Day in November 361
33. The Week the Beatles Arrived 369
34. The Mountain That Follows You Around the Town 379

Acknowledgements

I felt compelled to write about my childhood in the Mill Valley of the 1950s and 60s in an attempt to recapture those elusive memories of a life which seemed so permanent at the time but which is now gone forever.

These stories reflect my memory of events and began as a series of online essays entitled *Miller Avenue Musings.* They seemed to attract a small and interested audience so I decided to self-publish this collection.

In trying to remember the Mill Valley of old I have been greatly aided by childhood friends as well as many people I didn't know as a kid. I would like to thank: Tad Alvord, Augie Belden, Ernie Bergman, the late Julia Bergman, Jerry Boore, Shonnie (Berry) Brown, Toby Byron, Alex Call, Brian Collett, Chuck Collins, Corky Corcoran, Cheryl Cleland Dennett, Jon Diedrich, Barry Eldridge, Alan Eshleman, Carol Eshleman, David Gilliam, John Goddard, Tom Harper, Gene Heyman, Tony Houston, Robin Jackson, Pam Kroner, Cheryl McDavitt, Bill McIntyre, Jan Mettler, Judith Moore, Debbie (Riva) Nelson, Mary Norstrum, the late Glen Pritzker, Robin Pritzker, Alex Robertson, Dan Smith, Ed Smith, Renato Sottile, Ray Sterios, Mark Symmes, the late Jim Tamburini, Linda Tamburini, Christie Trapp, Frank True, Abby Wasserman and Richie Wasserman.

Some of my memories are fairly accurate but many not so and the people listed above have helped me enormously in fleshing out many details with much more clarity than I was able to manage. For that I am grateful.

I also owe a debt of gratitude to my sisters, Nell Myers and Kate Thornton as well as my brother, Jim Myers for confirming or denying all the explications I threw at them. From the Dreyfus family I owe thanks to Jared and his two sons, Adam and Christian as well as his wife Genie. From the Hallinan family I was aided enormously by Danny and Ringo (Conn).

My wife Clare acted as my editor for which I give heartfelt thanks. I must also thank my good friend Bonnie MacLean who convinced me that I should put my stories into book form. And I must express my gratitude to author Gareth Mottram, my nephew-in-law, who introduced me to Createspace and guided me through its complexities.

John H. Myers
London 2018

Introduction

The Bearville Massacre

The smoky aroma of eucalyptus bark wafted in off the Pixie Trail as the young boy dipped his hand into one of the two large cardboard boxes which sat on the flat surface of the garage roof. The first box was full of teddy bears and the second was empty.

He lifted a medium sized brown teddy out of the box and looked into its innocent button eyes. He spoke.

"Name?"

"Cubby Bear," the other boy answered in what they both recognised as bear voice.

"Crime?"

"Breathing."

"Sentence: death by hanging."

He took the twine noose he was holding, put it around Cubby's neck and dangled his body over the edge of the roof. After a moment he pulled the bear back up, removed the noose and put its body into the empty box. He then reached into the first box and took out another stuffed animal.

"Name?"

"Lamby L. Lamb."

"Crime?"

"Snoring."

And so the grim ritual proceeded. The first box contained the thirty odd inhabitants of Bearville, the town which my brother Jim and I had invented, nurtured and played with for the previous eight years.

Cubby had been the first teddy to arrive in our household. He emerged from inside a bright and beautiful package on Christmas morning, 1953 at 10 Seymour Avenue. The main thing which distinguished Cubby from the others who followed was that he was brand new.

Bearville was about to become a reality due to those family friends who were inclined to give us castoffs. Stuffed creatures of all descriptions began appearing at 10 Seymour. Grumpy was a worn and considerably bigger brown bear and Lamby L. Lamb was a sizeable slightly off coloured cross between a lamb and a white rabbit with a pink nose.

Each creature was christened and a variation of the bear voice was assigned them as they entered this new, ever evolving community.

The population increased and activities abounded, such as the bears taking a trip to the movies. The seating area was my parents' bed, which had to be neatly made to accommodate such an occasion. The audience sat on top of the pillows facing the end of the bed where an imaginary movie screen stood. We had a small plastic case with a clear dome on top which we used as a popcorn machine. The film which was invariably screened was *The Man In The Raincoat*. This consisted of a kind of puppet show with much finger walking around the screen area while Cubby would sing the song which we'd heard on the radio. The crowd went wild. Bearville loved going to the movies.

Another new teddy arrived who we named Pandora Panda. Pandora was black and white and very beautiful. Cubby was immediately smitten. Before we knew it, they were getting married and the wedding also happened on my parents' bed.

These events were carefully stage managed by Jim and I and were often observed by our sisters Nell and Kate.

The emotional dynamic between my siblings and I was a delicate thing. If boredom descended on my soul, the first instinct I followed was to torment my oldest sister Nell, which was easy to do. She was a very self contained person who always seemed to be reading a book. She loved the *OZ* books and had them all. She loved the *Mary Poppins* books and had them all. She loved the *Nancy Drew* books and certainly had many. I did not read books. The sight of all those words put me off but I loved to look at her books and gaze at the illustrations. I particularly liked the *OZ* pictures.

One picture I particularly enjoyed had a beautiful woman in a salon full of mirrors with a variety of different interchangeable female heads she could try on like hats.

The greatest advantage of Nellie's preoccupation with reading was that she didn't really have much experience of boredom whereas I was constantly washing up on that particular shore and when I did, I'd sneak up behind her and give her a fright. I was very good at sneaking quietly and she was usually too absorbed to notice me coming.

My sister Katie was a different creature altogether. She was the diplomat of the Myers family, always looking on the bright side of things and mediating in any conflict. If one of us boys was in tears she'd take us by both hands and dance us around the room singing: "Katie-o, Katie-o, Let's all do the Katie-o."

Both Nellie and Katie collected trading cards which they'd purchase in packets of five at either Ben Franklin or Bennets, the two five and dime stores in Mill Valley. A pack cost a nickel and contained an odd assortment of different cards but each one was part of a set of three, four or five. There'd be three paintings of a similar landscape or garden by the same artist and you'd trade the doubles to friends for the ones you wanted.

Both my sisters had their own individual shoe boxes packed with trading cards and, though I never bought or collected them myself, I loved looking at them and recognizing the artists' styles.

My sister Nell also read *Screen Stories,* a monthly magazine which featured the synopses of about five new film releases each issue. Nellie also used to take me with her on Sunday afternoon trips to the Sequoia to see the new movies. The Sequoia changed programme twice a week and the Sunday to Tuesday fare was usually a bit more highbrow than the Wednesday to Saturday. I, however, went to both and also managed the Saturday matinee with brother Jim.

Jim was a year and a half younger than I and quickly outgrew me so it became clear from about age five that I would never be capable of physically bullying him. Also he was the handsome one of the two so one would guess that I should resent this soon to be towering sibling but I don't believe that was the case.

He did, however, refuse to follow any lead I might be giving. Whatever interests I had in the world were studiously avoided by my brother. I developed a passion for movies in general and horror movies in particular so Jim, therefore, collected baseball cards.

The only arena in which we shared a common interest and got on well was Bearville. If the bears weren't involved, we went our separate ways.

In fact there were lots of separate ways going on in our family but most of them seemed to overlap a bit.

My mother Beth used to play her classical records while cleaning the house and consequently we all became familiar with that music as well as the show recordings we had like *Oklahoma* and *Porgy And Bess.* Nellie and I seemed to go off in different musical directions as she collected movie soundtracks and I amassed pop 45s by Elvis Presley, Little Richard and Jerry Lee Lewis. But we all heard each other's records.

My father Blackie wouldn't allow us to have a television so a trip to one of the movie theatres in Marin County was always fun. At the Lark we'd see British films like *The Lavender Hill Mob* and *The Lady Killers,* as well as French and Italian movies. We'd also go to The Marin Theatre in Sausalito and the Tamalpais in San Anselmo.

Beth's love of New Yorker cartoonist Charles Addams bore a resemblance to her enjoyment of the movies of Alfred Hitchcock and a family outing was always in order whenever one of his pictures came out.

The first Hitchcock film I recall seeing was *The Trouble With Harry*. I didn't understand much of it but like many of the movies I saw with my folks, that didn't matter. I loved the look of it with all those autumn leaves and the music was exciting. *Rear Window* was a much more thrilling experience. Jimmy Stewart seemed such a nice guy and Grace Kelly was absolutely gorgeous. Watching them and Thelma Ritter become embroiled in the doings of all the neighbours on the other side of the apartment block was so involving and the humour of it was such fun that when the gruesome reality of what Raymond Burr was really up to dawned, it had an emotional power which was chilling. Hitchcock took delight in manipulating our feelings and we, as a family, enjoyed that experience.

To Catch a Thief was another one our family went to and the combination of gorgeous scenery, beautiful actors wearing lovely costumes and spouting witty dialogue cast its usual spell. My design eye was captivated by the picture used on the poster and in the ads of Cary Grant seen from above and behind on the rooftop overlooking a party of people below.

The San Francisco Chronicle was a daily arrival in the Myers household and it was divided into four sections: the news section, the Herb Caen section, the Peanuts section and the sports section.

I always dived for the Peanuts section first, so titled because Charles Schultz's cartoon strip had pride of place at the top and in the centre of its front page. The reason I turned here first was because of the movie ads. I absolutely loved them. On a Monday and Tuesday they were mostly small but come Wednesday as new films were about to open the ads would start getting bigger.

I was constantly drawing imitations of the movie ads and soon began to notice the difference in design between the various studios' output. The ads for a Fox movie had a certain look as did those for Universal International, Warner Brothers, MGM and Paramount. By way of contrast United Artists, Columbia and Allied Artists didn't seem to have a distinctive house style.

The Man Who Knew Too Much was a thrilling movie and I remember copying the picture in the ads of the guy in Arab dress, staggering towards Jimmy Stewart with a knife in his back, attempting, unsuccessfully, to reach it with his hand.

The last Hitchcock film I remember us going to as a family was *North By Northwest* and I was very pleased that Blackie and Beth didn't object to it on political grounds since the baddies were very clearly Russians or Eastern Europeans. It was such fun and I could no more follow the plot than count the hairs on my head but it mattered not a jot. I absolutely loved the musical score and gasped a sigh of recognition to see the four heads of Mount Rushmore which we'd visited in North Dakota on our way west to California.

By the time that *Vertigo* had come around, we were old enough to go to the pictures on our own. I saw *Vertigo* a few times. It was not really a film for our family though there were fun elements in it, like the fact it was shot almost entirely in San Francisco and the sight of Jimmy Stewart getting exasperated tailing Kim Novak's Jag around the city.

But it was a much darker film and, in places, a bit scary. I have no idea if Beth even saw it. My guess is she didn't.

Blackie and Beth were people of the left politically and this fact made our family different from the majority of the kids I knew at school. We were used to conversing with adults, something which was unusual among my school friends. Children were, largely, treated differently than we Myers kids. Our family was relatively poor in comparison to most of those around us but the great irony was that some of my parents' closest friends were very wealthy indeed. On the east coast there was Fred Field as well as Luke and Ruth Wilson and in California there was the Dreyfus family and the Hallinans.

In fact our house at 10 Seymour was bought for us by Babbie Dreyfus. It was never an issue like it would have been in a play by Ibsen or Tennessee Williams. It was an act of friendship which she was able to perform. Babbie had known Blackie and Beth in New York during the 1930s and they became very close for life.

One thing Blackie and Beth had in common was that both had turned their backs on religion. Blackie's family was a mix of the Protestant faith and Catholicism while Beth's were American Irish and solidly Catholic.

Blackie was a seaman by trade and had been one of the founding members and vice presidents of the National Maritime Union. The NMU was one of the more radical American unions of the 1930s and 40s. It had been strong and militant as it's fight for the rights they'd won was long and bloody.

Black was born Frederick Nelson Myers, one of seven children in a Brooklyn family. Though he was always short in stature, he grew up fairly tough and his nickname came about because of his striking black hair. By the time I was ten, his hair had turned silver. He told me that he never finished high school and shipped out at a young age. There was hardly a port on the earth he hadn't been to and he seemed very much a citizen of the world.

Unlike my father, Beth came from a fairly middle class Irish American family in San Luis Obispo and Myers folklore had it that, as a teenager, she hitch hiked across the country, settling in New York where she became a writer.

She gravitated towards the political left and before long was writing for the Daily Worker. It was on an assignment to interview Blackie that the two met and apparently the chemistry was instant.

They must have been an attractive couple as both were very good looking. During World War II Black was an advisor to the Roosevelt administration on labour relations and it wasn't until the war was over and Roosevelt was dead that the claws of anti-Communism came out with a vengeance.

Blackie told me that he simply had no idea that the red scare was coming. He didn't believe for a second what was about to unfold in the United States.

When the witch hunts began, the NMU was squarely in the government's target. The majority of the leadership, with the exception of president Joe Curran, were Communists. An election was held in the year of my birth, 1947, and Blackie and all the other reds were voted out of office. The government had taken his passport away so that he couldn't go back to sea.

Thus began a long series of different labouring jobs, each of which would come to an end after a visit from the FBI to inform his employer who he was.

Blackie and Beth, now with children to feed, went from being social celebrities to pariahs practically overnight.

People they knew well would walk past them on the streets of Manhattan without even a hint of recognition. The climate of terror spread like a disease across the nation.

Publicity hungry politicians like Richard Nixon projected the image of fearless crusaders fighting off the red menace. It's easy now to be amused by photos of Nixon solemnly examining micro-film found in a pumpkin on Whitaker Chambers' farm, but the reality across the land was that ordinary Americans became frightened.

Alger Hiss went to prison, as did the Hollywood Ten and the Rosenbergs were executed for treason. This witch hunt was very real indeed.

All four of us Myers kids were born at the Beth Israel Hospital in Manhattan but soon after Jim came along we moved up to Bethel, Connecticut. We also used to spend time at Fred Field's place, Red Hill, also in Connecticut. He too went to prison during this period.

The promise of work on the waterfront in San Francisco through the ILWU, the west coast longshore union of which Harry Bridges was president, gave the Myers family a reason to head west. An intimidating visit to our landlady in Bethel from the FBI meant we had to leave our house. We set off in a little car, a Willys, given us by Fred Field.

It wouldn't be a straightforward journey and the first extended stop was a house on White Bear Lake in

Minnesota where we spent the autumn and winter of 1951. We'd had plenty of experience of snow in New York and Connecticut but not quite like this. Our house actually backed onto the lake so that we could walk out onto it, frozen solid beneath a layer of snow at least five inches deep.

In May of 1952 when the snow had all melted, we made our way through North Dakota to San Cristobal in New Mexico where our friends Jenny and Craig Vincent had a ranch which seemed to be a place of retreat for wealthy lefties. We spent a glorious summer there and, by September, we rolled up through San Francisco, across the Golden Gate Bridge and into Mill Valley, the place where my sisters, brother and I would grow up.

Despite all the strains and anxieties which surrounded our circumstances, life in the Myers household was pretty good and I can remember, as a child, never wanting to be in any other family.

Unlike others of my generation who were able to enjoy television and radio programmes about the glories of the FBI, I found these government agents to be frightening in the extreme. Family folklore had it that Beth chased a pair of FBI men away from 10 Seymour with a broom. Their usual mission was to try and get my parents to tell them something which could be used against Harry Bridges, who the government was trying to deport on the basis of his supposed membership of the Communist Party. Harry, an Australian, was a regular visitor to 10 Seymour and they would never dream of betraying him.

The realities of the anti-red era gave rise to tremendous confusion within me about who was the enemy and who was not. Blackie was a virtual encyclopedia of colourful slang and he had a different nickname for every avenue of life. A bar was a gin mill, a tourist was a scenery bum, a not very intelligent Caucasian from the deep south was a scissor bill (actually pronounced 'sizzrabill') and on it went. The fact that most people in business had a "licence to steal" created a certain image with us children and one time, coming out of the Safeway in Mill Valley, my sister Katie announced with great pride that she had just stolen a packet of Life Savers. We were stunned to see the rage with which Blackie told her off. We, like she, thought he would be proud.

The contradictions in my parents' world view left us in a peculiar kind of limbo as to who was right and who was wrong. We didn't have too much confusion about agents of the state like the FBI, particularly as they all seemed to look and behave like Jack Webb on *Dragnet,* which seemed pretty scary. But what to make of the local police in Mill Valley was something less certain.

One of the problems with my parents was that they spoke

to us children as though we knew what they were talking about. This may have been polite but it was hardly constructive. I remember asking my mother about something to do with racism in the deep south and she replied: "Oh you know, honey. All that Jim Crow stuff." In a different life I might have challenged her to define her terms but my tendency was to shrug and move along. This is how the growing bubble of my educational ignorance began.

Unlike other parents, Blackie and Beth didn't take our education seriously. Perhaps they felt that, as the system was rotten, there was little point in preparing us to do battle within its confines. Jenny and Craig Vincent used to argue with them about involvement in the PTA. My parents felt that it was a waste of time while Jenny and Craig felt differently.

Beth would help me with homework in an emergency but not on a day to day basis, hence I tended to always leave it until the last minute. Because I didn't have what I would describe as gifted teachers in my elementary years, I got into the habit of coasting at school.

I was a day dreamer who would draw imitations of the movie ads on the top margin of my binder paper. For it was the movies that I seemed to be living for. Going to the Sequoia Theatre was always the most exciting thing I could ever do.

Occasionally on a visit to the pictures I might arrive after the film had begun which was always a bit disconcerting but all you'd have to do was wait for it to start again and simply see it over from the beginning.

It was Alfred Hitchcock who put a stop to such practices when Paramount released *Psycho* in 1960. One of the gimmicks Hitchcock employed was a policy of not admitting anyone into the theatre after the picture had begun. The master of suspense had always been a master of showmanship as well but with *Psycho* he came into the limelight in a way not seen before.

All the ads and posters featured pictures of him announcing the fact that no one would be allowed in after *Psycho* had started. It was a very clever tactic and it worked a treat.

I went off to see it at the Marin in Sausalito on a matinee day, not really knowing what I was in for. I was aware that it was black and white, unlike every other Hitchcock film I'd ever seen. I also knew there was a murder but not much more. The ads showed photos of Janet Leigh in her bra and John Gavin with his shirt off. Some also had a somewhat shocked looking Tony Perkins but the copy was very minimalist: "A new and altogether different screen excitement!"

I was, by now, thirteen years old and pretty conditioned to scary movies. I prided myself on never closing my eyes or looking away but I had never really been truly terrified by a Hitchcock picture. Made anxious perhaps but not actually frightened. I was not prepared for the experience I was about to have.

All the exposition from the opening was unsettling. Marion Crane stealing the money and leaving town was upsetting and unpleasant. That ghastly drive when she encountered the policeman followed by the pouring rain and finally her arrival at Bates Motel.

I never knew Bernard Herrmann's name as a kid but his music was always my favourite and here it was so powerful an influence on the audience, every bit as intense as the visual images. The music hammered home the anxiety of Marion's flight. It also alluded to the doom she was hurtling towards.

To say I was shocked by the shower scene doesn't quite put it strongly enough. I found it to be an emotional assault on the audience and it left me stunned. When I was quite certain that the murder was over, the one thought which came into my mind was that my mother Beth must not see this movie.

Psycho was brutal. I remember reading of a woman who threw a whisky tumbler at Hitchcock in a restaurant, shouting; "That's for scaring the hell out of me with that goddamned Psycho!"

Not long after seeing it I read Robert Bloch's novel, but for years I remained happily innocent of the fact that it was based on a real life incident. The conversations between Norman and his mother unsettled me and made me contemplate the regular exchanges my brother and I had with the teddy bears.

We'd both walk into a room and I would say something to Grumpy who would then answer via Jim's voice. Now admittedly these were teddy bears and not rotting human corpses but to me there was a parallel.

I suppose we'd reached a turning point. Jim and I agreed that the time had arrived to put Bearville away. We settled on the following morning for the execution and when that time came we took the two boxes up on the roof. As each bear was executed, they were then deposited in the *dead* box.

What happened to them after this I cannot recall. But the art of ascribing voices and personalities to those who cannot speak was not finished in the Myers household just yet.

The Myers family in New Mexico. From left: Nellie, Jimmy, Beth, Katie, Blackie and Johnny.

Back row from left: Beth Myers, Blackie Myers, Jenny Vincent, Craig Vincent. Front row: Johnny Myers and Katie Myers.

These two snapshots were both taken at the same Location: Cibola, the ranch in San Cristobal, New Mexico which belonged to my parents' good friends Jenny and Craig Vincent. The two and a half months we lived at the ranch was the last stop we made before the final drive to Mill Valley.
The year was 1952.

Chapter 1

A Hostage To Nostalgia

The Myers family arrived in Mill Valley in September of 1952. My father Blackie was driving the big black DeSoto which had brought us all the way from San Cristobal, New Mexico.

My sisters Nell and Kate sat in back with my mother Beth while my brother Jim and I were in the front seat, weary from many long hours on the road.

Coming into town on Miller Avenue, Blackie took a left at the 2am Club and began the climb up Montford.

The first house we moved into was on Madera Way off the Panoramic Highway, about halfway up Mount Tamalpais. When the fog would roll across from Stinson, we would get it first before it cascaded down into the valley below.

Madera Way was certainly the steepest road I had ever encountered in my five year old life and I remember feeling giddy about the almost vertical nature of it. The house was nice in a Hansel and Gretel sort of way and we were surrounded by deep, dark forest.

My mother Beth would take brother Jim and I up this impossibly steep road each morning to see our sisters Nell and Kate off on the yellow bus which took them down to Old Mill School. It was the number 2, driven by a man named Vic. Beth was tickled by the inaccurate imitation of her that Jimmy and I would shout as we waved: "Goodbye mine honeys. Goodbye mine sweeties."

Then we would gingerly walk back down Madera Way to our house which sat off to the left.

We only lived there for the first six months and had arrived in Marin County after a long and complicated journey across the United States. In my short life I had already lived in Greenwich Village where all four of us were born, in Bethel, Connecticut where we had a lovely wooden house, in White Bear Lake, Minnesota where our home backed onto the lake, frozen solid in the winter of 1951, in Rapid City, North Dakota where we rode on burros and slept in motels, in Denver, Colorado where we spent time with cattle, horses and actual cowboys and finally in San Cristobal near Taos, New Mexico where we stayed with our good friends Jenny and Craig Vincent who had a wonderful ranch up in the mountains.

I hadn't even begun grade school and yet my siblings and I had already seen Mount Rushmore, the Black Hills of Dakota, the Carlsbad Caverns, the Grand Canyon, the Painted Desert and the Petrified Forest.

My introduction to the world of nostalgia was born, I believe, out of my yearning for the things which no longer surrounded me in the beautiful hills of Mill Valley. Things like snow, the autumn leaves of New England, the incredible underground world of the New York subway, the smell of the lobbies in Manhattan apartment buildings and the aroma of sage in the New Mexican desert. All these memories and more accompanied me in a constant reverie throughout my childhood.

Blackie's first job when we moved into Madera Way was working as a painter on the Golden Gate Bridge. I remember being intrigued by the existence of elevators in the bridge's towers which the workers would take up to the various levels. While he was working on the bridge, some poor fellow fell to his death. This shocked us all and was, I believe, the reason he quit the job.

It was in March of 1953 that we moved to our new house much further down the Tamalpais slopes at 10 Seymour Avenue. It had three stories and a big patch of land below.

The house was a gift from Babbie Dreyfus who lived with her husband Barney and three sons up in West Blithedale Canyon. She had grown very close to Blackie and Beth in New York in the late 1930s. When we arrived in Mill Valley, which was Babbie's home town, she quietly took it upon herself to purchase the house and property and hand it over with no strings attached. I didn't know this as a child but did notice that I never heard a bad word about Babbie ever.

The Myers family was always financially poor but we were wealthy indeed in the quality of our friendships.

The house stood below Seymour Avenue, a short, gravelled dirt road which ended abruptly at the wooden turnstile where the Pixie Trail began. At the other end across Molino was a bank of mailboxes and a set of steps. All the hills around us had steps like these which descended between the houses down into the valley below.

One neighbour we encountered was Mrs Hunsinger who lived at number 6 Seymour along with her Lassie-like dog, Jeanie.

She was an Australian whose house was a treasure trove of exotic things from all over the world.

"Call me Hunsie," she commanded on our first

meeting. And we always did.

All four of us Myers kids spent many hours at Hunsie's where never a dull moment passed. She was a stamp collector with books full of them in bright colours from all corners of the globe. Spears, swords and exotic weaponry of all sorts could be found in wicker bins. And behind every artifact was a story which she was always happy to tell us.

It was Hunsie who had christened the stretch of undeveloped land just beyond Seymour Avenue as 'The Pixie Trail.' This was because, she explained, the pixies always came out at night to have their parties there. The proof of this was the profusion of pixie hats, eucalyptus acorns, which, along with strips of bark from these trees, carpeted the ground.

Hunsie was the perfect neighbour for four young children to visit as she catered to the very different imaginations of all four Myers kids.

A favourite treat that Hunsie made for us was what we called road cookies. This was actually shortbread but the dough had been squeezed out through a syringe which gave the pastry long grooves. They were delicious.

As a fan of any comic strip I could find, I was pleased that Hunsie took the Examiner. As a Hearst paper the Examiner was banned in our house. There were several demons constantly referred to in our family and William Randolph Hearst was one of them. So it was a novelty to be able to see this forbidden fruit as it had different comic strips to the Chronicle.

The downstairs of Hunsie's house was where her guests would sleep and it opened out onto the garden which was a fusion of the orderly and the wild. She had plum and apricot trees which bore fruit each year. We ate plenty.

We were only a few minutes walk away from the local playground at the corner of Janes and Molino. It had been dug out of a hillside and was kind of like a large rectangular crater that you could look down into from either of the roads above.

Not long after we moved there I met one of our neighbours, Dennis Brogan, whose house was just off the footpath down to Una Way. A year older than me and considerably bigger, Dennis had reddish coloured hair and a freckled face which seemed to curve inwards like the drawing of a quarter moon.

I first met him on a lazy afternoon in the playground when

a steam roller was parked in the middle of it. I guess the surface was being re-laid or it could be that it was being laid for the first time. We were new in the neighbourhood so the playground's history was unknown to me.

Dennis suggested we play on the motionless steam roller. My instinct was not to touch the thing at all.

"What's the matter?" he asked. "Are you chicken?"

Such a challenge proved effective and we both climbed up onto it. He positioned himself in the driver's seat and began fiddling with the various controls, while I sat nervously at the side and watched him.

At six years old I was a tiny child and Dennis was a big kid. I was inclined to do whatever my new friend wanted me to do.

We pretended to be driving around on this thing which I would have enjoyed a lot more had I not felt so nervous. The junction of Janes and Molino had three stop signs and the sound of vehicles slowing to a near stop then accelerating was the background noise to our activity. I have no memory of how long we played on this damned thing, but at some point one of the cars screeched to a halt up on Molino. A man wearing a white shirt and tie jumped out, screaming: "You kids get off that thing or I'll call the cops!"

Within the blink of an eye, Dennis leapt off the tractor, ran up the hill and was gone. He left me, standing next to this machine all alone, looking up at the man on the road who continued his tirade, making me feel like a six year old criminal.

"Do you have any idea how much these things cost? This is city property. If you were to do any damage... any damage at all to this tractor your parents would be held responsible!"

It seemed like he went on and on berating me until he finally ran out of things to say. He was clearly very angry about what I and the now absent Dennis had been doing and I guess he worked for the city of Mill Valley in some capacity.

So after what felt like a lifetime of being shouted at, he finally got back in his car and drove away. My walk back up Molino to Seymour was somber and the phrase which reverberated all the way home was: "I'll call the cops!"

Both Blackie and Beth were sitting in the kitchen as I got to our house. They seemed to be in a particularly jolly mood and didn't comprehend the depth of my trauma at all. They laughed it off, assured me I hadn't done anything wrong and told me I had nothing to worry about. Blackie referred to the guy as a dildock with nothing better to do than bawl kids out.

Of course my parent's judgment was soothing, but I remained traumatised by the incident. As I lay in my bed that night and for several nights after, the shouted phrase:

"I'll call the cops!" echoed to make me wince into my pillow.

When I saw Dennis again the incident was never referred to and the tractor wasn't there any more.

This time I was on the swings and he had a large brick in his hand as he climbed up the steps of the nearby slide. My memory of his idea is hazy but I think he wanted to see if he could miss me with the brick as I was swinging the other way. Why on earth I should have gone along with this hairbrained concept I have no idea but I suddenly felt the full weight of this brick on my forehead and fell to the ground, bleeding and in considerable pain.

Muriel Johnson, a friend of my parents, had the house on the playground's eastern border. She heard me crying and immediately ran out to my aid. Once again Dennis ran across the playground, up the hill and was gone.

Muriel took me into her house and cleaned me up. On this occasion representations were made to Dennis's mother who wouldn't believe a word of it, claiming her boy was too much of an angel to do such a thing.

It's at this stage that I must attempt some kind of explanation about Dennis who, sadly, is no longer alive to defend his reputation. Though he had a younger sister, he was a bit like an only child. His mother Jean worked in the city and she and his father were divorced. I only met his dad a few times and certainly didn't find him very friendly. I think he lived in Sausalito and never looked at all happy whereas Dennis's mom seemed a jolly sort.

The third installment in this saga involved my brother Jim and, again, I'm at a loss to remember what precisely the experiment was but the outcome was that Jimmy's finger was almost cut off with an axe.

There were lots of things we did with Dennis that didn't result in trauma and agony but I don't recall many of them. I guess he was just big enough and old enough to be a bit of a bully. I was microscopic in size and, though Jim was taller, he was two years younger than Dennis who carried on being a fact of our lives on Seymour Avenue.

The playground continued to be the hub of local activity for Jim and I over all the years we lived on Seymour. It was where we learned to ride a bike and was the place we played sports like softball and touch football with the friends we made in the neighbourhood so it was as important to me as the Pixie Trail.

But unlike the Pixie Trail, I didn't go to the playground to be alone. It was a place you went to be with others and there seemed to be a significant difference between the two for me for, being alone, had become important.

Chapter 2

Going To Homestead School

When we arrived in Mill Valley from points east I was only five but my sisters Nell and Kate were older so they enrolled straight away in 5th and 3rd grades at Old Mill School.

After our move down from Madera Way to Seymour Avenue, I spent a week in a kindergarten class at Alto but then it was decided that I would stay home until Jim and I could start together at Homestead School.

Sometime during the summer of 1953 I had a trip to the city with my mother Beth on my own which was very exciting. It may have been for a visit to Kaiser Hospital but I'm pretty sure that some shopping also happened. I was taken for the very first time to one of the big movie theatres on Market Street. It was The Paramount and the movie was *Shane* starring Alan Ladd.

Coming in from the afternoon light, our eyes weren't adjusted to the darkness and we had trouble seeing where to sit. When we finally got seated it became clear that the movie was almost over. Young Brandon DeWilde was shouting the name "Shane" over and over as the main character rode off into the distance on his horse.

There was something wonderfully disorienting about coming into a movie late for, in addition to the difficulty of seeing where you were going, you really had no hope of understanding the story. Unlike today's cinema-going which has separate showings, all we had to do was watch the whole thing over again.

Before this outing I had only been to movie theatres in Marin County with my family and the Paramount's size impressed me. Although my mother would attend the pictures with us all as a family, this was the only time I had ever been to the movies with her alone and it felt special.

I obviously was not unique in considering my mother to be the most important person in the world. In my young life she was the one who was always there in times of agony, joy and indecision and my attachment to her was intimate both physically and emotionally. When I would return from the Pixie Trail, my hands coated with the dust of history,

Beth would magically produce a hot wash cloth and within a flash my fingers and thumbs were crystal clean. It was the most familiar relationship in my life. The first time I had to leave that snug cocoon was when my brother and I went to Homestead School.

Our first day was exciting and terrifying in equal measure. Both Jim and I had brand new clothes on and Beth had packed us each a lunch in identical brown paper bags with our names written on in pencil.

Jimmy was starting kindergarten and I was going into first grade with Mrs Spalding. Beth came with us and we all walked down to the playground where we turned right on Janes then down to Montford where the school sat. As we entered through the main door we were greeted by the principal, Miss Grimm, who was charming to my mother and said hello to both of us. After a brief chat it was time for Beth to leave us. It was touch and go whether we would cry or not but as it turned out, neither of us did.

Once she was gone we walked straight through the door leading out onto the playground, full of noisy children playing. We just stood around, clutching our lunch bags and watching.

When the bell rang and it became clear which line I should join for Mrs Spalding's class, I did so. Suddenly I felt excited to be there. The little boy in front of me in the line had a hat on. For some reason, I lifted this kid's hat off his head then, immediately dropped it back in its place. I don't believe this upset him and I guess I didn't notice the approaching noise of a lady's high heeled shoes. Suddenly my arm was grabbed forcefully and this eagle-headed woman was glaring angrily into my face. "If I ever see you do that again," she said sternly, "I'm going to spank you! Do you understand?" I nodded sheepishly and she went away.

The woman who accosted me was Mrs Lewis who taught third grade. I soon learned that only those pupils whose parents gave permission could be spanked by the teachers. Blackie and Beth certainly gave no such permission along with the vast majority of the parents. It was a slightly sad minority who were the regular recipients of corporal punishment at Homestead School.

Mrs Spalding was a tall handsome woman with dark hair and a fairly smiley face most of the time. She probably got through that first week without administering any corporal punishment but then some poor fool committed a minor crime and was chased up and down the aisles until caught. The child was then dragged to the front of the class where Mrs Spalding sat down, bent the kid across her knee and, wielding a ruler, proceeded to angrily paddle the kid's backside while the entire class watched, stunned by the display.

The result of these occasional spankings was an atmosphere of terror. The fact that I knew I wouldn't be spanked didn't lessen my fear of it and one couldn't help identifying with the poor souls who were getting it. Another element was the disproportionate fury of the teacher administering the punishment. Mrs Spalding would begin the paddling angry faced but with each blow her facial rage would intensify so that she was a hellish mask by the time she finally stopped.

A young lady in my first grade class had a learning difficulty which rendered her unable to speak publicly and when she found herself incapable of saying her pledge of allegiance, Mrs Spalding took a yard stick to her and broke it across her bottom.

There were no male teachers at Homestead and the place was run, presumably, along the lines dictated by Miss Grimm. I accidentally witnessed Miss Grimm administering an after-school spanking to an older boy in one of the class rooms while I was dawdling on my way home one day.

Betty Grimm was a dark haired woman somewhere between forty and fifty. She was short, trim and good looking. She also bore an uncanny resemblance to the film star Joan Crawford. It was her eyes which seemed to have the same intensity as Ms Crawford's.

Although I tend to remember the strict side of her, all the

class photos of Miss Grimm portray her smiling in an endearing manner and when she was in a jolly mood she would refer to her collective flock as "her little chickadees" which must mean she'd been a W.C. Fields fan at some point which can't be a bad thing.

Early on I had an encounter with Miss Grimm in the hall just outside her office when she told me to let a little girl go first through a door while I held it open.

"Remember," she said in a matter of fact voice, "It's ladies first and it always will be."

Among the children I went to school with there seemed to be an almost ideological division of opinion on corporal punishment. If their parents practiced it, then the children of those families almost certainly believed in it. The opposite seemed to be true of the families which didn't embrace corporal punishment.

The Myers family was out of step with so much of the American way of life in the 1950s that it was like we lived on a different planet. A phrase which summed up many American parents' view of children was: they should be seen and not heard. This was definitely not the case in our household, nor the Dreyfus's or Hallinan's. All my parents' left wing friends treated their kids like people and tended to respect their points of view. I never heard of any beatings or spankings.

In fact there was an invisible barrier which existed between the world of my parents' friends and society as I viewed it through the prism of Homestead School.

I don't know if corporal punishment was carried out at the other schools. I'm pretty sure it didn't happen at Old Mill or we would have heard about it from Nell and Kate. All of the grade schools were little islands, isolated from each other. It wasn't until 7th grade that we finally mixed with students from Park, Tam Valley and Strawberry.

So I don't know if Homestead was unusual. My first three teachers there: Mrs Spalding, Mrs Dempster and Mrs Lewis, were all ruler-wielding disciplinarians and for me it was counter productive because it made the learning environment a scary place to be. Any excuse to stay off school and I would grab it.

As for corporal punishment in the Myers household I got one spanking from Beth after almost pushing brother Jim out of a second floor window and Blackie gave Jim and I the occasional smack on the backside but that was nothing like the regime at Homestead. My sisters, on the other hand, glided like angels through childhood without any such interference.

My lack of enthusiasm for school probably fed my passion for the things which really interested me like movies, comic books, radio and popular music.

By the time I began at Homestead I had already become a fairly regular moviegoer, either with my family or in the company of my older sisters. One of the first movies I remember seeing at the Sequoia was *Houdini* starring Tony Curtis. I loved this film and fell madly in love with Janet Leigh. It was in glorious colour and featured Harry Houdini escaping every form of imprisonment possible until the end when he couldn't get out of the box. I was terribly upset by the ending.

Another movie I enjoyed enormously was *Calamity Jane* with Doris Day. The songs were thrilling and she was just gorgeous in her buckskin jacket and rebel hat. Doris Day joined Janet Leigh in my growing list of beautiful women I fell in love with at the movies.

We probably wouldn't have gone to the pictures as often if we'd had a television and when we went it was usually to movies of a fairly high standard: *Stalag 17, Miss Sadie Thompson, From Here To Eternity*. We also went up to The Lark to see mostly foreign films.

I don't believe a Sunday evening ever arrived without a feeling of dread that I had to go back to school the next morning.

There were, however, compensations. Hot dogs were served on a Thursday. Beth would give us each the thirty cents to order two hot dogs which were prepared by volunteer mothers in the staff room. The aroma began seeping through the school about 10:15 and by lunch time everyone was ravenous and anxious to get their hot dogs, beautifully wrapped in waxed paper.

Our normal lunch on the other days usually consisted of a bologna sandwich on white bread with French's mustard. This was accompanied by a piece of fruit and three of Beth's homemade chocolate chip cookies wrapped in wax paper. Little cartons of milk were provided by the school.

Of course there were other things about Homestead School which were good. Those first three teachers taught me how to read, write and do basic arithmetic so I did actually learn something useful from them. But given a choice between sitting in class with Mrs Lewis and anything else I would always rather be riding shotgun with Doris Day on the Deadwood Stage or travelling with Uncle Scrooge and his nephews to far away lands.

And so a pattern developed of living for those hours when we weren't in school. The three o'clock bell on a Friday afternoon always held the glowing magic of a weekend full of promise. Though that promise often crumbled into boredom and worse it still never lost its allure for my fevered imagination. Whatever was going on outside the confines of Homestead School had to be better. Didn't it?

Chapter 3

Of Monsters And Scoundrels

It was on a visit to the Hallinans' in Ross that I first heard about *The Beast From 20,000 Fathoms*. Danny Hallinan, who was not yet five at the time, had been taken to see it by his older brother Ringo and, as we sat on the massive porch of their mansion one afternoon, he told me about it in great detail.

"The scientist looks out of the diving bell and sees the beast coming towards him through the water. He describes it over the microphone to the people up in the boat. It comes closer and closer then it opens its mouth."

"Then what happened?"

"The line went dead."

A moment of silence descended upon us both then, as if on cue, Danny plunged into another description.

"The Beast comes down this street and a cop starts shooting at him. He lowers his head and eats the cop alive. You see the guy's legs dangling out of his mouth. Then he shakes his head back and swallows him whole."

There was more and Danny enjoyed telling me all about it for I hung on his every word. The giant monster emerging from the ocean at night to wreck a lighthouse. The same beast destroying a fishing boat. The sighting of the creature by an injured scientist as he lay, helpless, in an arctic wasteland. The images Danny conjured up were so exciting to me that I immediately longed to see this movie.

Yet I never did see *The Beast From 20,000 Fathoms* until many years later and so it gained within my soul a mythic, legendary quality. Danny was very lucky to have an older brother who would take him to see such films.

The closest I ever got was a clipping of an ad for the movie from the Chronicle. It showed The Beast, a large dragon-like monster with jaws dripping and nostrils fuming, rampaging angrily above an amusement park with a ferris wheel and roller coaster. Down on the ground tiny men and women ran screaming in horror.

This clipping became my constant companion each night as

I went to sleep. It stayed on my bedside table for what must have been weeks and every night I would gaze at it longingly. If Jiminy Cricket were to have appeared at my bedside to grant me a wish it would have been to see *The Beast From 20,000 Fathoms.*

This was my very first encounter with a monster movie and my passion for the concept would grow. At the same time my parents and their friends were having a pretty scary time politically as the agencies of the federal government regarded them all as dangerous subversives.

Vin and Vivian Hallinan were friends of my parents but they existed in a very different world to the Myers family for, unlike us, they were extremely rich and lived a life that most people could only dream about.

It's an interesting thing about the American left that deep and lasting friendships can be found between people from different economic and social classes. The Myers family was, throughout my childhood, financially poor in comparison to most of my friends at school. At home we never ate steak or butter and Blackie always drove an old car. He also wouldn't let us have a television.

One of Blackie's great strengths was a total lack of concern about social status. At a time in American history when keeping up with the Joneses was truly a way of life, he couldn't have cared less about owning the latest gadget or the flashiest vehicle.

Among our school friends there was much mirth about the Myers kids having no television but I never heard a word on the subject from our rich friends like the Dreyfus's or the Hallinans.

A visit to the Hallinans' always aroused conflicting emotions in me. A thrilling kind of excitement was contrasted with a dread of danger. Whether you were out in public with them or in the privacy of their palatial home, danger was never far from the Hallinan boys. The fights they would erupt into were usually between themselves but not always.

When we were staying the night, Blackie would drop us off and the drive into Ross was, in itself, like a visit to a different planet. Ross was the wealthiest enclave in Marin County. There were plenty of rich folks all over Marin but nowhere else had such a concentration of them in one small area.

Vin and Vivian had six sons, five of whom were practically adults, leaving the youngest, Danny, somewhat isolated. He was in the same age bracket as Jimmy and I. It was for this reason that we would be invited to stay over as often as we were because, within the leafy estates of Ross, the Hallinans were viewed as leftist radicals by their wealthy neighbours. None of them would allow their snooty offspring to play with Danny.

Vincent Hallinan was a famous criminal lawyer who actually ran for president on the Progressive Party ticket in 1952 and had spent six months in federal prison for contempt of court while defending Harry Bridges.

Vin was a physically striking man of Irish descent with wavy dark hair and rugged good looks. He was tough and he raised his sons to be tough too. He didn't drink, never smoked and was a physically fit, committed athlete.

In addition to being excellent swimmers, the boys were all taught to box and play American football. Each was given a nickname: Butch, Kayo, Tuffy, Dynamite. The two youngest sons had problems with their nicknames. Conn was christened Flash but didn't like it so after seeing John Ford's *Stagecoach,* settled on Ringo after the Ringo Kid. The youngest son, Danny, was given the name Dangerous and, for a variety of reasons, it never stuck at all.

Vivian was without doubt the most glamorous and beautiful woman I had ever laid eyes on. She had just the right combination of natural good looks, impeccable dress sense and, of course, the money, to make herself movie star gorgeous. Even in her bathrobe with cream all over her face, Vivian exuded glamour coupled with intelligence and wit.

In fact the Hallinans were a very original bunch. Vin swore like a stevedore but was highly educated and given to quoting the classics.

Their house in Ross was a mansion with pillars on the porch overlooking a massive expanse of green. On one side of the enormous lawn was an artificial lake and at the other end a huge swimming pool and gymnasium. The house was every bit as grand as Tara in *Gone With The Wind*.

Vivian had become, over the years of her marriage to Vin, an extremely successful buyer, seller and manager of apartment buildings, mostly in San Francisco. By the time we met them, Vivian was the richer of the two but they were both millionaires. They had a maid who cooked and cleaned for them and a meal at their table was like eating in a fine restaurant.

Vin might have remained respectable as far as the establishment was concerned but for the fact that he decided to defend Harry Bridges, the president of the west coast longshoreman's union, the ILWU in federal court in 1949.

The government was determined to convict and deport Harry, an Australian by birth, claiming he had lied in stating he didn't belong to the Communist Party when he became an American citizen.

In the end, Harry avoided prison but Vin did not. While we were in New Mexico on our way west, Vin was serving six months at McNeil's Island for contempt of court and came out just in time to do some campaigning for his presidential bid against Eisenhower and Adlai Stevenson.

Now as a six year old I picked up snippets of all this but didn't really understand what was going on at all. Blackie and Beth would speak about Vin's case like we knew what they were talking about but most of the time I didn't.

My oldest sister Nell wore a 'Hallinan For President' button at Old Mill School and found herself very much in the minority.

Vin's presidential candidacy gave a focal point to the American left at a time when it was under serious attack. He spoke out eloquently against the Korean War and the Cold War and gave voice to many issues which the newspapers of the day were sweeping under the carpet.

The media barely reported his campaign at all and it didn't come as a huge shock to anyone that Vin and his running mate Charlotta Bass, who was black, didn't win in 1952.

But while the media may not have been paying much attention to the speeches of Vincent Hallinan, the same cannot be said of the FBI. Under J. Edgar Hoover's guidance, his agents, who had Vin and Vivian under constant surveillance since the Bridges trial, studied their finances thoroughly and turned what they found over to the IRS.

In March of 1953 the government indicted both Vin and Vivian for income tax evasion. Though I, as a six year old child, was unaware of this fact as Danny regaled me during the summer months with tales of *The Beast From 20,000 Fathoms,* both his parents were deeply involved in preparing their defence in federal court.

In the case, which lasted eight weeks, the prosecution made a great deal of the Hallinan lifestyle and the fact that the pool and gym were both claimed as business expenses. Family members on the payroll, donations to organisations deemed pro-Communist and even Vivian's fur coats, jewellery and shoes were examined in detail.

Near the end of the trial Vivian, who was convinced they were both going to jail, laid out a plan. She would go straight to prison and Vin should appeal, a process he could string out for a few years and by the time it was decided against him, she'd be out and, in this way the boys would not be left alone.

When the jury's verdict was delivered, however, Vivian was found not guilty while Vin was convicted on five counts of evading $37,000 in taxes. He was sentenced to eighteen months in jail as well as having to pay fines, costs and penalties totalling $622,000.

I recall Beth saying they were determined to get Vin. "If they can't get you on anything else, they can always get you on tax evasion." The idea of a friend going to prison meant nothing shameful in our household. Blackie had spent plenty of time in jails across the country during strikes. While we were living in Connecticut, our close friend Fred Field was sentenced to nine months in federal prison for refusing to divulge the names of contributors to the Civil Rights Congress Bail Fund. Another friend, Alvah Bessie, spent a year in prison as one of the Hollywood Ten.

Interestingly Vin was of the opinion that, in the light of the political hysteria of the time, his sentence was a lenient one. For that reason he didn't mount an appeal. Prison held no great terrors for Vin as he was a tough guy but it did disrupt the family. Both Butch and Kayo soon found themselves in trouble fighting and one of Vivian's prize property acquisitions, the Clay Jones Building in San Francisco, had to be sold to pay the fines and to fund the inevitable legal battle that Vin would mount to keep from being disbarred.

As he went off to McNeill's Island again, Vivian rented out the house in Ross and moved with the boys into one of her properties in the city.

There was only so much of this that I knew about but things were discussed around the dinner table. Nellie and Katie were aware of Vin and Vivian's situation as the tax evasion case was reported daily in the Chronicle.

It was a frightening era for the children of left wing parents. Lillian Hellman dubbed it *Scoundrel Time* in her book of the same title. The persecution of the left in the early 1950s was an easy bandwagon for opportunist politicians to climb on. The climate of terror whipped up by HUAC and Senator

Joe McCarthy meant that the most ridiculous accusations would be taken seriously by the media and, in turn, by the general public.

The greatest casualty of the whole red scare was the consciousness of the American people. Proper debate can only occur in an environment where people aren't afraid to speak their minds and the whole business frightened everyone too much for that to happen.

I came to love my movie monsters. They frightened me but I enjoyed the thrill unlike the fear I encountered from the scoundrels. Knowing that Vin, Fred Field and Alvah Bessie had all gone to prison meant, to my young mind, that Blackie and Beth could also be taken away from me as well.

When the Rosenbergs were executed it sent a terrifying message to the families of the left. Looking at a photo of the Rosenberg children in a magazine after their parents had died in the electric chair, I thought the same thing could happen to Blackie and Beth.

Unlike my beloved monsters, this fear was no fun at all.

Chapter 4

An Illustrated Access To Classic Literature

As a young boy I had an almost phobic aversion to the sight of a page of type. Whether it was the first page of a novel or a lengthy article in a magazine, all those words looked impenetrable to my child mind.

Now it wasn't because I had any problem reading the words but rather that I didn't want to. My sister Nell would look at the same page and see stories like *Ozma Of Oz,* but I would see hard work that I didn't want to do. My mother was constantly leaving newspaper and magazine clippings for my attention which I resolutely ignored.

It was this aversion which led me instead to the

comic book. Comic books had brightly coloured covers with alluring illustrations and I took to them with gusto. *Walt Disney's Comics And Stories* was one of the first I ever bought from the Bus Depot and I found it along with many others on the lower section of the display case just inside the Throckmorton entrance. The upper section was mostly magazines and another, slightly different looking comic book: Classics Illustrated.

It may well be that my mother Beth bought the first of these for me in an attempt to kick-start my reading. Classics Illustrated produced comic book versions of very old books by authors like Charles Dickens, Victor Hugo or William Shakespeare with a back catalogue of 167 titles. The covers of the comics had an oddly dignified look: beautifully painted colour pictures of high drama from different periods of history. I went for the more exciting covers: the bullet shaped rocket leaving the earth in Jules Verne's *From The Earth To The Moon* or a man in a pith helmet about to be trampled by a giant rampaging elephant in H. Rider Haggard's *King Solomon's Mines*.

In the upper left hand corner of each cover was a yellow rectangular box containing the distinctive *Classics Illustrated* logo. Below this box was the yellow image of an open book superimposed over the illustration with the comic's number on the left page and the price on the right: 15 cents. It was expensive. Every other comic book cost a mere dime but these elevated-looking periodicals dared to be different and succeeded.

A beautiful summer's day during vacation time would find all four Myers kids sitting out in front of the house with our reading matter. Nellie would invariably be sitting in the sunshine with an open book in her hand. Katie too would have a book or a magazine while Jim and I would be engrossed in one of the many comic books that made their way into our house.

I have learned from those older than I that one of the main uses of *Classics Illustrated* comics was for older students to avoid reading the originals for exams but that played no role in my enjoyment of them.

I found them to be portals to worlds of adventure in lands I would otherwise know nothing of. *The Hunchback Of Notre Dame* took me to Paris; *Oliver Twist* introduced me to London and *Crime And Punishment* played out in the dark side of St Petersburg.

My mother cleaned the house with the record player on and among her favorite pieces were Beethoven's *Fifth Symphony,* Schubert's *Trout Quintet* and Rimsky Korsakov's *Scheherezade.* I associate all this music with the reading of the Classics comics in our yard but mostly it's *Scheherezade* that I think of. The opening movement was titled *The Sea* and it had all the terror and majesty of a massive ocean surrounding you with its sound.

As I'd lose myself within the pages of these illustrated worlds I was also soaking up the music. After the dramatic opening, *The Sea* calmed down and a solo violin, representing Scheherezade herself, weaving her tales, played a gentle but passionate passage which took us further into this highly charged and emotional music as I travelled with the charmingly illustrated Tom Sawyer: getting into a fight with a strange boy, white washing the fence and falling in love with Becky Thatcher.

The Classics comics appealed to me in the same way as the Saturday matinee and my mother's background music provided the soundtrack. There was adventure, heroism and, with stories by H.G. Wells and Jules Verne, science fiction as well.

Classics Illustrated was the invention of Albert Kanter, the American son of Russian Jewish immigrants whose passion for classic literature led him in 1941 to publish the first of the series, *The Three Musketeers.* He soon found there was a huge market for his comic books which changed their style several times before I finally encountered them in the early 1950s.

I would surrender to each comic book like a movie, giving it my total concentration. The sight of Lou Cameron's superb illustration of *Dr. Jekyll* staring into the mirror while holding the foaming goblet and seeing the hideous face of *Mr Hyde* staring back was enough to make me read the box below and turn the page.

Cameron masterfully set the scene as the eerily ugly Hyde made his way through the brothels and bars of London while rats nibbled on apple cores in the foreground and drunks lay unconscious in the gutter.

There was one sequence which began with a beautiful young servant woman gazing out of her window at night and seeing two male figures approaching each other on the street below. She recognised the little man as Mr Hyde who had, on occasion, visited her master. As they met at the bottom of the page, the taller gentleman tipped his hat in a friendly gesture to Hyde.

When you turned the page over, it was filled with one enormous and shocking illustration of Hyde swinging his knobbly walking stick at the man's head, knocking him backwards towards the viewer. This picture had all the drama of a 3-D movie.

Once he was down, Hyde began jumping up and down continuing to beat him with his stick until he was dead. The final panel of the episode after Hyde walked away was the servant lady lying unconscious in a faint on the floor.

This same artist, Lou Cameron, also produced the drawings

for H.G. Wells's *War Of The Worlds* with stunning Martian machines which stalked the earth's surface on silver tripods. A death ray projected out of the glazed head piece while metallic tentacles dangled from its bulbous chest unit.

The Martians were angry octopus-like creatures who operated their machinery with a ruthless efficiency.

The spectacle on offer in both these comic books was every bit as exciting as a movie and with *The Trout* or Beethoven's *Fifth* in the background, all the more so.

Cameron seemed to specialise in vapours, whether they were the steam rising from a foaming liquid or wisps of cloud crossing in front of a full moon. When characters smoked, the fumes wandered around the room with great purpose. Sometimes his perspectives went a bit off but he was a truly fine illustrator.

Norman Nodell was another good artist who brought Jules Verne's *Journey To The Center of the Earth* to life in spectacular fashion.

The splash page featured his illustration of a charred note with ragged edges reading: 'Go down the crater of Sneffel, that the shadow of Scartaris softly touches before the beginning of July, brave traveller, and you will come to the center of the earth. I did it. -Arne Saknussemm'

Nodell's almost photographic renderings of the craters in Iceland were beautifully realised and he dramatically captured the darkness that young Axel felt when he got lost and his lamp burned out. As the light in the lamp went out Nodell resorted to colourless, tinted line drawings of the panicking Axel tripping and falling.

Nodell also illustrated Washington Irving's New England tale of *Rip Van Winkle.* It was coupled with *The Legend Of Sleepy Hollow* which featured Ichabod Crane, the village schoolmaster, a wonderful character with long spindly legs, giant bat ears and a little pony tail under his three-cornered hat. Ichabod's final confrontation with the headless horseman was more than a little spooky and highly dramatic.

Another Nodell comic was Victor Hugo's *Les Miserables* which, though gruesome and grim, had an exciting vitality to it. *Classics Illustrated* never gave me a light experience and in this way it provided a proper antidote to the cosy comics of Walt Disney. This was particularly true of Dostoyevsky's *Crime And Punishment* which was illustrated by Rudolph Palais. The world of St. Petersburg seen through the eyes of Raskolnikov was a moody and murderous place. Palais, who was clearly influenced by the 1935 film in which Peter Lorre played the doomed Raskolnikov, made his tragic main character look like Lorre. He also made Alyona Ivanovna, the old woman he murdered, very much like an old witch. In fact she may have been the inspiration for the Old Witch in the EC horror comics of the early 1950s.

The murder itself was gory and was followed by another when the elderly pawnbroker's stepsister returned to the flat unexpectedly. But the true drama of the story was Raskolnikov's relentless descent into paranoia.

So while Archie and Veronica were sipping sodas through a straw and Huey, Dewey or Louie were consulting the Junior Woodchuck Manual, Mr Hyde was beating some poor bastard to death in the street and Raskolnikov was murdering the old woman with an axe.

It's no wonder that some issues of *Classics Illustrated* came under the microscope of Dr Frederick Wertham in his book *Seduction Of The Innocent*. This was the tome which formed much of the evidence presented to Senator Estes Kefauver when his committee investigated the comic book industry and its effect on juvenile delinquency in the early 1950s.

But while the storm stirred up by these hearings put Bill Gaines's EC horror and crime comics out of business, *Classics Illustrated* sailed through without any controversy at all. There was, of course, a big difference between the types of comics EC ground out and the ones published by *Classics Illustrated*.

EC had a range of titles like *Tales From The Crypt, Vault of Horror, The Haunt of Fear* and *Crime Suspense Stories*.

I was too young to even know that these comic books existed and I feel certain that my mother Beth would have found them horrific and destroyed them as I'm sure that a censorious eye was cast over all our reading material and if anything beyond the pale came across the threshold we'd have known about it.

My explorations of *Classics Illustrated* continued. The ultimate tale of unforgiving isolation was Daniel Defoe's *Robinson Crusoe*. Once Crusoe found himself shipwrecked and got organized on the island, the time passed dramatically. Every page saw the news that another several years had gone by. As a seven, eight or nine year old boy I wasn't capable of comprehending that much time passing. A year to me was a lifetime so for Crusoe to spend the best part of thirty years alone was utterly incredible to me. True he had the dog, but the dog died. He also came across Man Friday who he taught to speak English. I suppose it was somehow educational for me to confront such realities as time passing. Goofy, Donald and Mickey all lived in a zone where no-one aged and the passage of time didn't seem to occur.

Throughout my childhood there were moments when I would leave home in a temper vowing never to return but I would only ever get as far as the Pixie Trail before I realised that home was where I belonged, so stories like *Robinson Crusoe* and *Swiss Family Robinson* about people cast away from the worlds they belonged in were terribly exciting to me.

Mary Shelly's *Frankenstein* was a ghastly tale in

which the doomed Victor Frankenstein created his monster early in the story then spent the rest of it steeped in regret as he watched his creation murder every person he loved.

Tragedy seemed to mingle with happiness in most of the tales. Quasimodo's love for the beautiful Esmeralda who he rescued dramatically in *The Hunchback Of Notre Dame,* Jean Valjean's persecution in *Les Miserables, Rip Van Winkle* falling asleep a young man and waking up extremely old, Captain Ahab's grim determination to hunt down and kill the white whale *Moby Dick.*

None of these stories left my young mind unchanged. They seemed to challenge everything I took for granted in my life.

The titles I added to my collection included *Hamlet, The Three Musketeers, Ivanhoe, Julius Caesar, The Jungle Book, Macbeth, Great Expectations, Treasure Island, Mutiny On The Bounty, Don Quixote* and *The Invisible Man.*

I would return to reread each of these comic books as the years passed though I never did read the original novels.

When I discovered that the part of London where I resided was for many years the home of Daniel Defoe I made a stab at reading *Robinson Crusoe* but found the prose impenetrable.

So the reading matter of my childhood in Mill Valley was at the lower end of the cultural scale. MAD Magazine made me howl with laughter, Uncle Scrooge took me on fantastic journeys to far off lands and *Classics Illustrated* opened a dungeon door to deep tragedy and mysterious adventure. I enjoyed it.

Chapter 5
From 3-D To CinemaScope

My enchantment with the world of the movies when I was five and six years old was immediate. At the Sequoia Theatre everything excited me: the posters out front, the red carpet and velvet curtains inside, the popcorn, the cartoons, the previews of coming attractions. Every time I'd go to the pictures with my family the experience would cling to me like bubble gum and yet the only souvenir I'd ever have of the movies I had seen would be the ads in the newspaper.

Now the business of advertising is to make us want things we might not need and even savvy individuals fall prey to this most seductive of arts. My father had an expression about things without substance. He'd call it sky meringue and somehow I feel that phrase describes many of the products promoted by Madison Avenue in the early fifties.

Movie advertising had more in common with carnival and circus promotion than it did with soap powder and breakfast cereals but they knew how to penetrate my consciousness and could sell me sky meringue any day of the week.

The first striking example of my being sold a great big plate of steaming hot nothing was 3-D which I became aware of as I gazed across the movie pages in the Chronicle early in 1953.

Younger readers will be used to the term 3D without a hyphen but back in the early fifties there was almost always one between the 3 and the D. Films like *Fort Ti, Man In The Dark* and *Second Chance* had banners across the tops of the ads reading: *3-Dimension.* They all had pictures of movie screens with actors and other images emerging out of them.

3-D in the movies was a craze during the early fifties which came and went very quickly. Hollywood was in serious trouble due to the growing popularity of television. Suddenly on Thanksgiving of 1952 an independently produced movie in 3-D called *Bwana Devil* opened in Los Angeles to sensational business in spite of the fact that every critic in the country panned it. Huge lines snaked around corners past posters depicting a lion leaping off the screen: "A lion in your Lap! A lover in your arms!"

Bwana Devil's enormous success at the boxoffice

became front page news coast-to-coast and it took no time at all for the major studios to jump on the bandwagon. Warner Brothers went into production with *House Of Wax* and by early 1953 a plethora of movies in 3-D rolled out across the nation.

The stereoscopic process, however, was not without problems as it required expensive projection equipment to be installed and patrons needed to wear special glasses. This was all very well for the major exhibitors in big cities but something of a budget buster for the smaller theatres who simply couldn't afford it.

I, of course, knew none of this. I was six years old and all I saw were these wonderful ads in the paper with pictures of men fighting to the death in precariously high places and beautiful busty women leaning provocatively out of movie screens.

As wonderful as it looked, I only actually saw one film in 3-D at the Sequoia and I don't even recall its title. It was a western in black and white for which we had to wear Polaroid glasses and, though I couldn't admit it at the time, it was a boring movie. I couldn't admit it because I wanted to love it. Now, had I seen *House Of Wax* at this time it would have been a different story as that was full of colour and spectacle.

There were a couple of reasons why the 3-D fad came and went so quickly. First was the greed of the studios who demanded avaricious terms from those exhibitors who had already gone to the expense of installing the special projection equipment to show the films. The second was the shoddy quality of most of the 3-D movies which flooded the market by the summer of 1953. While *House Of Wax* and a few others had been of a high standard, the same could not be said of the rest and by September the public appetite for 3-D began to subside. People complained of getting headaches from the glasses and stopped turning out in great numbers.

Warner Brothers had planned to shoot all their films in what the trade described as 'depthies' but as the summer boxoffice turned poisonous they discreetly shelved plans to film *East Of Eden* and *A Star Is Born* in the stereoscopic process.

Hollywood, in trying to find a new way of luring the public out from in front of their television sets had, for that brief time, thought 3-D was the answer. But, as it became clear that it wasn't, they kept their people working on the problem and 20th Century Fox came up with a system partially inspired by another cinematic innovation called Cinerama.

Cinerama was a new filmic experience which had debuted sensationally in New York a few months before *Bwana Devil's* great opening. It required three projectors, a curved screen and stereophonic sound. On Market Street in San

Francisco the Orpheum Theatre would soon be converted to show *This Is Cinerama* which famously opened with a roller coaster ride. I went to see it and it was exciting but there were two lines between the three projected images on the screen so that it wasn't one seamless picture.

Spyrous Skouras who was heading up Fox at the time told his technicians to design something like Cinerama but cheaper. The process they came up with was given a brand new name: CinemaScope.

CinemaScope as portrayed in the advertisements was a horizontal screen which looked as though it wrapped around you like Cinerama. The reality was nothing like that. It was simply a rectangular picture which was longer than it was tall. Up until that time the image on movie screens was almost square but the shape of CinemaScope was like a letter-box.

The first movie released in this new format was *The Robe*. I remember seeing this at the Sequoia and I was as excited about seeing CinemaScope as I was about seeing *The Robe*.

Before it got to the Sequoia *The Robe* opened at the Tamalpais up in San Anselmo, advertised in the Independent Journal as an 'Exclusive Marin County Showing.'

'The Tamalpais Theater,' read the ad, 'Takes pride in announcing that it has been granted the privilege of bringing to the theatregoers of this area the first motion picture in CinemaScope - THE MODERN MIRACLE YOU SEE

WITHOUT GLASSES!'

Even at six years old I already knew the music which accompanied the 20th Century Fox logo with its searchlights set against a night sky. But for the opening of *The Robe* the Fox edifice and searchlights were superimposed instead on a red velvet theatre curtain and the music was that of the movie's score. The credits rolled in beautiful shiny gold letters and when they were finished the curtain opened, unveiling not only a scene of Roman gladiators but CinemaScope itself.

'This new-dimensional photographic marvel,' the ad in the IJ trumpeted, 'Will bring you the greatest story of love, faith and overwhelming spectacle ever brought to the screen.'

Now I grew up in an atheist household and this was definitely not a film my parents would want to see in a million years but my sister Nell, being a bookworm, had read the Bible and loved its stories and, though *The Robe* was not from the Bible itself, it was about the garment Jesus Christ was wearing at the time of his crucifixion.

Richard Burton played Marcellus Gallio, a Roman Tribune who supervised Christ's execution and then became haunted and ultimately converted to Christ's cause. The screenplay was co-written by Albert Maltz, one of the blacklisted Hollywood Ten, under the pseudonym John B. Sherry.

As it turned out, what passed for my Biblical education

occurred exclusively at the Sequoia. Hollywood in the 1950s ground out a steady diet of Christian religious epics.

One of the great excitements of *The Robe* for me was Jean Simmons who I fell madly in love with. The end of the film with her and Richard Burton marching nobly to their deaths was repeated at the beginning of the sequel *Demetrius And The Gladiators* which Fox managed to get into movie theatres by the following summer. It too was in CinemaScope which, unlike 3-D, went on to become something of an industry standard for many years.

There were still a few 3-D movies to come: *Hondo, Dial M For Murder* and *Kiss Me Kate* but the dawn of Cinemascope marked the beginning of the end for the Depthies. There was, however, another stereoscopic experience which I found just as alluring: 3-D comic books.

During the summer of 1953 as the 3-Dimensional movie craze reached its climax the comic book equivalents began appearing in magazine racks. Each comic had its own special glasses made of cardboard with one red lens and one blue. They looked so cool and the pages inside were not printed in full colour like other comics.

What you saw in a 3-D comic without the glasses was a blurry picture printed in red and another practically identical one in blue. Certain elements in the foreground of each frame were printed in the one position, red on blue like the frame outline but the background imagery would be separated sideways, red from blue by as much as an eighth of an inch sometimes. This created the illusion of depth when you looked through the glasses and was very striking.

The 3-D glasses were an exciting thing on their own though they were only worn for reading the comic books unlike in movies like *Back To The Future* where one of the villain's gang had them on all the time.

These exciting looking periodicals, however, all cost 25 cents each and that was prohibitive. As comic books were a mere dime, to pay two bits for one was out of the question. Also you couldn't exactly read them at the bus depot because you needed the glasses which could not be removed without damaging the comic book.

I did only buy one 3-D comic and that was *Batman* which came with special Batman glasses which you had to punch holes in and tie a string through to keep them on your head. The effect was fun but the truth was that I didn't really like Bob Kane's illustration style. I loved the imagery of the *Batman* costume and the bat-shaped logo. I also enjoyed the searchlight signal which somehow stopped on nothing up in the sky with a plate-like projection of a bat. But the story lines got on my nerves and they always seemed to end up in these amusement parks where everything was full of gigantic furniture.

The reality though was that reading these comic books was a formula for getting headaches. Before too long the craze was over and 3-D of any kind vanished forever. At least that's how it seemed. When I was a bit older Warners re-released a double bill of *House of Wax* and *Phantom of the Rue Morgue* complete with the glasses. I went and loved both movies.

The truth is that I was enchanted with the depiction of 3-D in the advertising but my actual experience of it in its heyday was practically nonexistent. It was something which was happening inside movie theatres I never entered and comic books I couldn't afford to buy. This, of course, made it unattainable and therefore deeply exotic.

I never really wised up to the carnival barker which was the movie business. During the 1960s I fell under the spell of William Castle, a flimflam man if ever there was one. I never missed one of his films though I could see that his gimmicks were much better than his movies. More about William Castle can be found in chapter 24.

It was that ludicrous promise of something fantastic which made me surrender my money. Sometimes it was terrific fun but many times it was disappointing in the extreme. So I became a little more savvy in making my choices…but not a lot.

Mill Valley Days

Chapter 6

A Cultural Link To Life In Manhattan

The Myers house at 10 Seymour Avenue was never short of reading material. Our bookshelves were well-stocked with an interesting mix of classic literature, modern fiction and leftward leaning political works, many written by friends of my parents.

Our coffee table was always festooned with magazines and newspapers. We took the San Francisco Chronicle daily, the pages of which often mingled with left-wing weeklies like The National Guardian and The People's World.

But the magazine which could always be found in abundance on our coffee table was The New Yorker which arrived in the mail every week.

Both my parents were a bit like political refugees in the warm hills of Marin County. They had little to do with the social side of life in Mill Valley though they were far from friendless. It's just that all their close friends were, like them, of the political left and the early 1950s was a pretty scary time to be of that persuasion.

The reason we had come west in 1952 was that my father Blackie was simply unable to keep a job for more than a few months before the FBI would turn up to inform his employer of what a dangerous radical he was.

Blackie was indeed a radical trade unionist and a sailor by profession. He had been, for much of the 1930s and 40s, a vice president of the National Maritime Union, a prime target of the federal government in the post-war era.

An election was held in the year of my birth and all the left-wing executives of the NMU, Blackie included, were voted out of office. In addition to this the government had taken his passport away so that he couldn't ship out. This meant he had to do any job he could get in New York as he had a family to feed.

We moved from our apartment on West 12th Street in Greenwich Village to another on West 105th Street. We were at this location when my brother Jim was born. Our next move was to Bethel, Connecticut.

Blackie carried hod, washed windows and dishes but no matter what the job was, the men in the Brooks Brothers suits would turn up to finger him to his employer who would then let him go.

We had been living in Bethel for almost two years when my parents got word of the chance of employment on the waterfront in San Francisco through the longshore union, the ILWU, whose president was Harry Bridges. Harry and Blackie were both hardened veterans of the often violent and brutal struggle to build the American trade union movement.

Our time at Bethel had been wonderful. We lived in a beautiful wooden house with a big porch surrounded by a sloping lawn on a hill. We had snowy white winters and would spend idyllic summers at our friend Fred Field's beautiful estate at Red Hill.

I only ever heard Fred referred to as 'Fred Field' so I didn't know, as a child, that his full name was Frederick Vanderbilt Field and that his embrace of socialism made him a class traitor in the wealthy and powerful world from which he came.

Before we left Connecticut, Fred was convicted in federal court for refusing to divulge the names of contributors to the Civil Rights Congress Bail Fund of which he was a secretary. Fred and the other trustees were ordered to give the names of those who had contributed to this fund. He refused and was sentenced to nine months in a federal penitentiary which he served alongside Dashiell Hammett, the creator of *Sam Spade* and *The Continental Op.*

Now before I get too wrapped up in historical data, I must return to The New Yorker magazine. It was probably the most important cultural link, certainly for my mother, to the life she and Blackie had lived in Manhattan throughout the 1930s and 40s.

Beth was a writer. She was a published novelist and had been a journalist on The Daily Worker and had met my father when assigned to interview him at the NMU.

The anti-Communist witch-hunts of the post-war era turned Blackie and Beth's world upside down. In a short space of time they went from being popular folks about town to pariahs. People they knew well in Greenwich Village suddenly didn't know them at all.

So while Black did a variety of labouring jobs in Manhattan, up in Connecticut Beth wrote furiously and produced several novels which there seemed to be a market for.

She was never proud of these books as she claimed they were all done for money but each one was in print throughout my childhood and seemed to sell reasonably well. Titles like *The Enchanted Land, The Steady Flame* and *The Doctor Is A Lady* would arrive in boxes from her agent as they were published.

While we were still living in New York, Beth and Blackie collaborated on a book based on his adventures as a seaman which was published in 1948 under the title *Home is the Sailor*.

Beth was constantly reading. She always seemed to have a book, magazine or newspaper in her hand and whenever I would have to write something for school her criticism was always constructive and helpful.

I think it was the quality of the writing which kept her reading The New Yorker and she was terribly amused by what she thought of as snobbish prose. Much of the magazine's output was of the socially lofty variety.

The reviews tended to presume that those reading the magazine had all the advantages of a good education so there was no need to talk down.

Practically all of the movies we went to as a family in Marin County were ones which The New Yorker had recommended: *Androcles and the Lion, The Lavender Hill Mob, Knock On Wood.*

Their movie section bore the subtitle: 'Films of more than routine interest are described in this section.' The vast majority of these were foreign language European films. Hollywood had to pull an impressive rabbit out of its hat to be included in the New Yorker's film list. Needless to say there was never a mention of *Creature from the Black Lagoon* or *The Beast from 20,000 Fathoms*.

The editorial page was titled 'The Talk Of The Town' and featured a beautiful illustration of an aristocratic looking gentleman wearing a monacle and writing with a quill. A cluster of tall buildings rose from a grassy landscape and an owl sat in the foreground. The text below this heading always used the royal "we," even though it was clearly from the typewriter of one person.

At the time that the House Un-American Activities Committee (HUAC), under the chairmanship of J. Parnell Thomas, was holding their 1947 hearings in Hollywood, 'The Talk Of The Town' stated: "This magazine traffics with all sorts of questionable characters. Our procedure so far has been to examine the manuscript, not the writer; the picture, not the artist. We have not required a statement of political belief or a blood count. This still seems like a sensible approach, although falling short of Representative J. Parnell Thomas's standard."

By the early 1950s with the emergence of Senator McCarthy, the red scare was more difficult to circumnavigate yet The New Yorker seemed to remain above the fracas though I'm sure they were no longer able to use pieces by people condemned by the committee.

My oldest sister Nell, sharing Beth's passion for literature, was also an avid reader. As I had an aversion to what I considered to be 'too many words,' I didn't read any of the text of the magazine but would scan each page, lingering on the cartoons, some of which left me mystified and many others which made me laugh out loud.

I particularly liked their cartoonist Charles Addams who became a Myers family favourite. Studying his somewhat gruesome output was a very rewarding exercise. His illustrations were rich in detail and style and I could spot an Addams cartoon immediately. His signature was always the same and read 'Chas Addams.'

Like all those in The New Yorker, his cartoons were in black and white but they were not mere pen sketches. Each was an intricate painting with fine components and subtle shading.

Often it took a bit of time to figure out the gag in an Addams cartoon but he rarely disappointed; the little girl in the grim family had cut out a string of paper dolls all of which had two legs except for one which had three. I remember gazing at this for some time before spotting the three-legged doll.

As time went by Simon & Schuster published a collection of Addams cartoons from the New Yorker entitled *Homebodies* and it immediately found its way onto our bookshelf.

The television sit-com *The Addams Family* didn't happen until the 1960s so throughout the 1950s he was only known to those who read the New Yorker.

The covers of the New Yorker were always in full colour and usually depicted life on the east coast. Golden autumn leaves and snow-covered parks alternated with illustrations of the many cultural activities on offer in Manhattan and always from an interesting viewpoint: the musicians in an orchestra pit, seen from the brass section or a nicely painted picture of people in a museum. Another cover featured a close-up of an orchestra's conductor at an outdoor concert experiencing the first few raindrops. Emblazoned across the top of each cover was the subtle but utterly recognizable logo.

In a subconscious way, seeing The New Yorker arrive in the post every week, triggered some kind of awareness in me of the city I was born in. I have a clear memory of knowing that every child in my class at Homestead School had come into this world at Marin General Hospital and that I was the only one who had been born elsewhere. It gave me a feeling of pride though I don't ever recall it being an issue.

On lazy walks home from school in good weather I would daydream about sights and sensations I'd experienced in another part of the world. Some days it would be snow in Connecticut, others it was descending into the Manhattan subway with its underground tunnels and trains.

It wasn't that I was unaware of the beauty of Mill Valley - I clearly enjoyed it and spent much of my young life alone on the Pixie Trail - but somehow it was just something I took for granted. There was no snow in Mill Valley. Nor were there subway trains and it was the clear memories of these experiences which often dominated my thoughts. It would be a good many years before my nostalgic tendencies shifted its focus from childhood in New York to childhood in Marin County.

Chapter 7
A Curious Connection To *On The Waterfront*

By the summer of 1954 the promise of work on the San Francisco waterfront for my father Blackie had not yet materialised. We had been in Mill Valley eighteen months and he was now in business for himself delivering dry cleaning for a shop down on Locust Avenue. He did this in a bright red Ford panel truck he'd purchased. He even had cards printed by our friend Wally Kibbee which read: Fred Myers, Dry Cleaning.

This was my first summer vacation from

Homestead School and among my diversions was regular attendance at the Sequoia Theatre seeing such movies as *Demetrius and the Gladiators, The Caine Mutiny* and *Susan Slept Here.*

In July my sisters Nell and Kate went off with the Hallinan boys and their mother Vivian to stay at the family's cabin up in Mather. Vin Hallinan was still in prison on tax evasion charges and it's possible that his going to jail was one of the reasons that Harry Bridges and the other executives of the ILWU were reluctant to let Blackie work on the waterfront. The government had come down hard on Vin for defending Harry and possibly the union was wary of giving them any more provocation.

My mother Beth, in addition to raising four Myers kids was also a published author and her agent in New York regularly sent a big box with copies of the latest novel. During that summer it was *The Doctor Is A Lady,* all about Enid Barnes, a beautiful young general practitioner from a wealthy background who set up her medical practice in a small town in Connecticut and had to fight for acceptance by the locals.

This was also the summer that the movie *On*

The Waterfront came out. It opened in San Francisco in August and didn't make it to Marin until October when it played at the Rafael. It was in early 1955 that it finally came to the Sequoia.

The trailer caught my attention in a way different to other movies as it had to do with working men on the docks and that was close to home. I recognized the clothes and look of the stevedores on screen as familiar and real.

My habit of drawing copies of the movie ads in the Chronicle continued and I was particularly taken by the photo of Marlon Brando and Eva Marie Saint running down an alley being chased by a big truck.

The movie was a huge success at the boxoffice and has become a classic, primarily for the acting but the political world of my parents had much more to do with this film than I could possibly realise at the age of seven.

I was aware of Senator McCarthy and of HUAC and that Harry, Vin and all my parents' close friends were considered dangerous radicals by the establishment. Certain things like the Rosenbergs being executed brought this reality home in a chilling way.

I knew that my father had been a vice president of the National Maritime Union in New York and that he'd been blacklisted. I was also aware that the FBI was not regarded fondly in our household. But there was little evidence for me to understand my parents' situation. I'd seen a few press photos of a younger Blackie but neither he nor Beth advertised their past. In conversation things would come up which I would find surprising like famous people that they knew. Blackie knew Billie Holiday, Paul Robeson and Woody Guthrie.

On The Waterfront was written by Budd Schulberg produced by Sam Spiegel and directed by Elia Kazan. It told the story of Terry Malloy, a sad ex-boxer working on the Hoboken docks as a longshoreman and doing dirty jobs for Johnny Friendly, the gangster in charge of the crooked waterfront union. When Malloy reflected on his complicity in the murder of a friend, his conscience began bothering him and he ultimately testified against Friendly.

Though this film was made on location in New Jersey the previous winter, its genesis went back to the late 1940s when playwright Arthur Miller and Elia Kazan attempted to get Miller's screenplay of *The Hook* produced at Columbia Pictures.

Arthur Miller and Elia Kazan had worked together on a few projects, most significantly the Broadway production of *Death of a Salesman* which Kazan had directed.

The Hook was based on Miller's research into the real life murder and disappearance of Pete Panto in the late 1930s. Panto was an activist from the Brooklyn docks fighting the corruption in the east coast Longshoremens' union.

Harry Cohn, the head of Columbia Pictures, wanted to make *The Hook* but said he had to clear it first with Roy Brewer, the right wing head of the stagehands union, the IATSE, who acted as an advisor to the big studios on subversive content. Brewer suggested they should make the villains Communists rather than gangsters.

"You don't want to give the impression," Brewer said, "That your picture is a plea for the support of Bridges, do you?"

Although Kazan seemed open to the idea of making the villains Communists, Miller was adamantly opposed and ultimately withdrew his script.

So *The Hook* never got made but during that trip to Hollywood Kazan had introduced Miller to Marilyn Monroe, who the writer would fall in love with and eventually marry.

Another important development was Kazan's decision, in 1952, to name names. His testimony before the committee was seen by the left as a betrayal and it drove a wedge between him and Miller.

Budd Schulberg used the same source material of Pete Panto in writing his screenplay for *Waterfront* but did not bend to Columbia's desire to make the gangsters Communists. Schulberg, by this time, had also been a friendly witness before HUAC as was the actor who played Johnny Friendly, Lee J. Cobb.

When I first came to London I met Elliott Sullivan, an actor who was named by Cobb and he described the last time he'd seen him. He said that Cobb had thrown his arms around him at a party and told him how much his friendship meant to him. Elliott subsequently learned that he'd already named him.

To use the vernacular of the day, this movie was written by a stool pigeon, directed by a stool pigeon and starred a stool pigeon. And the story was a thinly disguised justification for being a stool pigeon.

The other actors in the picture, like Marlon Brando, Rod Steiger and Karl Malden, were too young to have been involved in the political world that Kazan, Schulberg and Cobb had been such a part of. They had indeed all been committed leftists and each adapted potent justifications for their testimony.

While Kazan and Miller were developing *The Hook*, the director wanted to meet my father. This was accomplished through the writer Walter Bernstein who introduced him to Blackie.

"He asked me if I could help him meet Blackie Myers," said Bernstein in his chapter of *Tender Comrades (by Patrick McGilligan and Paul Buhle)*. "I knew Blackie slightly and we went down and met him and some of his merchant seamen friends in a bar one afternoon. We drank and talked about politics for a few hours. But Gadge (Kazan) actually did want to meet these guys. After we talked, as we were walking away, Gadge said to me how much he admired them, and how this was the side that he was on. That was his sincere view."

Bernstein who was subsequently blacklisted himself could never forgive Elia Kazan because he felt that he was probably the only one in his position who could have made a difference by standing up to the committee.

Bernstein found the movie a total justification for Kazan's, Schulberg's and Cobb's testimony. "When I saw *On The Waterfront* later on, all I could see was a rationalization for his (Schulberg) and Kazan's informing."

Most actors will, on the other hand, rave about Brando and Steiger's scene in the back seat of the taxi cab. Brando did win an oscar for this role but he, too, could never forgive Kazan for his betrayal.

I learned from my sister that Pete Panto, who's body was ultimately found in the river, had also been a good friend of Blackie's, so the source material was very close to home.

But life seems to move too fast for history to ever catch up with the realities of the present. All I remember Blackie saying about this movie, which he took me to see at the Sequoia, was that he knew the guy it was based on.

The performances in *On The Waterfront* were indeed very good and Brando definitely deserved his golden statue. Lee J. Cobb also was stunningly good as Johnny Friendly and the same goes for Karl Malden, Rod Steiger and Eva Marie Saint. It's a genuinely moving and moral story which is much easier to enjoy if you don't know any of the details from behind the scenes.

All those who named names had to live with what they had done and some were more successful at it than others. Kazan didn't look like he had any problems about it while others, like Clifford Odetts and even Lee J. Cobb apparently found it difficult to live with the guilt.

Another friend of my parents who Cobb had named was Alvah Bessie who eventually wrote a novel called *The UnAmericans* which featured a character partially based on the actor.

Alvah had quit his job as a journalist covering the Spanish Civil War and joined up to fight Franco with the Abraham Lincoln Brigade and, like many of his friends, wound up badly blacklisted in the anti-red hysteria that followed the second world war. One of the many phrases coined by HUAC was a description of people like Alvah as 'Premature Anti-Fascists,' the implication being that no decent American had a right to be anti fascist before World War II.

It was in this topsy turvey political landscape that I grew up. I don't remember hearing anything about politics from my friends at Homestead School. It just never came up but that was not the case when we were socialising with my parents' friends. People like Barney and Babbie Dreyfus, Tom and Grace Cox and countless other adults all had strong political opinions and expressed them. Needless to say they were mostly in contradiction to those I'd read in the Chronicle.

The Chronicle regularly ran headlines using phrases like 'Reds' or 'Commies' and such jargon was very upsetting to me at a young age.

It truly was the era of the scoundrel. People like Richard Nixon and Ronald Reagan built their political careers on anti-Communism and a vast majority of American citizens went along with it. So there was me. Listening intensely to Marxist rhetoric one minute and howling with laughter at Road Runner cartoons at the Sequoia the next.

Chapter 8

Coonskin Caps at Bennett's Variety Store

There must have been kids whose parents told them all about fashion and popularity. How else would boys know when boody cuffs were in or out as they invariably were from time to time throughout my young life?

I make this observation from the standpoint of someone who grew up in a family that considered such topics to be totally insignificant and not worthy of discussion.

Because my folks were not remotely well off, our clothes tended to be practical rather than fashionable. At the beginning of each school term my mother would take my brother Jim and I to Mosher's and buy us each a new pair of brown shoes. I don't recall any debate about the shoes' colour. It was always brown and they started out looking pretty good but after a week of the kind of punishment a young boy puts his footwear through, the leather became scuffed and the toes began to turn up. This always upset me.

I admired the attire of adult men. The toes on their shoes never turned up so why did mine? And something about the brown leather which took such a beating in the playground and out on the Pixie Trail just made these shoes look like hell. Goofy's shoes turned up. Clowns' shoes turned up. My shoes turned up.

Men in movies and magazines wore sharp suits with ties and their shoes were flat. I guess the real problem was that all of my role models were adults. Whenever there were kids in a movie they were always winy and annoying. I thought of myself being like film stars such as Kirk Douglas and Cary Grant, not high-voiced freckle-faced children.

Fashion didn't really play a significant role during my early years at Homestead School, at least not in a straight-forward clothes-conscious way. The 1950s in America, however, was a storm centre of conspicuous consumption and one of the forces driving this machine was conformity. Keeping up with the Joneses was a way of life embraced by at least half of the people I went to school with.

The Myers family stood back from this parade as it passed by for a variety of reasons, the main one being political. Both my parents were extremely left wing and, like many of their friends, were experiencing the difficulties of blacklisting during this rabidly anti-Communist era.

Blackie and Beth made no attempt to fit into the society we were growing up in. They had nothing to do with the PTA or any social gatherings in which they had to mingle with other parents. They had plenty of good friends with whom they spent a lot of time but the parents and teachers at Homestead School were not amongst them.

By the winter of 1954 I was in Mrs Dempster's second grade class and I had already discovered the delights of after-school visits to the record shop up by the Sequoia Theatre. The lady there was very friendly and would allow my friend Glen Pritzker and I to listen to the latest discs in a special booth. We'd hear *Three Coins in the Fountain* by Frank Sinatra and *This Ole House* by Rosemary Clooney. I particularly loved *Mr Sandman* by the Chordettes because the instrumentation and the vocal harmonies conjured up images of a magical cloud land in my mind.

We were aware of the shows on television because of the ads ABC, CBS and NBC ran in the Chronicle.

In order to see what was on TV, we would turn to Dennis Brogan and watch them at his grandfather's house down near the playground. The earliest shows I remember seeing were the first episodes of *Disneyland* on ABC.

The programme would open with an animation of Tinkerbell spreading fairy dust across the screen as the title appeared to the sounds of Cliff Edwards singing *When You Wish Upon a Star*. The announcer would tell us of the four worlds, one of which we would visit that week: *Frontierland – tall tales and true from the legendary past, Tomorrowland – promise of things to come, Adventureland - the wonder world of nature's own realm. Fantasyland - the happiest kingdom of them all.*

Then Walt Disney would come on and introduce that week's subject in his folksy and friendly manner. He'd always pick up a book from his desk and show it to us. He seemed like such a nice guy. It was lucky for me that my parents hadn't bad mouthed Mr Disney to us at all. In fact they must have made a decision not to, because he was a notorious anti-Communist and anti-trade unionist who had been a friendly witness before the House UnAmerican Activities Committee when it came to Hollywood in 1947. Disney had actually named names to the committee. Blackie and Beth were not shy about mentioning others who had done this, like Ronald Reagan, but Disney somehow got special dispensation, for we, as a family, always went to his movies and never a bad word was spoken about him.

The first *Disneyland* I remember seeing at Mr Brogan's was entitled *Operation Undersea* which took us behind the scenes of filming Jules Verne's *20,000 Leagues Under the Sea.* I knew the story from the *Classics Illustrated* comic book and seeing James Mason as Captain Nemo fighting the giant squid fascinated me.

The following week was the debut of *Davy Crockett – Indian Fighter.* Davy was played by Fess Parker who was tall, handsome and attractively low key. He and his sidekick Buddy Ebsen spent much of this episode making General Jackson's Major look foolish. Crockett wore a coonskin cap with a tail that hung down his neck. One thing which endeared him to viewers was his unpretentious manner and refusal to be intimidated by the military brass. He did things his way and was not going to be told otherwise.

One of the hit films of 1954 was the sci-fi giant ant epic *Them!* which starred James Arness. Disney's casting people screened this Warner Brothers picture for Walt thinking he would want Arness to play Crockett. Instead Disney spotted Fess Parker playing a small role as a pilot who had been incarcerated in a mental hospital after reporting a giant queen ant flying in the skies.

Though Parker was a Texan and had been raised on a farm, he couldn't ride a horse and was actually a highly educated young man more interested in drawing room comedies than cowboy films. But he took the role which made him into a huge star.

I don't suppose Walt Disney had any idea just how successful this show was going to be. The marketing strategy of the *Disneyland* television program was to lay the foundations for selling the theme park which was under construction at that time, but *Davy Crockett* took off like a rocket. By the time the next installment, *Davy Crockett Goes to Washington,* aired in January 1955, the country had gone wild for it and kids were buying coonskin caps, buckskin jackets, Davy Crockett lunch pails and goodness knows what else, all marketed with zeal by the Disney corporation.

I remember kids coming to school wearing coonskin caps and carrying Davy Crockett lunch boxes. It was in February that the last show, *Davy Crockett at the Alamo,* came on the television. It was the last one because he got killed in that battle, but it was only the beginning of a marketing phenomenon which was amazing to behold.

In March three separate recordings of the Davy Crockett song came into the top 20. Written by the film's composer George Bruns with words by its writer Tom Blackburn, *The Ballad of Davy Crockett* sung by Bill Hayes came in at number 5, while Fess Parker's version arrived at number 15 and yet another performed by Tennessee Ernie Ford came along at number 20. By the next month Hayes was number 1, Parker number 5 and Tennessee Ernie was at number 9.

I had mixed feelings about this whole thing. On the

one hand I thoroughly enjoyed the shows and found Fess Parker's Crockett to be a charming character indeed. I did, however, come from a family of non-conformists and the sight of the lemming-like rush to buy anything associated with the show left me downright *plum flummeried.*

My brother doesn't remember this but I think the pair of us began making the case for the trail-blazer Daniel Boone as someone who was also worthy of attention. We'd say this to anyone who would listen. Not that anyone would. The Davy Crockett marketing machine was a mighty beast indeed. Entire displays at Bennett's, Ben Franklin and Safeway were given over to the sales of Crockett merchandise.

Who knows? Maybe Blackie and Beth would have bought us a Davy Crockett lunch box if we'd asked for one, but it became a matter of principle not to want one.

This was probably my first experience of being outside the magic circle of mass conformity. It certainly was not to be the last.

Chapter 9
Radio Nights At 10 Seymour

In a strange way my parents, Blackie and Beth, lived in another time and place from the Mill Valley I was growing up in during the 1950s.

Blackie, in particular, had nothing to do with a huge slice of American life during that era. He never, to my knowledge, ever ate a hamburger with fries or drank Coca-Cola. I don't think he even considered what they sold at C's Drive-In to be food at all.

My mother Beth probably knew more about what was going on culturally than my father because she read so much but she too stood at a distance from the world we existed in.

America during the 1950s was a very conformist society and my parents were not of that persusasion.

When the winter season came around we were not allowed to put up our tree until Christmas Eve when all around us had them decorated with lights on days before. Electric lights on our tree were forbidden. And then, of course, there was the business of the television.

Blackie would not allow us to have a television set. This was the early 1950s and, with a few notable exceptions like the Symmes family, I don't remember any of the kids I went to school with not having one.

It was, after all, the era of the television but, though we had to make do without one, our family was not culturally deprived. We had the radio, gramophone records, The New Yorker magazine each week and the Chronicle every day. Plus my sister Nell always bought *Screen Stories* magazine and we all made regular visits to the Sequoia and other movie theatres in Marin County.

My father had no interest in the trinkets which we often associate with the 1950s. The wonderful American travel writer and humourist Bill Bryson has described his dad inviting neighbours into their house in Des Moines to admire the new fridge or mixer or some brand new gadget. His descriptions run so contrary to the lives of Blackie and Beth that I find it charming in the extreme. For a start my parents never discussed products. If products had ever been discussed in our house I would probably be able to tell you what the make of our radio was.

Most discussions around the dinner table were political in nature and it gave us kids a window onto the capitalist society we were living in.

We had a very diverse record collection which included popular classics of my mother's choosing like Beethoven's *Eroica.* In addition there were cast recordings of Broadway shows like *The King And I* and *Sound of Music.* Jazz was represented by Fats Waller and Louis Armstrong. And, of course, there was also the radio.

One evening each week, Nellie, Katie, Jimmy and I would all gather up in my parents' bedroom at the top of our house and huddle around the radio. It was an old model, certainly from the 1940s. Sitting close to it in the semi-darkness, the light from its dial display reflected on our faces as we sat, totally engrossed by the four or five dramatic and entertaining programmes which played one after the other on KNBC.

The Whistler was creepy. The sound of a man whistling an eerie tune preceded this weird voice saying: "I am the Whistler and I know many things for I walk by night." He would then introduce a tale of treachery and deceit which always had an uncharitable twist at the end. It wasn't pleasant but it was certainly engaging.

The Lone Ranger was exciting and somehow reassuring. "By special recording," the hearty announcer thundered, "General Mills, the makers of *Wheaties,* the breakfast of champions and *Cheerios,* the oat cereal ready to eat, presents *The Lone Ranger!"* Then it was a full orchestral performance of the William Tell overture and a shout of "Hi Ho Silver!"

Fibber McGee and Molly was funny and featured the Great Gildersleeves whose voice I loved for its deep bass quality.

This was usually followed by *Rocky Fortune* starring Frank Sinatra. Each programme began with a blaring bluesey trumpet and Sinatra would introduce his story as the hapless *Rocky* who drifted from job to job and always found himself embroiled in some criminal intrigue. Sinatra signed on to do a fairly long season of these shows but turned his back on them when he won his 1954 Oscar for *From Here to Eternity,* making his dramatic show business comeback.

The most exciting programme of the evening, however, was *Dragnet.* Walter Schumann's unforgettable four notes, *Dom-da-dom-dom,* ushered us into a world of danger where all the voices were serious and scary. Jack Webb spent most of the thirty minutes sounding serious and scary as he took us through that week's case, tracking down and arresting criminals.

Webb was something of a pioneer in radio drama and *Dragnet* was his creation. You'd often hear him and his colleagues lapsing into irrelevant chit-chat in an attempt to simulate realism. They also worked hard at dramatising the tedium of police activity.

The late Stan Freberg made wonderful fun of *Dragnet* on his Capitol recording of *St George and the Dragon-Net* where he zeroed in on the irrelevant chit-chat beautifully. The disc went to number one in the charts.

The announcers on *Dragnet* all had the same dispassionate quality as they delivered lines like: "The story you are about to hear is true. Only the names have been changed to protect the innocent."

Each week's episode played out on a landscape of our imaginations. The sound effects painted pictures for us. Every footstep was crystal clear as were the opening and closing of doors, the breaking of glass and many other noises which we might not even have noticed if it was a film we were watching.

After the initial *Dom-Da-Dom-Dom,* one of the scary male voices would tell us: 'You're a detective sergeant. You're assigned to robbery detail. A store clerk has been murdered, shot to death in a robbery. The holdup man is described as tall, well-dressed. He escapes in a taxi cab. Your job….Get him.' *Dom-Da-Dom-Dom! Dom-Da-Dom-Dom-Dommm….*

Then came the ad for Chesterfield cigarettes which changed the tone completely with its persuasive pitch for smokers to switch because of virtues such as 'mild flavour' and 'quality.'

Next Sergeant Friday told us: 'It was Thursday, 8.29 pm. We were working out of homicide. My partner is Ben Romero...'

The reality was that this was highly dramatic radio and we never missed an episode.

The criminals usually had a very ordinary quality about them which was probably innovative at the time. Webb's character, however, was constantly occupying the moral high ground and sharing his somewhat bigoted opinions with the audience.

At the end of the programme, after all the heavy drama, Webb would lighten up and come out of character to deliver his personal endorsement for Chesterfield cigarettes stressing again their mildness and quality (See chapter 25).

All these programmes had full orchestral accompaniment unlike some lesser shows which featured only an organ playing the music. I surmised that it was one sign of quality radio to have more than an organ to guide your emotions through the twists and turns of the tale being told.

It was truly wonderful that we were able to experience radio in this way for, in reality, this was not the era of the radio at all. *Dragnet* was, by this time, already a television programme as were most of the mainstream radio shows, so we were actually getting in on the last chance to hear old-time radio before it vanished forever.

Whenever I had to stay home sick from school I would lie in my parents' bed and listen to *Art Linkletter's House Party* which was a kind of light headed chat show. He had a friendly voice and an easy manner and I always enjoyed listening to him.

I also used to listen to Arthur Godfrey who had a talent show. Godfrey was a slightly peculiar phenomenon. With the voice of someone with a permanent cold he'd plod his way through this talent show making these odd, unfunny jokes which made the audience roar with laughter. His main sponsor was Lipton Tea and because he was such a huge success he could get away with making gentle fun of the products he'd advertise which practically nobody else did in the 1950s.

Of course we knew nothing of the historical circumstances which had made such huge stars out of these people. We were only experiencing them in the vacuum of their current popularity. It turned out that Godfrey was also something of a pioneer in the broadcast industry as he was one of the first to speak in a folksy, conversational way at a time when most people on the radio announced in a stiff and inflexible manner.

I think all the virtues of good radio can be heard in the 1950s recordings of Stan Freberg. The combination of inventive writing, fine music, sound effects and strong characters take you into a special zone which simply wouldn't exist if you could see what was happening.

I used to think that I could tell by the sound of a man's voice on a record or radio whether or not he had a moustache. Of course I was always miles off the mark but the fact was that my imagination was made to work by the lack of visuals.

It was Sara Wilcox at our local record store, Village Music, who first played Freberg for me when he brought out his parody of Harry Belafonte's *Banana Boat*. The Freberg recordings of the 1950s made wonderful fun of everything that took itself seriously in that monochrome era and half a century later my own kids love listening to them.

Freberg also had the finest musical accompaniment in the business: Billy May, George Bruns, Les Baxter and Billy Liebert. Jack Webb himself actually lent Freberg the services of *Dragnet* composer Walter Schumann for his first parody of that show.

One of the regular targets for the Freberg machine were the rock and roll records which were pushing jazz out of the top 40. He produced masterful lampoons of *Heartbreak Hotel,*

The Great Pretender and *Sh-Boom*.

Every year on Christmas Eve, I'd join my sisters and brother on a long walk through Mill Valley to each of our family friends' houses to deliver presents, sing carols and drink hot cocoa. On one of these occasions in the early 1960s, when we got to the Dreyfus house up in Blithedale Canyon, we were handed a present by Babbie and Jared. It was a Capitol LP entitled *Stan Freberg Presents the United States of America.* It wasn't long before I knew this record by heart and right up until Jared's death in 2011 we would quote lines from it in our emails to each other.

In a strange way it was the limitations of radio which made the performers work that much harder to create a world that you couldn't visit through any other medium except imagination.

It's only the historically curious who now have any idea of what the radio era was like. FDR's fireside chats, Orson Welles sending the nation into a panic with his Mercury Theatre production of *War of the Worlds* and weekly visits into people's homes by stars like Bing Crosby, Jack Benny and Bob Hope who all gave the impression to listeners that they were close personal friends.

Radio still has a tremendous power but we now have television and the internet which tend to eclipse this amazing medium which saw our predecessors through the Great

Depression and the Second World War.

It is, however, a unique form of storytelling which I continue to find exciting perhaps because, as somebody once said: the pictures are better on the radio.

Chapter 10

Learning To Live With The Fear

Films can have the power to terrify and before I was old enough to be tantalised by the concept of being frightened at the pictures, I stumbled, almost accidentally, into some of my deepest and darkest fears in the flickering shadow world of the cinema.

During my childhood the Sequoia Theatre would put on a special matinee of *The Wizard of Oz* in the summer months and from 1953 onwards we saw this movie every year.

My mother Beth took all four of us kids to the film that first time. The Sequoia was full of children and the opening, with it's sepia-tinted monochrome, immediately connected with the audience. We saw Judy Garland's Dorothy trying to tell Aunt Em all about Miss Gulch's threats to her little dog, Toto, and not being listened to by anyone.

The set of the Kansas farm was not realistic looking and gave the movie a surreal quality which made me feel uneasy.

As Judy Garland sang *Somewhere Over the Rainbow,* with Toto perched on the tractor seat, she seemed to express our childish longing to see other lands and to get away from the strictures of an adult world.

The sight of Miss Gulch pedalling up the unreal-looking road on her bicycle to the sound of worrying music, gave witness to the unease I was experiencing.

"That dog's a menace to the community," she tells Aunt Em. "I'm taking it to the sheriff and see that it's destroyed."

Margaret Hamilton's performance as Miss Gulch was so uncompromising. She was a stern, cabbage-faced old bat and wasn't about to be sweet-talked around by anybody.

Dorothy's grief at surrendering her beloved dog to be "destroyed" was very traumatic and left the young audience at the Sequoia in no doubt about who was good and who was bad.

But, as we all know, Toto escaped out of the basket and scampered back to Dorothy. Then the two set off on the dusty road to surreal adventure.

Originally released by MGM in 1939, *The Wizard of Oz* was something of a flop at the boxoffice when it first came out but as the full house at the Sequoia every summer showed, it later found its audience with children of all ages.

Its blend of the violently frightening and the strangely unreal never allowed us to settle down and get comfortable. The intensity of the cyclone, grinding away on the horizon as doors flew off hinges, was genuinely unnerving. I was particularly upset to see Aunt Em become hysterical when she couldn't find Dorothy as all hands made for the storm cellar.

Dorothy's trip in the house flying through the cyclone was the stuff of scary dreams and it's not for nothing that lines like: "Toto, I don't think we're in Kansas anymore," have infiltrated the language as a way of describing anything oddball.

The full colour world that Dorothy entered as she opened her front door was anything but realistic: weird giant flowers in the foreground and cartoon-like mountains in the distance. Then when Glenda turned up in her giant bubble and the munchkins came out... well, you get the idea.

This was a movie of emotional extremes and after all that disturbing stuff with the cyclone, the munchkins celebrated by joyously singing *Ding Dong the Witch is Dead,* dancing and marching around the set with all the choreographic brilliance befitting a big budget MGM musical.

But their liberated joy was short lived as a red cloud of smoke exploded in their midst and the wicked witch of the west emerged from within it, clutching her broomstick and cackling menacingly.

This first sighting of the wicked witch, with her green face, black hat and scorching voice terrified me so badly and so immediately that I burst into tears and had to be taken, screaming, out to the lobby by my mother. I was six years old and I can't remember this ever happening before or since.

Beth sat with me on the sofa down by the ladies' room. When I'd stopped sobbing, she explained that Margaret Hamilton, who played the witch, was someone she and Blackie knew in New York and that she was a very nice person. This cut no ice with me but I did go back in and didn't cry again.

I never missed the annual showing of *Wizard of Oz* and never cried again. Margaret Hamilton's witch continued to frighten me but I guess I was learning to live with my fear.

I was also frightened by a Little Rascals short at the Saturday Matinee called *Mama's Little Pirate* in which the kids discovered a cave with an enormous treasure chest. As they broke the lock on the chest, out spilled this mountain of coins, jewels and treasure. The children began gleefully filling their pockets. They then found another door which took them into a giant's kitchen. By the time they got around to worrying about being there, the giant returned with a large goose he was presumably going to cook for dinner. He closed the door behind him.

He was tall, bearded and wore a Robinson Crusoe-type outfit. He also carried a big club and mumbled in a very deep voice. He didn't see the children at first as they hid under the table. Then when his back was turned they scrambled up the chimney above the large cauldron he was presumably going to cook the goose in. Up in the chimney the children tried to be still but the main character, had stuffed his pockets so full of coins that they burst open. The coins began falling into the pot, alerting the giant to their presence and making him very angry. One by one he dragged the struggling children down out of the chimney and hung each one up on a hook. This clearly was a child-eating giant. He was going to cook those children and eat them. That notion terrified me to the core.

Visitng the Lark, which was smaller than the Sequoia and didn't have a balcony, I encountered another manifestation of my deepest fears whilst watching *Hans Christian Andersen*.

Danny Kaye was particularly enjoyable for young children as he was childlike, gentle and very funny. The movie was charming with wonderful songs like *Inchworm* and *Thumbelina* but there was one scene in which Hans and his assistant, Peter, arrived in Copenhagen and set up shop in the town square by the statue of the king. While Peter climbed up on the statue, Hans sang his song to the crowd, advertising his skills as a shoemaker and the crowd fell under his spell. Suddenly two police officers appeared and placed him under arrest for allowing Peter to climb on the statue. "Run Peter," shouted Hans as Peter dashed away.

It was the power of the state in the form of the police arresting Hans which scared me. My parents and their friends were all considered dangerous subversives by the federal government and I'm sure this informed my reaction to the scene.

All of these films frightened me spontaneously and caught my vulnerable feelings by surprise. How much that gave rise to my later passion for scary movies I don't know.

Another annual event at the Sequoia was a late night showing of *Dracula* with Bela Lugosi and *The Phantom of the Opera* starring Claude Rains. This double bill showed up every year at Halloween and because it was late at night, I never got to go but I always saw the trailers and became familiar with Bela Lugosi saying: "I am....Dracula." My imitation of this phrase became very tiresome for my brother Jim.

I spent an awful lot of my youth in movie theatres and the experience of a darkened cinema is a very intimate one: just you, your soul and the characters in the story being told.

On our way west we lived about six months in Minnesota and while there we visited a friend of my father's at a warehouse of some kind. There our family watched a 16mm film which showed a group of white hooded Ku Klux Klansmen by a roadside at night, stopping cars and checking them. They pulled one man out of his car and there, by the side of the road, they tarred and feathered him then threw him off a cliff. The camera was stationary and the entire footage was shot in a single take. I have no idea whether it was a real-life documentary or if it was staged but this film had a profound effect on me and gave me something of a morbid preoccupation with the Klan.

Another film I saw with my parents at the Lark was Walt Disney's *The Living Desert* and it gave me a lifelong terror of tarantula spiders. Just why these eight-legged arachnids should frighten me so profoundly I don't know but they did.

I learned later that it was Disney himself who decided the spider should be the villain of the piece and this must be why the film's composer gave us scary music every time it made an appearance on the screen which, in turn, conditioned me to find them scary.

Movies are a powerful medium and the effect on young minds can be unpredictable. In time I would seek out movies

I knew would scare me and by seeing them I guess I was attempting to toughen myself up. I knew I would never be a hard guy in the conventional sense, because I was so small. Because of the political climate of the times I was growing up in, I did find that fear was my constant companion. I was always afraid that my parents could be arrested. I was also afraid there was going to be a nuclear war. Every time a jet from the airforce base up on Mount Tam broke the sound barrier I would think the worst had just happened (see chapter 29).

So maybe, I thought, sitting through a scary movie was a way I could make myself less vulnerable. It's probably no more ridiculous than thinking you should hide under your desk in a nuclear attack.

Chapter 11

Duckburg At The Bus Depot

Though I was never a reader of books, my mother Beth, in addition to being well-read herself, was also a published author. She constantly said to me: "When you finally start reading, darling…"

What would follow would be a pitch for a particular book she hoped I'd one day read. I'm not certain why I had this aversion but, with a few exceptions, I didn't begin reading books until about halfway through my twenties.

Both my older sisters Nell and Kate read books while my brother Jim and I read comic books.

We didn't read any old comic books. Our favourites were *Uncle Scrooge, Superman, Walt Disney's Comics and Stories* and *Classics Illustrated.*

The Disney comics were published by Dell while *Superman* came out under the DC banner and *Classics Illustrated* were something different for, unlike the others which all sold for a dime, these slightly elevated-looking publications cost fifteen cents.

I bought most of my comics at the bus depot, so called because it was where you purchased your tickets for the Greyhound buses which ran to and from the city every hour. When I first began frequenting the bus depot, the counter was tucked inside the Throckmorton entrance to the left but sometime around the middle of the 1950s the whole place was redesigned and the new counter stood straight ahead of you as you entered from Throckmorton. This made much more space for bookshelves and it also meant that the racks holding the comics were directly opposite the counter so that the ladies behind it could keep an eye on the boys, for it was mostly boys, who were always looking at and reading the comic books.

"Put the comics up, boys," was the constant refrain of Margo and Brun who worked there. Margo was big, blonde and quite chubby while Brun was short, brunette and pencil thin. Neither was terribly friendly to the boys though I got special treatment, probably because I spent so much time there that they got used to me.

The titles were many. Most of the famous cartoon characters had their own comic books: *Donald Duck, Porky Pig, Mickey Mouse, Bugs Bunny, Woody Woodpecker.* Then there were cowboys like *Roy Rogers,* super-heroes like *Superman* and also *Archie & Veronica, Nancy* and *Little Lulu.*

I read them all at the Bus Depot but the ones I actually paid money for were very few. These ones, like *Uncle Scrooge,* I kept and collected.

The world you entered within the pages of an *Uncle Scrooge* comic was special indeed. He lived in Duckburg and we'd invariably find him inside his money bin, a mammoth square edifice with a massive dollar sign chiseled into its facade. He could often be found counting his lucre or even bathing in coins. He was a benevolent miser of epic proportions and the adventures he took us on were usually to do with some great treasure to be found or an outstanding debt to be settled.

Always assisting him was his nephew Donald Duck who, in turn was uncle to Huey, Dewey and Louie. Why these three were nephews and not offspring I never knew. Perhaps it was because Donald Duck started out in the cinema cartoons as a notoriously bad tempered fellow and it may have been thought that he didn't have the patience to be a parent. However in the *Uncle Scrooge* stories, Donald was a model of calm behaviour in stark contrast to his wealthy uncle who squawked at the drop of a pin.

Huey, Dewey and Louie, who addressed their uncles as 'Unca,' were members of the Junior Woodchucks, an organization like the Boy Scouts, and they referred regularly to the Junior Woodchuck Manual, a small book of encyclopaedic proportions which was called upon to solve all problems, great and complicated.

I must have wondered who the guy was that wrote and illustrated these glorious comics but such information was not on offer. The only name on the front page was that of Walt Disney and it didn't take a degree in mathematics to figure out that Walt Disney would never have the time to write and draw all this material which appeared every month. In fact Walt couldn't even write his signature in the style designed by his artists and his cartooning days were way back when.

It's only subsequently that I learned that our terrific storyteller and illustrator was Carl Barks who apparently used National Geographic magazines and the Encyclopaedia Britannica as inspiration for his adventure stories.

The yarns almost always involved a mystery which had to be solved and Mister Barks employed many cinematic devices in his storytelling. Shadows played a big part and the cast of characters was always colourful.

Usually the villains of any *Scrooge* story were the Beagle Boys, a gang of crooks who did nothing sartorially to disguise their malevolent intentions. With prison numbers across their chests and thin black masks to cover their eyes, the Beagle Boys were straightforward grinning baddies. They were, as their name implies, dogs, though completely humanoid except for their noses and ears which gave their caninity away.

The humanization of the animal kingdom was a regular feature of Walt Disney's cartoon characters who all had the regulation three fingers and a thumb and wore white gloves. White gloves didn't feature in the Barks drawings as the ducks' digits were white already and the Beagle Boys didn't wear any gloves over their three-fingered hands.

The clothing the ducks wore constituted an odd compromise between the natural world and that imagined by Disney's artists. Donald wore his sailor's hat and top but nothing else while the three nephews sported jumpers and little baseball-type caps. Scrooge's attire consisted of a top hat, a smart-looking jacket, spats over his webbed feet and a pair of spectacles perched on his bill. And the whole ensemble had the smart finishing touch of a walking stick.

The ducks seemed to fall into a special Disney category when it came to clothing, as almost all his other creations like Mickey Mouse and Goofy wore trousers of one sort or another. But the ducks had their bottoms exposed. Presumably this was a subject that Walt and his colleagues discussed in some detail somewhere along the line. Actually the idea of getting trousers over a duck's lower parts does seem a bit impractical but then putting a pair of pants on a dog is equally ridiculous. The Disney solution to the dog problem in Goofy's case was to dispense with his tail and give him a human body unlike Pluto who remained wholly canine and naked. Only Pluto's teeth were humanoid. I suppose the Beagle Boys were somewhere in between and, who knows? Perhaps they had tails curled up underneath their trousers.

You didn't pick at an *Uncle Scrooge* comic, rather you surrendered to it like a movie, making the journey with them all the way.

In the *Scrooge* comics I recall encountering foodstuffs I'd never heard of like Scones and Hard Tack. Exotic locations were almost always visited such as the Isle of Colchis in *The Golden Fleecing,* when Scrooge was abducted and flown off by a flock of Larkies, Barks's version of the Harpies of Greek mythology.

The Larkies were particularly exotic and their introduction to us, disguised as men with beards in Arab dress, made for a wonderful surprise when they finally exposed themselves as these heron-like women.

They had come to Duckburg aboard their ship, The Argo, and each of the Arab men had names like Eikral Senga which was Larkie Agnes spelt backwards.

Barks packed his yarn with plenty of clues along the way such as the Arab man saying: "Come aboard the 'Argo' and we'll talk it over with my sis - I mean brothers."

It was Scrooge's desire to have a coat made out of gold which led to him being followed by the 'man' in Arab dress who then produced a sample of golden wool from the Isle of Colchis.

McDuck's greed leads him into a trap, when the Larkies got him and Donald on board the Argo. Then, carrying the ancient vessel with ropes, they flew off into the night. Huey, Dewey and Louie arrived at the pier to see the Larkies lifting The Argo up into the night sky.

The style of illustration that Barks employed in the *Scrooge* comics was very simple and remarkably consistent and the detail was always worthy of scrutiny. The background drawings were not on the scale of *MAD Magazine*, but you could always find interesting things happening behind the main story. Barks was also expert at suggestive illustration, creating the illusion of detail on piles of coins or a forest of trees in the distance.

In most *Scrooge* comics there would usually be a shorter tale about Gyro Gearloose, a goose-like creature who was an inventor. Amongst his inventions was this miniature skinny robot, only a few inches tall, with a lightbulb for a head. This tiny guy was never referred to but you could spot him in practically every story box. Gearloose never acknowledged his presence nor made mention of him but this little fellow was almost subliminally crucial to each of the stories, helping the inventor solve problems along the way.

I don't remember what relationship, if any, connected Gearloose to Uncle Scrooge. It looked like he, too, lived in Duckburg though the humanoids in his stories had human ears rather than dogs' ears. In actual fact Barks seemed to make up his anatomical rules as he went along.

In *Land Beneath the Ground,* Uncle Scrooge had a shaft dug beneath his money bin to guard against earthquakes and discovered a vast underworld of giant caves where the Terries and the Fermies rolled themselves into balls and actually caused the quakes he feared.

In *The Son of the Sun,* Scrooge and his nephews flew to the mountains of Peru to find Inca gold before his arch rival, Flintheart Glomgold, got there first.

The *Scrooge* comics didn't shield their young readers from many of the uglier elements of human nature like avarice and envy. Also Scrooge's shortcomings were never disguised. It seems to have been a fact within the stories that Donald was a duck of modest means along with the nephews and that, having a fabulously wealthy uncle didn't bestow them with any particular advantages in life. Unlike greedy humans in the real world, the ducks were not motivated to demand a share of his groaning fortune.

It appears that both Uncle Scrooge and Duckburg were totally invented by Barks while working on *Donald Duck* comics. He began his career at the Disney Studio in 1935 as an In-Betweener for $20 a week. This meant that he drew the animation cells between the extreme actions of whatever cartoon character was being brought to life, which produced a realistic illusion of movement. Before too long Barks began contributing gag ideas for the cartoons and was soon promoted to the story department.

By 1942, however, Barks found that his sinuses were being irritated by the studio's air conditioning system and he quit his job. He got himself a little chicken ranch out in the desert and whilst trying to establish himself as a chicken farmer, began doing freelance comic book work for Western Publishing who were doing *Donald Duck* comics for Disney.

It was in such an environment that he wrote and illustrated all the *Uncle Scrooge* comics. It does seem incredible that this talented man produced all this amazing work for roughly $11.50 a page. Considering that the comic books sold in the millions it is equally amazing that he never bore any kind of grudge against Walt Disney. His attitude towards Disney was that he was the boss and had given him a good job at $20 a week during the depression and the fact that all of Barks's stories went out under the Disney name didn't seem to bother him at all.

Again I'm surprised that we in the Myers household never heard any of the bad news about Walt Disney from our parents. We certainly heard plenty about William Randolph Hearst, the Dulles brothers and many other devils who shared Disney's political views.

For all I know, my parents might have even read my *Scrooge* comics. My sisters certainly did and, again, I think a gently censorious eye was cast over all our reading material. Although I never spied such activity I know that when I began reading *MAD* with a passion that Blackie read it too.

I looked forward to the monthly editions of *Uncle Scrooge* in the same way I looked forward to the Saturday Matinee. It always guaranteed a wild adventure that took me somewhere exciting and exotic. I can only guess that I didn't consider the Pixie Trail or Mount Tamalpais to be exciting or exotic enough. There was always a better adventure lurking within the pages of a glossy-covered comic book.

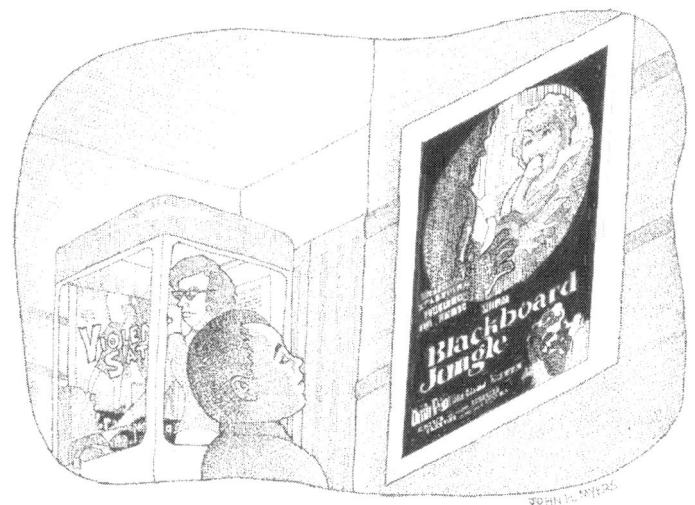

Chapter 12

Mister Daddy-O Visits The Sequoia

Many of us have certain memories burned into our consciousness: where we were when we first learned that president Kennedy had been shot or what we were doing the night of the first moon landing. I wonder how many of you can recall the very first time you ever heard rock and roll music.

When I was in grade school the ritual of going to the movies with my family was an exciting experience and sometime in June of 1955, the Myers family in its entirety went to the Sequoia to see *Blackboard Jungle*.

I was always in a whirlwind of excitement about going to the movies. We set off about 6.15pm and arrived at the parking lot by the Bus Depot soon after. We easily made the second feature at 7pm.

As it was a weeknight, there was no line for tickets and while Blackie bought them, I studied the posters for the next feature in the glass boxes which were on either side of the inner part of the Sequoia's tiled forecourt.

We then moved as a group through the open door into the carpeted lobby where Larry Counts stood, wearing a tuxedo, ready to take our tickets.

Larry Counts was a short stocky young man with blond hair cut in a flattop style that required the kind of hair which actually stood up on top. As he was about to take the tickets from Blackie, a young guy with greased back hair and sideburns walked briskly into the lobby from the street and proceeded up the red carpeted steps towards the auditorium. Counts turned quickly away from us, followed him up the steps and said in a loud, aggressive voice: "I told you not to come back!" Before the other guy could say anything, Counts grabbed him violently and frogmarched him down past us and out the door onto Throckmorton. He then returned to us and, without making any reference to the incident we'd just witnessed, tore our tickets in half. I was stunned by what I'd just seen.

Throughout my early childhood I never saw much in the way of physical violence between people I thought of as adults. I saw plenty of adults fighting in the movies but not in real life, so something like this upset me but I don't recall any comment about it from Blackie, Beth or my siblings and before we knew it we were at the candy counter.

Unlike the meager stipend Jim and I would get for the Saturday matinee, on this kind of family occasion Blackie bought us something good in the way of *Pogey Bait.* I had Junior Mints from the right hand side of the counter where everything cost ten cents.

A particular perk of going to the Sequoia with your folks was that you could sit upstairs with them. The upstairs was strictly for adults and it was the only place people could smoke. As you climbed the carpeted steps, the first four or five rows were the comfortable seats called the loges but my parents never paid the additional twenty five cents to sit there. They occupied the row along the back wall where the projection booth was.

When the lights went down the second feature *Cult of the Cobra,* began. It was called the second feature because it was the bottom of the bill even though it was shown first. It was a mildly engaging low budget affair which had Faith Domergue as a young woman who turned into a cobra to kill a load of ex-GIs who had defiled a tomb in some Middle Eastern location which, in reality, lay in the backlot at Universal International. It wasn't quite a horror movie and it certainly wasn't art but it passed the time interestingly enough.

The routine at the Sequoia was always the same. There would be previews of the next two movies and maybe a cartoon followed by a short intermission. Then the lights would go down for the main feature.

When *Blackboard Jungle,* began there was a written prelude which scrolled up the screen all about the importance of education and the dangers of juvenile delinquency. "The scenes and incidents depicted here are fictional. However, we believe that public awareness is a first step toward a remedy for any problem. It was in this spirit that *Blackboard Jungle* was produced."

While the speech was scrolling, a slightly jazzy military drum played. As soon as the words faded we heard a different but similar kind of drum beat and, as a blank blackboard appeared on the screen, this clear voice began singing "One, Two, Three O'clock, Four O'clock Rock..." and the title appeared on the blackboard.

The sound of this song was totally infectious. The rhythm made you want to get up and dance. It continued in the background after the titles were finished and we watched Glen Ford as Mr Dadier arriving at the school somewhere in New York for his interview as a teacher.

I was hearing two things for the very first time: Rock

and Roll and *Rock Around the Clock*. I was eight years old and I had never heard music like it before.

I was by this time a pretty regular hanger-outer at the record shop just inside the Sequoia building. Sara Wilcox who ran it not only tolerated my presence and that of my friend Glen Pritzker, but seemed to encourage it by playing us any records we wished to listen to in the booth. At this time there were three different versions of *The Ballad of Davy Crockett* in the top 40 along with at least two of *Unchained Melody*. Sarah Vaughan had a terrific record of *Whatever Lola Wants* and Nat King Cole sang *Darling Je Vous Aime Beaucoup* but I had never heard anything like Bill Haley's *Rock Around the Clock*.

The movie was a disturbing experience. Based on a novel by Evan Hunter, who also wrote crime fiction under the name Ed McBain. Although the teacher Mr. Dadier, was a tough World War II veteran he was up against a classroom full of knife wielding bad guys led by the very scary Vic Morrow. Early on his rowdy pupils changed his name to Daddy-O.

The guy we saw Larry Counts throw out of the Sequoia lobby was certainly what you would call a juvenile delinquent but the class that Mr Dadier had to teach in this movie was like nothing that even existed in Mill Valley. Of course I was only a second grader and too young to know much about such things but Nellie was in the seventh grade at Alto and Katie in fifth at Old Mill so I did hear about JDs from them.

Juvenile delinquency was probably the most significant sign of class distinction there was in Mill Valley. Hard guys or greasers tended to be those people who came from homes where education was not considered important. Their main interests were cars, hanging out at C's Drive-In and being tough.

But life in Mill Valley was not polarised the way it was in *Blackboard Jungle.* Poor Mr Dadier and his colleague, who had his entire collection of Bix Beiderbecke records smashed by Vic Morrow and his thugs, were truly engaged in a war. An early manifestation of this was the near rape of a pretty female teacher in the school library on the first day.

Dadier got beaten up real bad but in true Hollywood cowboy fashion he wouldn't give up. He was going to break through to this bearpit of a classroom. He even got called on the carpet by the principal for using racist expressions in class. He did use racist expressions but only in the context of a lecture on intolerance.

This movie was the first one that Vic Morrow ever made and it was the picture which propelled Sidney Poitier into stardom. Poitier played Miller, the one person in the class that Dadier tried to co-opt. But while we sensed a streak of virtue in Miller it was plain that Dadier's truly immovable enemy was Morrow whose character, West, was deadly in his hatred for the teacher and who was deeply involved in serious drug addiction and criminality.

Though constructed in a classic Hollywood fashion, *Blackboard Jungle* was a moving and important film tackling hot issues like race, drugs and class at a time when most movies side-stepped anything controversial as a result of the red scare. It was hugely successful at the boxoffice and also became the vehicle which introduced rock and roll into the lives of a generation.

The song *Rock Around the Clock* had been discovered by Glenn Ford's son Peter, who was an R&B enthusiast and haunted his local record shops in Hollywood, collecting discs, most by black artists. *Rock Around the Clock* was a B-side by Haley which hadn't clicked at all.

Screenwriter and director Richard Brooks was visiting the Ford household in the run-up to shooting and heard young Peter playing the disc. Brooks borrowed the record and never returned it. The next thing Peter knew it was in the movie.

Pandro Berman, the film's producer at MGM paid $5,000 to use the music three times in the film and in July of 1955 *Rock Around the Clock* by Bill Haley & His Comets hit the number one spot in the Top 40.

Blackie and Beth took us regularly to movies which were probably considered "adult" fare. Often I wouldn't fully understand them but I had no problem with *Blackboard Jungle.*

On the drive home my mother talked about *Rock Around the Clock* and how much she liked it as did Blackie. It had the same qualities as a good big band swing record and Bill Haley's voice was clear as a bell with fine diction so it didn't exclude my parents as would Elvis in a year's time with his slurred lyrics and pelvic sexuality.

Bill Haley and his Comets were actually a very mainstream band. Haley cut a deal with producer Sam Katzman to make a quickie film for Columbia using the song as its title and, though they did have other hits, Haley's career, touring the world really only existed because of *Rock Around the Clock.* He also didn't seem interested in sharing his success with the Comets who remained on meagre wages while he enjoyed a huge bounty of financial reward. By the time the movie was filming, three of his musicians had walked and their replacements mimed to the discs that had been recorded with the original band.

There's a jolly, innocent quality to *Rock Around the Clock* which cannot be found in much of what followed in its wake. Rock and Roll soon became inextricably linked with the phenomenon of juvenile delinquency. Both *Blackboard*

Jungle and Katzman's *Rock Around the Clock* were at the centre of the unfolding controversy.

A few disturbances at movie theatres showing *Rock Around the Clock* made for lurid headlines about rioting teenagers and the public outrage made both these movies big grossers at the boxoffice.

Clean-cut Pat Boone got in on the act with *Ain't That a Shame* and a new artist named Chuck Berry burst into the charts with *Maybelline.* And though the 1955 hit parade was still dominated by the likes of Les Baxter and Mitch Miller, the tide of rock and roll was definitely rising.

It made the younger generation different from the parents who had preceded them. This new jungle music had a wild, animal quality unlike the smooth Glenn Miller sound which our parents enjoyed so much. And yet Glen Pritzker and I still listened to Perry Como and Doris Day records but our folks couldn't do that in reverse. Putting up with Elvis and Little Richard was simply beyond the pale for them.

And so the seeds of a later, more fundamental cultural revolution in the 1960s were planted, I believe, in this generational divide brought about by rock and roll.

The Pied Piper had visited the Sequoia in the form of *Blackboard Jungle* and the children were soon to follow.

Chapter 13
An Ice Cream Sandwich On Evergreen

At the corner of Evergreen and Miller on the border of Homestead Valley stood four airplane-hangar-like constructions which housed the Miller Avenue Shopping Centre. There was a supermarket, a pharmacy, a liquor store and a small post office.

For reasons I shall never know, this was the only place in Mill Valley where I could purchase a Borden's ice cream sandwich which was one of the great confectionery delights of my childhood.

There were other brands of ice cream sandwich to be had up at the bus depot or the Mill Valley market but they lacked its superior qualities.

The Borden's sandwich was rectangular, between six and seven inches in length, perhaps two and a half inches wide and approximately an inch and a bit thick. It came tightly wrapped in yellow waxed paper, decorated with the smiling cartoon of Elsie the cow and the thing that made them superior to the other brands was that the chocolate biscuit, which made it a sandwich, was sufficiently soft so that when you took a bite, it came away as one piece.

The other brands, the names of which I cannot recall, were square and the biscuit was hard so that when you bit into it the ice cream would squish out the other side. This was a most unsatisfactory experience and, after a few minutes you'd have a serious mess on your hands.

You had to have ten cents in your pocket to partake of a Borden's ice cream sandwich but it was always worth it. You'd find them in those big freezer boxes which you'd dip into for popsicles and other frozen delights.

Now a popsicle was not as exotic as a sandwich and cost a nickel. They consisted of two almost separate rocket shaped cylinders of frozen flavoured water on a pair of wooden sticks. The entire confection came inside a kind of transparent paper bag with the two sticks protruding at the bottom.

Certain vendors of popsicles had a knife especially designed for cutting the two cylinders in half, presumably so it could be shared by two children. That was an odd concept. Obviously you couldn't fit both halves of a popsicle in your mouth too easily but I don't recall very much benevolence when it came to sharing your treats with others.

Of course advertisers made great play of the virtues of sharing. The *3 Musketeers* bar was originally supposed to divide into a trio of separate sections to share with your friends but, by the time I was buying them, the commercials showed you how to break them in two, giving one half to your friend. I guess this was wishful thinking on the part of the advertising copy writers for I certainly guarded my confectionary with a feral intensity and don't recall sharing it with anyone unless I had to.

Buffalo Bob did this on *Howdy Doody.* He'd lean forward with a *3 Musketeers* bar, unwrap it before our very eyes and then break it in half and show you the inside as the camera zoomed in, all the while prattling on about how good it was for you and how we should ask our mom to buy us one.

Candy bars at this time cost either a nickel or a dime and simple economics kept me in the five cent category, hence my gravitation towards the *3 Musketeers* bar. Manufactured by the Mars Corporation, it consisted of a sizeable slab of fluffy but solid nougat covered in milk chocolate, the top of which was wavy and thicker than the sides or bottom. I would gently bite away whole sides of chocolate from the nougat which extended the eating experience considerably.

Also in the nickel category was a *Big Hunk* which again was nougat but much thicker and hard. It had nuts and honey in it and was a real slow chew. Other nickel bars were *Tootsie Roll, Baby Ruth* and *Butterfinger.*

Chewing gum was a slightly different experience to eating candy bars. In addition to *Dubble Bubble* which was pink Bubble gum, there was also *Bazooka* which I didn't like the taste of as much as *Dubble Bubble* and the little comic strip inside the wrapping wasn't as good either.

One of the virtues of bubble gum was being able to blow bubbles with it when you weren't busily grinding its sugar content into your teeth.

My favorite brand of non-bubble chewing gum was Wrigley's *Juicy Fruit* which cost a nickel for five individually wrapped sticks. I enjoyed the ritual of pulling the tab on the compact shiny packet, removing the top and pulling a single stick out. The packaging was neat. You'd slide the silver foiled stick out of its paper sleeve then unwrap it. The dry stick of gum had a soft film of sweet powder on its surface and you'd either chew it as you fed it into your mouth or roll it up into a tootsie roll shape and sink your teeth into it.

Chiclets, made by Adams, were a different kind of gum

altogether. They came in a small cardboard box with a tiny window, through which the candy coated lozenges of gum could be viewed.

The claims that advertisers made for these products during the 1950s now have an amusing quality to them but it's important to remember just how persuasive they were. All these authoritative adults with perfect diction telling small children watching television about the virtues of whatever product they were selling in a very aggressive way. *Dentyne* gum was sold on the basis that it was good for your teeth even though it contained sugar.

Dentyne was something different again. The individual sticks were much tinier than the others and were packed vertically rather than horizontally like Wrigley's. The gum tasted wonderful but how on earth it was supposed to be good for your teeth was a mystery.

The one obvious consequence of eating all these sweet things was tooth decay.

The various maladies of childhood were always so absolute when they struck. The swirling nausea of a stomach ache was, I felt, the worst ailment there could possibly be in the world until such time as it was replaced by a throbbing headache. Whatever the discomfort, it was always the worst. The same applied to toothache and as for visiting the dentist, that was a descent into hell itself.

The first dentist our family went to in Mill Valley was Dr Danford, whose office was up on Lovell just above Litton Square. I have no specific memories of Dr Danford but I do recall that he came in for some seriously negative publicity within the Myers household. My oldest sister Nell remembers being told by him that if she didn't cry while he drilled her teeth she could have some candy afterwards and, so insistent were the phone calls from his office demanding payment of his bill, that Blackie went to the trouble of paying it in person. He delivered the entire amount in pennies.

Our next dentist was Dr Bortfeld who operated from a small office above the variety shop opposite the Brothers Tavern on Locust.

I never liked a visit to the dentist. I hated injections and that shot of novocaine was simply terrible. The needle would stingingly pierce your gums and then after a few minutes you'd be overcome by a deranging numbness which put you into a state of painful disorientation. After your mouth was no longer able to perform any function you wanted it to, the scraping, digging and drilling began and it seemed to go on forever.

I probably could have spared myself some of the time I spent in the dentist's chair by not eating quite so many sweet things containing large quantities of sugar. Doesn't that sound sensible? Of course no such idea ever occurred to me in the entirety of my young life.

Our friend Mark Symmes, who was in brother Jim's class at Homestead and lived up on Molino, was paid an extra bit of allowance by his mother Betty if he didn't put sugar on his cereal in the mornings. I can recall chortling at the idea of this at the time but I suspect that Mark never suffered the kind of nerve grinding agony which I endured at the hands of our doctors of dental surgery.

My frequent visits to the dentist, however, had no impact on my intake of candy bars, sticky sweets and sugar on my breakfast cereal.

The morning routine which I observed with a ritualistic zeal went something like this: the cheerios were poured into the bowl. The milk was then added until the little circles began to rise. A spoonful of sugar was sprinkled across the top surface of the cereal. This top surface was then submerged in the milk with my spoon. A second spoonful of sugar was applied. By now the cheerios had taken on a softer chewy quality and I ate them briskly for, if I left it a few minutes more, they would get soggy. The remaining milk which was now swimming with sugar received another small helping of cheerios to mop it up.

I didn't like the taste of unadulterated milk. My mother would insist on us drinking a glass of milk with our supper each night and, in order for me to comply with this, I would stir in a spoonful of Hershey's chocolate sauce making it chocolate milk.

So the concept of not putting sugar on my cheerios each morning was totally incomprehensible to me.

After breakfast it was off to school with the packed lunch my mother prepared for each of us. My sisters went to Old Mill and left earlier than Jim and I. A brown paper bag with my name written on it stood on the kitchen table alongside brother Jim's. Inside was usually a bologna sandwich on white bread with *French's* mustard, wrapped in wax paper. In addition there would be a piece of fruit and three of my mother's home made chocolate chip cookies, also wrapped in wax paper.

We would walk up the steps to Seymour and out through the wooden turnstile onto the Pixie Trail. As soon as we'd come to the path down the hill we'd break into a run and a combination of gravity and sure footedness guided us as we ran down to the lower trail, across Janes Street, through the Purvis's garden, across Janes again and down Cherry Blossom Lane to Homestead School.

Apart from the three chocolate chip cookies in my lunch bag, nothing actually loaded with sugar passed my lips throughout the school day.

When it was time to come home, my brother Jim and I

would usually cover the same ground but, because it was all uphill, we might vary the route by wandering up Montford then taking Janes along to where it met Sunrise and climb up through the vacant lot into the playground.

If, however, we happened to have any money on us, we would postpone our ascent altogether and walk down Evergreen to Linden Lane where there was a little shop called Homestead Store. Here we could purchase individual sticks of red licorice for a penny. I preferred the red licorice to the black as it was sweeter. The licorice sticks stood in tall glass jars. You could also buy Dubble Bubble gum for the same price and no shortage of other sweet and wonderful tasting candies.

The red licorice was very chewy and you weren't able to eat it quickly. It would cling to your teeth and gums for a long time. It is a wonder to me at this later stage of my life that I have any teeth left in my head at all.

Armed with our red licorice or whatever else we had the money to buy, we'd then turn left on Montford and walk up to the base of Molino where we'd take a right. The beginning of Molino was the biggest and baddest hill in our neighbourhood.

Climbing hills to get home was something I never looked forward to and any diversion from this grim reality was heartily embraced. Confectionery of any kind tasted wonderful and provided just such a diversion. Candy bars, chewing gum or ice cream could always keep me putting off the big hike home.

As an adult now I'm so grateful for my childhood in Mill Valley. The network of steps leading down into the valley from every elevated location provided splendid access to the mountain for hikers from all over the world and it has taken me all these years to finally recognise just what a paradise we grew up in.

It's very easy to say 'Those were the days.' I had a good musician friend in London in the early 70s who used to wonder why we never said: 'These are the days.'

Chapter 14

Escape To The Matinee

Growing up in an atheist household in Mill Valley had many good things about it but one thing we had little experience of was the kind of ritual associated with religion.

As our father Blackie would not allow a television set in the Myers household through most of the 1950s, going to the movies took on a much more sacred quality for me.

My earliest cinematic visits were with my family and we often attended the Lark up in Larkspur where we saw mostly European films.

From the beginning I got into the habit of giving the movie my full attention in an almost reverent way. I was always immediately intolerant of any distraction while watching a film. This presented no problems when seeing movies in a room full of like-minded individuals but I found, by attending the Sequoia for every Saturday matinee of my young life, just how intolerant I had become of those who didn't share my viewing habits.

Mind you, I never missed a Saturday matinee. My brother Jim and I were often first in line at the Sequoia Theatre well before the cashier emerged. The doors opened at 1pm and by that time the line behind us had snaked back up past Bennett's and El Paseo.

After we'd paid the quarter for our ticket we only had a nickel left over for what my father called *Pogey Bait,* so it was the left side of the candy counter for us. Over on the right side for a dime you could have Junior Mints or a Nestle's Crunch while all you could get for a nickel was Milk Duds, a box of Dots or one of those big suckers which were not great but lasted a long time.

Most of the kids who turned up for the matinee were there to relish a long moment of liberation from parental authority rather than to watch movies. Once this barking dog of a crowd was inside the Sequoia it became like a battle zone with spitballs and Ju-Ju Bees flying across the auditorium at alarming speed. The noise was deafening as all these kids screamed at the top of their vocal capacity. It was, from my point of view, hellish, but it was part of the price which had to be paid for a truly remarkable cinematic experience.

When the lights went down we'd get about five cartoons. The violence in these cartoons was always exaggerated. The likes of Tom and Jerry inflicted hideous wounds upon each other without ever having to deal with the consequences. The noise continued all through the cartoons.

There were usually a few ushers on duty during a matinee and they were constantly up and down the aisles shining their flashlights in the faces of kids who were misbehaving. I never received the glare of a flashlight and often wondered what happened to those children who were taken out.

After the cartoons came the comedy which usually meant *The Three Stooges,* another penalty you had to pay for the rest of the programme. *The Three Stooges* were, in my opinion, not funny at all. They were ugly and their violence was downright disturbing. I'm pretty sure that they didn't quiet the kids down either. That was the job of the serial.

Every week we'd get a new chapter of *Batman, Flash Gordon, The Phantom* or *Radar Men from the Moon.* Each chapter would finish with the hero being trapped in some calamitous situation. Batman was about to be crushed by a giant vice one week or the Phantom was sinking in quicksand. I think it was these idiotic cliffhangers, more than anything else, which kept me coming back week after week. Perhaps if I had discussed them with someone I might have become aware of being manipulated but instead I kept it to myself and really would worry that Batman might be crushed to death. When you returned the next week they simply showed you some detail which had been edited out at the climax, like Robin throwing a wrench into the machinery of the giant vice and jamming it.

The serials were always full of grown men wearing tremendously silly costumes. What did I know? It was good guys and bad guys writ large and I lapped it up with a ladle. By the time the serial came on the din of the crowd died down and everyone surrendered their attention.

The thing about the Saturday matinee was that all the movies were old and presumably cheap. Some of the cartoons dated back to the late thirties and forties as did the comedies, the serials and sometimes the main features. I think it was this weekly cinematic potpourri which gave me my taste for the vintage in popular culture. Women's fashions made a particular impression on me as the contrast between the 1940s and 50s was pronounced. Hair styles and ladies with shoulder pads were clearly of another time.

Before the main feature came on, the manager would bring a big colourful barrel on stage and call out ticket stub numbers. The lucky winners, of which I was never one, would then come up on stage and receive a goody bag. I often wondered what was in these bags. Birthdays were also celebrated but I never understood how these things were known about.

The main feature was the big event and it was always a movie of quality with genuine stars and good production values but a bit old. They showed a lot of westerns, war pictures and adventure films like *King Solomon's Mines*. Every so often we'd get a sci-fi movie which always gave me a thrill. We saw: *The Day the Earth Stood Still, War of the Worlds, Earth Vs The Flying Saucers, The Blob, The Space Children, Attack of the Crab Monsters* and *When Worlds Collide*. By the end of the main film the once-baying crowd of raucous children were mesmerised by the magic of the movies.

There were two alleyways either side of the Sequoia and as the words *The End* appeared on the screen, the young patrons would leap from their seats and crack open the exit doors on both sides, sending a blinding flash of daylight through the darkened auditorium as they ran out, squinting into the afternoon sun.

Movies always clung to me afterwards. Although my brother Jim was there with me for all the matinees he didn't feel there was anything to discuss once the experience was over so my reverie had to be a silent vigil on the long walk home.

We would wander up Throckmorton past Esposti's and Ben

Franklin's Five and Dime then turn left at the pet shop to take the steps up to Ethel. It was usually the main feature which I thought about while walking home. I wouldn't get around to worrying about the serial's protagonist until the next week.

Though I hated the noise and general behaviour of all those kids, I loved the matinee and before you knew it, Saturday had come around again and you went through the same ritual but with a fresh batch of films.

I don't know but I'd guess going to church wasn't quite like that.

Chapter 15

Glen's Top Ten

I have always been a collector and, as a young boy, I accumulated many 45rpm singles. The very first 45 I ever bought from the record shop near the Sequoia was Elvis Presley's *Hound Dog* which had *Don't Be Cruel* on the flip side. I bought it during the summer vacation of 1956 while I was between third and fourth grade at Homestead School.

I absolutely loved this record. Both sides were so exciting and very different from each other. I already had the LP *Elvis Presley* which featured *Heartbreak Hotel, Blue Suede Shoes* and lots of other great songs but these two were brand new and could only be had by purchasing this single.

Elvis was so cool. I would sing along with both sides of the record as well as the tracks on the LP though this had to be when no witnesses were around. All I had seen of Elvis performing was in photographs.

Though my father Blackie didn't allow us to have a television set, a cousin who stayed with us for a few months brought one with him and this occurred just in time for my sister Nell and I to watch Elvis Presley appear on the Steve Allen Show on NBC.

I began to put Brylcreem in my hair trying to look like Elvis. I even went so far as to comb my hair down into pathetic little sideburns in an attempt be like my idol.

At the record shop they had a booth where you could go and listen to pretty much any disc you asked for and I heard popular songs like *Sixteen Tons, Que Sera, Sera* and *The Great Pretender.* I soon began buying other singles like Carl Perkins performing *Blue Suede Shoes* and *Tonight You Belong to Me* by Patience & Prudence.

We had a record player which accommodated three speeds; 78rpm, 33⅓rpm and 45rpm. It had a special 45 attachment which was depressed around the main spindle and with a backward twist it would ascend to hold the single in place. American singles, unlike the other records, had a large hole. For the benefit of younger readers RPM stood for: revolutions per minute.

The 45rpm single had been designed and produced in the late 1940s by RCA Victor as an alternative to the heavy, scratchy and highly breakable 78rpm discs and they soon caught on. By the time I was buying records they'd become an industry standard and remained so until vinyl gave way to the Compact Disc.

My parents had a fair-sized record collection and music was played a lot in our house. In addition to the classical recordings my mother Beth liked, we also had Broadway shows like *Oklahoma, Finian's Rainbow* and *Porgy and Bess*. We listened to Fats Waller, Louis Armstrong, Ella Fitzgerald and when the movie *High Society* came out, the soundtrack became a big favourite in our house.

Although I was only *just* aware of the sociological controversy surrounding Elvis Presley's popularity with American youth, I did understand instinctively that this was music for me and not my parents. I never played my Elvis records within earshot of Blackie or Beth.

When I began the fourth grade my teacher was Mrs Blaugh who I actually liked. She brought history alive for me and I think I was probably a better student that year than I'd been to date. It was the year that "Under God" was inserted into our daily pledge of allegiance and nobody ever noticed that I never said it as we rattled through this morning ritual.

Mrs Blaugh, I soon learned, hated everything about

Elvis Presley and I guess most grownups did find him an unsettling phenomenon. He was considered lewd, vulgar and obscene by most of the adult population.

At school I was friends with Alex Robertson, Glen Pritzker and Billy Bowen. All three of these boys lived up in the hills above Tam High and I remember spending time with them all but it was Glen with whom I shared my passion for popular music and record collecting. Glen and I both examined all the details printed on a record label and regularly met at Village Music, where we'd pick up the latest Top 40 sheet. I can't ever remember anyone else with whom I could discuss the finer points. Like the fact that Elvis Presley's version of *Blue Suede Shoes* was infinitely superior to that of Carl Perkins, in spite of the fact that the latter had written the song.

Because I was a good singer and could do confident renditions of all the records I collected (Pat Boone, Elvis, Little Richard), Glen and I would fantasize about our grown up future with me as a performer and him as my manager.

Glen was a straight-A student and undoubtedly the smartest kid in class, whilst I was academically very pedestrian and spent most of my school time gazing out the window and drawing movie ads in the top margins of my binder paper. He also had an easy manner with the prettiest girls in class while I was very shy. He had a way of holding their attention which I didn't understand. And he was a talker. I don't recall any quiet times when Glen was around. It was as if he was constantly working things out intellectually.

I was a remarkably small child, always the tiniest one in class and this did nothing for my self-esteem in the romance department. I would never let on that I was, at this time and all through my years at Homestead, hopelessly in love with Lily Burris.

Lily was a pretty, dark-haired girl with freckles who I encountered in Mrs Spalding's first grade class. She was a little bit taller than me and maybe that was the problem. For Lily had no interest in me whatsoever and seemed to delight in brushing me off at every opportunity. I never got anywhere near her.

Glen, however, moved confidently among girls like Lily, Cathy Mibach and Mary Morrison and I never understood how he did it. Popularity was not something that I could comprehend and Glen was clearly popular.

Perhaps other families discussed such things as popularity but the subject never came up around our dinner table. My parents considered such concerns to be trivial in the extreme. So I found myself in the playground at Homestead School, wondering how certain kids behaved confidently and, inevitably, I would fall under their spell. Glen was such a person.

During our conversations about music, he would often speculate on the record charts and how they operated. I had a basic idea that the top 40 was compiled through sales but I don't think this caught my attention the way it did Glen's. He began following the progress of certain discs in the charts, copies of which we collected weekly from the counter at the record shop.

We both agreed that Elmer Bernstein's version of *Man with the Golden Arm* was superior to Richard Maltby's but the latter's came in at 17 while Bernstein's entered at 20. *Heartbreak Hotel* pushed Perry Como's *Hot Diggity* out of the number one spot while the Four Lads came in at 11 with *Standing on the Corner.*

The pop music of this time was very exciting because of its diversity. Big band, swing, rhythm and blues and rock and roll. Every week brought new records. *The Green Door* by Jim Lowe, *Friendly Persuasion* by Pat Boone, *Love Me Tender,* the title song of Elvis's first movie. Fats Domino's *Blueberry Hill* came out the same week as Bing Crosby and Grace Kelly singing *True Love.* Patience and Prudence followed up their previous hit with *Gonna Get Along Without You Now* and Harry Belafonte sang the *The Banana Boat Song.* These were all records I learned by heart.

Glen and I both liked the song *Young Love* which came out in two versions during the same week. One was by

Sonny James which was very good and came in at number 11. The other, by the actor Tab Hunter, was not so good and it came in at number 13. Tab, the super handsome movie star was not a natural singer at all. By the next week Sonny James had climbed to number 3, but Tab Hunter got to number 2 just below Elvis who stood at number 1 with *Too Much*. By the third week Tab Hunter was number 1 while poor Sonny James fell to number 8. Glen and I both agreed that Tab's status as a movie star was the only reason his record sold so well.

Tracking the progress of records in the charts gave Glen the idea of applying the same sort of system to his social life and he devised a Top Ten Friends list. I was very pleased to see that I occupied the number one position on his chart. Out in the playground he operated like a kind of pack leader with his flock following him around.

It must have been one Monday morning that Glen ran up to me in the playground with a worried look on his face.

"Myers," he said. "What's wrong?"

Perplexed, I asked what he meant.

"You've slipped. You're number two. What's happened?"

Thus began a process I was unable to have any impact on. Each day Glen would appear with more grim news. I'd dropped another point. The next day it was two points. I don't recall any frostiness on his part until the day he finally appeared with the news that I was now off the chart altogether.

"I'm sorry Myers," he said with solemnity in his voice.

From that day forward he never looked at me again. I would see him and the girls gathered around the playground bench talking, laughing and it was as if I was watching a movie. I'd become invisible.

Nothing in my life had prepared me for this experience and because it was to do with a subject my family would have considered unimportant, I don't believe I ever even discussed it with anyone.

My parents protected me from many things in life but the social manipulations of the playground at Homestead School were not on the list.

At the end of that school term Glen, being the very gifted student that he was, jumped a grade and I didn't see him again for many years. When we did meet again, the childhood agonies of the past had crumbled to dust and we were both able to laugh loud and long.

This had been my first experience of being an outsider. It certainly was not to be my last.

Chapter 16

Horrors At The Sequoia

The movies: going to see them and thinking about them, filled an enormous part of my life growing up in Mill Valley.

At the Sequoia Theatre I loved the posters outside, the red carpet inside, the curtains, the previews...in fact I loved everything about sitting there in the dark.

Sometime during the early 1950s I learned of the existence of horror movies and they became a kind of adjunct to this already intense passion of mine.

I was too young to have seen *The Thing* or *The Day the Earth Stood Still* when they first came around and I only knew about *The Beast from 20,000 Fathoms* because Danny Hallinan had told me all about it. I was also too young for *Creature from the Black Lagoon* and its sequel *Revenge of the Creature*.

The winter of 1955 was a particularly wild and wet one for Mill Valley and there was flooding down on Miller Avenue. All the way from the 2am Club to Tam High was under water.

During the winter months we also had our share of landslides and this year was particularly bad. On our way to school in our rain slicks and rubbers we'd regularly encounter huge mounds of earth in the middle of the road which had slid down the hill.

I was now eight years old and in third grade at Homestead with Mrs Lewis, a very strict woman who used to regularly beat students with a yardstick.

Glen Pritzker and I would often go uptown after school to hang out at the record store where Sara Wilcox would let us listen to the latest discs. At this time Tennessee Ernie Ford was number one with *Sixteen Tons* and I loved hearing it over and over. We also listened to *The Great Pretender* by The Platters, *I Hear You Knocking* by Gale Storm and *Memories Are Made of This* by Dean Martin.

The record shop, Village Music, was in the same building as the Sequoia Theatre and Sara never grew impatient with us ever. There was a little sound-proof booth we'd go into to listen to the records she'd happily play for us.

The Sequoia always showed two films which changed twice a week. Somewhere within an evening at the movies you would see previews of the next two pictures to be shown. I saw the trailer for *Tarantula!* at least twice and my goodness it looked scary and exciting: the giant spider crawling over a hill, a pickup truck spinning down the mountain, the enormous arachnid lumbering relentlessly towards us on the desert highway through the clouds of an explosion which hadn't stopped it.

I went to see *Tarantula!* at the Sequoia in that wet winter of 1955. I was already frightened of tarantula spiders thanks to the Walt Disney nature film *The Living Desert* which I'd seen up at the Lark. I don't think I had even been aware of the existence of spiders before that movie saddled me with a phobia that has lasted most of my life.

Tarantula! was good fun. Professor Deemer, played by Leo G. Carroll, invented a serum which caused giantism in animals and acromagaly (a hormonal disorder which distorts hands, feet and face) in humans. Amongst the bunnies and guinea pigs growing huge in his lab was a tarantula spider. A fight with a colleague resulted in the spider, now the size of an armchair, escaping into the desert.

The wonderful thing about this movie was that it was made in the style of a detective story. While we, the audience knew what had happened, John Agar and the others didn't, and watching them have to figure out the mystery was very engaging.

My blossoming arachnophobia did not interfere with my total enjoyment of *Tarantula!* and it whetted my appetite for more of the same.

The studio producing most of these films was Universal-International and another of their pictures that same year was *This Island Earth,* a sci-fi movie about visitors from a doomed planet with designs on our world.

While most of UI's 1950s sci-fi/horror fare was shot in black and white on budgets in the region of $200,000, *This Island Earth* was made in full colour for roughly four times that amount.

Spending the weekend up in Ross at the Hallinans' place, Jimmy and I, along with Danny and his brother Ringo, all went to see *This Island Earth* at the Rafael.

As had become my custom, I had followed the film's advertising in the Peanuts section of the Chronicle where all the movie listings were. Prominent in the lower right hand corner of the ads was the Metalunan Mutant, a giant insect-like creature with a testicular head and huge claws, seen assaulting beautiful Faith Domergue. On the poster there was an army of these mutants approaching in the background but on screen, presumably, the budget didn't stretch to more than one mutant appearing briefly at the end.

But the film was fabulous. Dr Cal Meacham, played by Rex Reason, was sent instructions and parts for building an Interocitor which turned out to be a hi-tech televisual communication device through which Exeter, played by Jeff Morrow, invited him to a scientific retreat. Curious but suspicious, Cal gets into a pilotless plane which flies him to a place run by men with enormous foreheads and startlingly white hair. They turned out to be from Metaluna, a planet being destroyed by warfare and the Metalunans had set their sights on Earth as their new home.

The Rafael was probably the swankiest movie theatre in Marin County. It certainly was the only one with a balcony which you had to climb carpeted steps to enter. Though it wasn't as big, it had the feel and look of one of the enormous movie houses on Market Street in the city.

Danny's mother Vivian drove us to the Rafael, but we all had to walk back to Ross, via San Anselmo, after the movie which was a considerable distance for boys of our age.

Staying at the Hallinans' place was always exciting. They were fabulously wealthy and lived in a mansion on a beautiful estate with a huge swimming pool.

Danny was my younger brother Jim's age but his five brothers were so much older than him that he was almost like an only child. Ringo was the only Hallinan son who paid us much attention when we visited and he was wonderful fun.

One time Jimmy, Danny and I were spending the night out on the massive lawn in sleeping bags when our chatter was interrupted by the sudden sound of something moving noisily through the bushes. Like a deer sensing danger, Danny immediately sat bolt upright with a look of terror on his face. Scary wild growling echoed from the woods behind their artificial lake. The crunching noises and growling came closer. Panic consumed us all and we scrambled to our feet. Of course it was Ringo but the performance was executed with such professionalism, complete with totally realistic wild animal sounds, that the experience was every bit as exciting as one of those scary movies.

Ringo, Danny and I shared a passion for scary movies while my brother Jim would come along but wasn't overly interested. Ringo regaled us with descriptions of *The Thing* - a tale of a malevolent, plant-based alien accidentally defrosted in the Arctic. Danny also told me all about *Them!* a movie featuring giant ants running amok in Los Angeles.

Another movie that Ringo took Danny to see in the city was *It Came from Beneath the Sea* in which Ray Harryhausen's giant octopus pulled down the Golden Gate Bridge. Danny told me all the details out on the porch but, years later he confided how strange it was for a kid so young to return from the movie across the very bridge he'd just seen destroyed.

The lure of these movies was very powerful. The sight of gigantic monsters destroying a major city or flying saucers arriving from outer space thrilled me with an intensity I could barely contain.

Of course they only showed a small number of horror movies at the Sequoia and they were vastly outnumbered by films like *The Private War of Major Benson, Pete Kelly's Blues, Love Me or Leave Me* and *The Seven Little Foys.*

Horror movies were considered very lowbrow in the 1950s and were hardly ever reviewed by the critics. My sister Nell used to get Screen Stories magazine each month and they never ran features on horror films though they did list a few in the back pages. The one exception was MGM's *Forbidden Planet* but that had a budget even bigger than *This Island Earth.*

The reality was that I actually saw very few of these movies. During a visit to my mother's relations in San Jose in 1956, the four of us joined our cousins to see *Forbidden Planet* which was wonderful. We'd already seen it at the Sequoia but it was fun to see again. The sound effects were eerie and the scenes where the invisible Id monster attacked the ship were dramatic. The flying saucer was excellent and Robby the Robot was a beautifully designed piece of machinery.

In between features they showed black and white previews

for a double-bill: *Earth Vs the Flying Saucers* and *The Werewolf.* Both these trailers absolutely thrilled me. Watching this guy turn into a werewolf before my eyes was the most exciting thing I'd ever seen and the sight of the saucers attacking Washington DC was amazing. In addition to the saucers there were these robot men with domed heads who shot rays out of their hands. The images from both these trailers blended into each other and resonated within my soul for years to come. I never got to see the actual films when they opened though *Earth Vs. the Flying Saucers* did turn up at our Saturday matinees a few years later.

A double bill which caught my imagination at the Sequoia was *World Without End* and *Indestructible Man* which starred Lon Chaney Jr. The posters for these films were full of allure. Movie posters always took the most sensational visual images from the film and intensified them. The sight of Lon Chaney Jr staggering towards you with a jagged halo of electricity surrounding his arms and head while wearing the face of a maniac conveyed the movie's plot effectively. The image of a giant spider attacking grown men on the poster of *World Without End* assured my attendance for both these pictures. But neither movie lived up to the poster.

In the early summer of 1956 another horror movie hit the Sequoia and, again, it was preceded by a trailer which convinced me I had to see it. *The Creature Walks Among Us* was so scary and exciting and the fact that I hadn't seen the first two *Creature* movies didn't make any difference.

The two actors from *This Island Earth,* Rex Reason and Jeff Morrow starred and the plot involved scientific responsibility and obsessive jealousy. The creature got his scales burned off early in the story which made him even scarier-looking than before.

The magic of these movies seared my consciousness with such strength yet I came away with no tangible evidence of the experience I'd had except for vibrant memories and a few clipped ads from the Peanuts section. Drawing these ads was something of an obsession for me and I remember the campaign for *The Creature Walks* with illustrations of the beast hurling a man's body overhead with his outstretched arms.

It soon dawned on me that not all the pictures ended up at our local cinema, for the Sequoia was just one of the small theatres where the movies played after their initial run in San Francisco. So I now scanned the film ads more thoroughly and kept a careful watch for what was opening in the city.

It became clear that to see some of these horror movies I would have to venture to Market Street in the city, all by myself. That would be a new and slightly frightening adventure which I would soon be embarking on.

Chapter 17

The Discovery Of MAD

I hadn't expected anything extraordinary to happen by tagging along with my older sister Nell on a visit to Erik Johnson's house next to our playground one Sunday afternoon in 1955. The visit, however, was to change my life forever.

Erik was the same age as Nellie and they had many things to talk about, so when we arrived, he pulled some comic books out of a drawer and suggested I look at them.

I was immediately taken by the title spelled out on the covers in pointy outline letters: MAD. They were comic books, not magazines. They were printed in full color and had a ten cent price stamp on the front.

Inside I lost myself in a version of *Alice in Wonderland* where Alice, beautifully drawn in classic blue dress with white stockings, chased the white rabbit down a hole and began falling, gracefully at first, then after turning completely upside down, she fell out of the frame and landed on her head with a **SPLAT!** Later when she encountered the rabbit again he had morphed into *Bugs Bunny*.

Getting into the rhythm of their story telling, I moved onto *Howdy Dooit,* a beautifully drawn take-off of *The Howdy Doody Show* in which Buffalo Bill had trouble controlling the children in the Peewee Gallery. With each frame the young crowd became more rambunctious until froth was coming out of their mouths. They then viciously attacked him. The next story was *Stalag 18* with fabulous cartoon likenesses of William Holden and other cast members from Billy Wilder's prisoner of war movie *Stalag 17*.

I was completely overwhelmed by these comics and sat in the corner reading them while Nellie and Erik talked about goodness knows what. I saw men, who, confronted by voluptuous busty women, transformed in a flash from sophisticated urbane fellows to drooling buffoons with extended tongues and eyes that bulged out of their sockets.

There was a parody of Disney called *Mickey Rodent* with perfect drawings of all the Disney characters. Mickey, who looked seedy and needed a shave, was jealous of the competition from Darnold Duck and lured him into a trap, locking him away from public view.

Examining the drawings closely I noticed all this amazing detail in the background: while Goony was telling Darnold he should be wearing trousers, there was a pet shop behind them with naked human men in the window. At one point when Darnold was talking to Mickey's girlfriend Minnie, he held his tummy with a look of nausea and told us in a thought balloon: "Somehow...the idea of a mouse with lipstick and eyelashes and a dress with high heeled shoes; A mouse, ten times bigger than the biggest rat...This idea has always made me sick!"

There was a story entitled *Poopeye* in which the drawings of Popeye and Olive Oil were every bit as good as the original. Another piece dealt with the movie *On the Waterfront* with perfect cartoons of Marlon Brando, Eva Marie Saint and Lee J. Cobb entitled *Under the Waterfront*.

How long we stayed I don't remember but I must have read these comics a couple of times through before we left. I came away with a conviction that MAD was for me and I had to have it. I had never seen anything which made fun of so many sacred cows in such an entertaining way.

After school the next day I went to the Bus Depot and asked Margo if she had a copy of MAD. She said they didn't have any at the moment but promised to keep one aside for me when it came in. Days became weeks and still no MAD arrived.

I stalked the Bus Depot for almost two months before MAD, at long last, appeared. But what I finally held in my hands was not the full colour comic book I had fallen in love with. No. This was a magazine, much bigger than a comic book. It had a detailed illustrated frame around the border and the word MAD was drawn in a kind of circus lettering with dropped shadows and serifs whilst inside the letters were pictures of these nymph-like women chasing four legged men who had hooves.

The cover was a slightly greyish white and in the upper right hand corner of the border art was a beautifully-drawn oval frame with the price twenty five cents inside it. Beneath this was a scroll containing the words: *Our Price.* Beneath that sat a little plaque with the word: *Cheap.*

I looked inside and all the pages were in black and white and in addition to the illustrations there seemed to be an awful lot of writing. So it was not a comic book at all.

Stunned and confused, I coughed up the quarter and took the new MAD home with me but, try as I might, at eight years old, I found too much of it to be simply over my head. I soldiered on for the next few issues but then stopped buying it for about a year.

I did, however, come across a Ballantine paperback of *The MAD Reader* at the bus depot which cost me thirty five cents and contained black and white reproductions from the comic books, printed sideways so it was a bit like reading a flick book but bigger. The cover utilised the original MAD logo and sported a black and white picture of a funny looking boy with jug ears. Most of my generation of Americans would soon know this boy as Alfred E. Neuman but I don't believe he had yet been christened.

The book had such treasures as *Superduperman, Starchie, Flesh Garden, Dragged Net* and *The Lone Stranger.* This book became my constant companion at bedtime.

In *Superduperman* Clark Kent was reduced from the mild mannered reporter of the *Superman* comics to a groveling, asthmatic copy boy who Lois Pain called a creep as she slapped him out of her way. Lois was stunningly beautiful with a tight skirt and big breasts. Her contempt for poor Clark was abjectly cruel.

In *Starchie* the clean-cut *Archie Andrews* was portrayed as a hardened juvenile delinquent who, with his equally delinquent friend Bottleneck, controlled the rackets at Riverdale High School. When the beautiful blonde Biddy threw herself at Starchie, the contents of her handbag flew out and we saw they consisted of a hypodermic needle, pills, reefers and playing cards. The style of illustration pulled no punches nor made any allowance for notions of censorship. This particular story was illustrated by Will Elder, one of three artists who became my childhood heroes. The other two were Wallace Wood and Jack Davis.

What I didn't know, as an eight year old boy, was that MAD was only one title in the sizeable output of EC (Entertaining Comics), a company which was a pioneer in the field of horror and violent crime comics. EC's comic books had become a target of Senator Kefauver's hearings on juvenile delinquency. William Gaines, the boss of EC appeared at the televised hearings in April 1954 and soon found the witch-hunt caused by his periodicals was so bad for business that it stopped publishing them and turned MAD into a magazine instead.

So I was stuck in a historically awkward situation. The comic books I'd absolutely flipped for were no longer being published and the magazine that EC was now putting out was a bit too adult for me. Of course I knew none of this and didn't have the presence of mind to simply ask Erik Johnson if I could have his old MADs.

Thank goodness, therefore, for *The MAD Reader*. In *Flesh Garden* I found a hero who was long on bluster and short on courage. In fact MAD seemed to specialise in exposing their heroes to be abject cowards in the face of danger. They delighted in debunking all notions of nobility and heroism.

A sequel paperback entitled *MAD Strikes Back* soon hit the stands and joined *The MAD Reader* on my bedside table. Equally terrific, it contained gems like *Prince Violent, Gopo Gossum, Ping Pong (as in King Kong)* and *Manduck the Magician.*

Now, however, I longed to see these stories in full colour as they were originally presented.

It was late 1956 when I began buying MAD the magazine again. It seems there was a palace coup within the EC empire and Harvey Kurtzman, the man who had created, written and edited the magazine, was fired and Al Feldstein took over as editor. One of the changes he made was to eliminate the illustrated frame around the cover page. Somehow the covers, now in full colour, became more accessible to me and I was soon hooked all over again.

I read MAD, the magazine, religiously for the rest of the 1950s and well into the 60s. I remember kids at Edna Maguire calling me sick for loving it. They were probably right. One of the things I liked about MAD was its claim to be mind-rotting trash. In a piece about children asking their parents what they did for a living, Wallace Wood drew this little girl sitting on Bill Gaines' lap while he says: "Your father's a crook, child. He publishes MAD Magazine."

One thing which never occurred to me was that MAD was totally a product of New York consciousness and it may have been the case that, without knowing it, I was responding to it so positively due to subconscious nostalgia. Nobody else in my school read it. In fact I think its sizeable readership at this time was predominantly adult.

My seventh grade history and English teacher, Mr Healy, told our class that his wife worked for an advertising agency and that it was considered the sign of a highly successful campaign to be parodied by MAD.

I didn't learn about EC's horror comics until my sister Nell was living on Greenwich Street in San Francisco in the early 60s and one of her flatmates had five issues including *Tales from the Crypt* and *Weird Science.* I immediately recognised the art work of Jack Davis and Wally Wood and encountered new names like Graham Ingels, who signed his works as *Ghastly.* I also discovered the work of Jack Kamen and Johnny Craig.

At some point during my junior year at Tam High I got talking in the bus depot with a senior who told me that he actually had a stack of MAD comic books at home. Had he been at all mercenary, he could have taken me for a bundle but this guy generously just gave them to me.

It was like taking possession of some mystical treasure that Uncle Scrooge and his nephews had searched the far corners of the earth for.

I was and still am a collector and my love affair with MAD

was just one of the early manifestations of this strange passion which consumed my soul. Some time during my high school years I drifted away from MAD and never read it again. What me worry?

Chapter 18

Mister Finney's Pods

I saw more than my share of sci-fi/horror movies throughout the 1950s and early 60s, but there was only one picture of this type which my father Blackie actually took me to see at the Sequoia: this movie was *Invasion of the Body Snatchers.*

The year being 1956, I had already seen *Tarantula!, The Creature Walks Among Us* and *This Island Earth* but my father had never shown the slightest interest in those films so when he offered to take me to this movie, I wondered what was up.

It emerged that Blackie had read the original story by Jack Finney in Collier's Magazine in November and December of 1954 and really enjoyed it. I was thrilled he was taking me to see an actual sci-fi movie.

I had seen the trailer for it at the Sequoia and it had excited me greatly though I was unable to glean from it what the body snatchers actually were. In the preview I saw lots of dramatic shots of Kevin McCarthy in a hysterical state running amongst cars on a night time overpass, being subdued by psychiatric nurses and hiding in a cave with beautiful Dana Wynter. There were crowds of people running in the street and the music was definitely alarming, but the closest thing to a monster I saw was a big seed pod bursting open in a greenhouse with lots of white liquid exploding from within it.

I doubt at this late stage I'll be giving away any great secrets by revealing that the body snatchers were, in fact, giant seed pods from another world which, when placed in reasonable proximity to a human being, would replicate exactly that person's body complete with their memories. The one component missing from these doppelgängers was human emotion and it was this lack of genuine feeling which alerted loved ones that something was not quite right with Uncle Ira or Becky's dad.

It was a hauntingly scary movie which stayed with me so much that I actually sought out and read Jack Finney's book *The Body Snatchers.* I bought a copy of the Dell paperback from the Bus Depot and enjoyed it a lot but realised while reading it that Santa Mira, the town in which it took place, was actually Mill Valley. Mention was made of names like Eberhardt and streets called Throckmorton and Sycamore.

Jack Finney actually lived in Strawberry with his family not far away from my later girlfriend, Janice Kaufman. Jan's family knew the Finneys and she told me that the author used several of his neighbours' names when writing *The Body Snatchers*. The psychiatrist who Miles referred his patients to was Dan Kaufman.

In the first week of January, 1955, Finney was visited by producer Walter Wanger, director Don Siegel and screenwriter Daniel Mainwaring. They wanted to discuss the filming and get a look at Mill Valley as it was Finney's model for Santa Mira. Location shooting in our town was soon ruled out as too expensive and Siegel and some Allied Artists executives decided instead to find locations near Los Angeles which resembled Mill Valley: Sierra Madre, Chatsworth, Glendale and Bronson Canyon provided most of the locations while a large proportion of the movie was shot in the studio.

The film, for me, still succeeds in creating fear, not with lumbering monsters but with a simple idea…the loss of humanity. The creepiest moment is when Miles kisses Becky and we see a close-up of her dead eyes staring back at him. She had earlier fallen asleep while he went off to investigate some beautiful music and the pods attacked while he was gone. Any fool could have told him never to split up in a black and white B-movie. My seventh grade History and English teacher, Mr Healey, picked holes in this scene because all the other transformations had taken at least 24 hours and suddenly here was Becky completely changed where she'd nodded off for a few minutes.

One of our closest friends in Mill Valley were the Dreyfus family who lived in a large house up in West Blithedale canyon. One of Babbie Dreyfus's cousins was Joe Thompson, a PR man who happened to do some work for Allied Artists, the company which produced the *Body Snatchers* movie.

Cousin Joe had given the Dreyfus boys a large promotional seed pod. Jared's older brothers, Dave and Tim, seeing potential mischief in the pod, selected a gullible friend to join them at the Sequoia one night to see the movie and, to sleep over at their house afterwards.

The night time walk back from the Sequoia to their house was spooky enough after watching Bambi and Thumper but, having seen this movie, it was decidedly darker and creepier than usual. As they walked up West Blithedale, surrounded by tall trees whose leaves cast haunting shadows on the road below, both Dave and Tim adopted a quiet, unearthly manner so that their friend became nervous. Arriving home it was suggested they should have a drink and the friend was asked to get some glasses from the cupboard. When he opened the cupboard door he saw the large seed pod which, of course, Dave and Tim had planted there.

According to Jared, this poor fellow became terribly distraught and was convinced that the premise of the movie was being played out in real life. Dave and Tim held their other worldly performance until they could contain themselves no longer and burst into hysterical laughter. The victim was, by then, so convinced of the pod's authenticity that they had to actually rip the papier-mâché seed pod to pieces to convince him it wasn't real.

Of course the movie was hugely successful and has since become a cult classic with much literature written about it.

On the strength of a Rolling Stone interview with Philip Kaufman, I went to see his remake in 1978 but found it lacking any of the qualities which made the original great. It was a beautifully-shot San Francisco movie with fine performances from an excellent cast and remarkable special effects; particularly masterful in its depiction of how the pods replicated the human bodies. It was also very creepy, as in the scene where Kevin McCarthy made a cameo appearance and is killed by the silent crowd. But where the Siegel original was set in the emotional landscape of the 1950s, this later film was made after Hippies, Vietnam and Watergate had ravaged the American psyche and the status quo had become much weirder than it had been in sleepy Santa Mira. Hence it was more difficult to undermine what passed for normal in the updated film version.

Also the story had none of the film noir mystique of Mr Siegel's film. As the credits rolled in the remake, we saw the spores leaving their planet and migrating to earth where we witnessed them landing and growing in San Francisco. In Siegel's film the invaders behaved like ordinary people while Mr Kaufman's pods were such obvious aliens straight off the flying saucer. I personally found it much creepier that Uncle Ira, who remembered every last detail of his niece's childhood, puffed his pipe and mowed the lawn.

There are two films which I feel perpetuate the creative concept of Jack Finney's original story and Don Siegel's film and they were both released in 1998; *The Truman Show* directed by Peter Weir and *Pleasantville,* written and directed by Gary Ross. In both these movies we find individuals bucking against an oppressive notion of conformity. Each of them also had chase sequences which echoed images of Miles and Becky fleeing Santa Mira.

I'm not a big fan of Hollywood remakes as most occur through a combination of corporate greed and creative sloth. I'm aware of other remakes of *The Body Snatchers* but I steer clear of them.

The Santa Mira of 1956 remains the only place worthy of Mister Finney's pods, though I suspect, judging by the behaviour of many of our town's current inhabitants, that he may have planted a few extra pods in the Mill Valley of modern times.

Chapter 19

Of Bartholomew and Babar

My aversion to reading proper books throughout my childhood didn't mean that I wasn't a sucker for a good story. The lure of an engaging yarn was always strong and pulled me in several interesting directions. In addition to movies and comic books, I also found these yarns within the pages of the children's literature we had at our house on Seymour Avenue. And there was a fine selection on our bookshelves. Dr Seuss was well represented as well as the *Babar* books which my siblings and I loved. *Eloise* was another character whose adventures we returned to time and again.

Dr Seuss alternated between stories written in verse and those told with no rhymes at all. Both included a generous array of fine idiosyncratic illustrations which clinched the deal for me. So long as the pictures were good, I didn't mind reading the words.

The emotional landscape of these stories was important as reading the book was a visit to a complete world which the author/illustrator had created for you and the reality for me was that I returned to these books over and over again so they had to stand up to that kind of scrutiny.

The world Dr Seuss created in *The 500 Hats of Bartholomew Cubbins* was an old-fashioned European-looking kingdom called Didd.

The story opened with King Derwin surveying his domain from a balcony in his palace. The view was spectacular with many mansions and towers in the foreground giving way to more humble housing and farmers' huts in the far away fields. On the next page we saw Bartholomew Cubbins, sporting his red hat, staring up at the glorious palace from his family's hut on one of those far off fields. Straight away the kingdom of Didd existed for me in no uncertain terms.

Dr Seuss's style of illustration was beautifully eccentric though his anatomical accuracy was non-existent. His horses resembled something between a llama and a cow. In fact all his creatures lacked Nature's grace. His cats were strangely non-feline and his dogs had practically nothing canine about them. But they were all charming in the extreme and when he actually invented creatures he was out of this world.

The real name of this author/artist was Theodor Seuss Geisel. After a good education at Dartmouth, he managed to find employment in New York City as a cartoonist specialising in commercial art. By the time World War II came along, Geisel had established himself as an anti-fascist political cartoonist under the name Dr Seuss, a pseudonym he began using in college.

His first children's book *And to Think That I Saw it on Mulberry Street* was turned down by every publisher in New York. It wasn't until he bumped into a college chum who worked at Vanguard Books that it finally came out in 1937. The subsequent titles all sold reasonably well but his huge success came with *The Cat in the Hat* in 1957.

We must have had almost all of the Seuss books and they were wonderful without exception. I found *Bartholomew and the Oobleck* strangely spooky.

Set again in the kingdom of Didd where the same monarch, Derwin, was bored with the weather and wanted something new to come out of the sky. It was the magicians who gave me the creeps. Once summoned they walked slowly through an underground tunnel from their distant mountain cave chanting something about the magic they could perform. There were seven of them and they all had beards and long peculiar hats. They also had a little cat who wore a hat like theirs and joined in the magical chanting which helped produce the Oobleck.

For those unfamiliar with this yarn, Oobleck turned out to be a horrid green slime which stuck to everything. In both the Batholomew Cubbins books King Derwin made the Journey from being extremely silly to some kind of enlightenment.

Geisel was a very accomplished artist who seems to have been self taught. He employed different techniques for different stories. Most of his rhyming tales were accompanied by line drawings with simple colours but those set in kingdoms involved more complicated pictures executed on illustration board with tinted wash. These were drawn in black and white, sometimes in charcoal, with one colour keyed in. In *The King's Stilts,* the page boy's trousers were red as were the king's robes and stilts while all the background was monochrome.

Unlike King Derwin, the monarch in *The King's Stilts* seemed to be a benevolent sort who worked hard but enjoyed running around his kingdom on stilts when his toil was done. His kingdom, named Binn, existed in the valley of an island surrounded by ocean. The only protection the valley had from being flooded by the impending sea water was a barrier of Dike Trees which grew along the shore, holding back the torrent with their heavy interwoven roots.

Geisel's picture of the Dike Trees protecting the valley island of Binn from the ocean is a fine example of his eccentric imagination at work.

All his stories benefit from these wild jumping-off points: Horton the elephant agreeing to sit on the egg of the silly bird Mayzie; Bartholomew Cubbins finding that each time he takes off his hat another appears; Young Gerald McGrew populating his zoo with armies of invented animals including 'a Nerkle, a Nerd (it's possible that this word was a Geisel invention) and a Seersucker too!'

One little conceit of Geisel's illustration style which evolved through the books was the teardrop horseshoe eyes. In the first books some characters had them but by *The Cat in the Hat* they'd become a Seuss trademark, every bit as recognisable as Disney's three fingered white gloves. As someone who was constantly drawing I would copy these teardrop eyes.

Another series of children's books my siblings and I returned to time and again were those about *Babar* and his wife Celeste. Babar and Celeste were elephants who dressed in human clothing and happened to be the reigning monarchs of their benevolent kingdom.

Again text and illustrations came from the same source which was the Frenchman Jean de Brunhoff. It seems his wife, however, was responsible for the first stories but never took professional credit for them.

The world these elephants lived in was very exotic. Babar was king and Celeste his queen. His usual attire was a green suit and he wore a gold crown on top of his head. Like the early books of Dr Seuss, the Babar series first appeared in the 1930s.

Where Babar's fortune came from was never clear but he seemed to build Celesteville with his own funds and set up a society where everyone had a function and all the elephants seemed to co-operate with each other.

In *Babar the King,* he and his wise old friend Cornelius were gazing at the lake, populated by pelicans, flamingos and Ibis. Babar tells the old elephant that this is the place he would like to build their town. "Our houses will be in the midst of flowers and birds."

Zephir the monkey was playing with Arthur, a young elephant cousin of the king and queen, when they saw a long train of dromedaries bearing luggage on their humps. They were bringing all the things Babar had bought on his honeymoon abroad.

"Now," pronounced Babar, "We shall be able to build our town."

Calling a meeting of all the elephants, he addressed them: "In these bales and trunks I have presents for all of you. I will give them to you as soon as we have built our new town." Then the elephants set to work constructing Celesteville under the guidance of their king.

Seeing the illustrations of this work in progress was deeply satisfying for us young children: the elephants felling palm trees and methodically stacking the logs while others toiled with picks, shovels, saws and axes.

Before long the new town was built and the elephants each had a house of their own, laid out in even rows above the lake where many enjoyed a daily swim.

Though many have criticized the *Babar* books as a thinly disguised tribute to French colonialism, I looked at the elephants' world through different eyes and saw something which looked like a socialist society.

The pictures were wonderful: the elephants lining up to receive their presents from Babar, the inhabitants of Celestville going about their daily business gardening, cooking and cleaning the streets. The children, including Arthur, an elephant and Zephir, a monkey all went to school under the tutelage of the Old Lady.

But it wasn't all cozy and nice. Bad things did happen. The Old Lady was bitten by a poisonous snake. The sight of this frail older woman with a swollen arm being taken to the hospital was shocking. "I cannot tell till tomorrow whether she will recover," said the doctor to Babar.

Then old Cornelius' house caught fire and he too went to

the hospital. Babar went to sleep and had a nightmare in which a load of ghastly creatures with names like 'Misfortune,' 'Disease' and 'Ignorance' all visited him in his bed. Just as this was all becoming too much for young readers, Babar heard the sound of flying elephants with names like 'Goodness,' 'Hope' and 'Patience' who chased the ugly spirits away. Both the Old Lady and Cornelius recovered and all was well by the end.

In *Babar and his Children,* Celeste gave birth to triplets, two boys and a girl. The boys were named Pom and Alexander while the girl was called Flora.

The first bit of drama occurred when Flora swallowed a rattle in her crib, turning red faced and wide-eyed. Zephir saved the day by pulling the rattle out of her throat with his hand.

While Arthur was out with the triplets pushing their carriage, he got distracted by the soldiers parading and didn't notice the carriage roll off down the hill. As he and the nurse chased the runaway pram it hit a turtle and stopped suddenly, propelling little Alexander head first over a cliff. Luckilly he landed in a tree where two red squirrels (this was a European story after all) returned him safely to Babar and Celeste.

Alexander suffered further trauma when he sailed out onto the lake in a boat which was Cornelius' derby hat. He was almost eaten by a hungry crocodile but luckily Babar was fishing in a nearby boat and threw his anchor into the jaws of the ferocious beast.

My practice of copying the illustrations in all these books was very rewarding, particularly in *Babar and Father Christmas* which featured a double page multi-level picture of Father Christmas's underground toy factory with pully operated elevators which took his helpers to the different floors. This picture held a special fascination for me with its ant-farm view of all the different activities happening simultaneously.

As a small child I was astonished and delighted the first time my mother took me down into the New York subway. There was something magical about descending those special steps on the sidewalk which took you down into another world beneath the streets where there were bright lights, turnstyles, trains, policemen and gum machines. A subterranean society which delighted my senses and was burned on my consciousness forever. This illustration of all the floors of Father Christmas's toy factory thrilled me in the same way.

An entirely different world was to be found within the pages of an *Eloise* book. She was a very rich little girl whose parents never featured as she was looked after by her English nanny and her only friends seemed to be the employees of the hotel she lived in, the nanny and her little dog.

The day-to-day world of this very rich, spoiled young lady was the Plaza Hotel in Manhattan where she fluttered from distraction to distraction without ever encountering a playmate her own age.

The Myers family never stayed in expensive hotels or dined in fine restaurants so the lifestyle of Eloise was well outside of our experience. True we did have rich friends who were very generous in sharing their advantages but on a day-to-day basis we weren't used to places like the Plaza Hotel so it was extra exotic for us.

These stories were written by Kay Thompson with illustrations by Hilary Knight.

Kay Thompson was something of a show business phenomenon in that she was an actress, singer and director with a successful career in movies as well as on the stage. The character of Eloise evolved as a bit of schtick she would do with her friends socially. One of these friends was D.D. Ryan, a glamorous editor on the magazine *Harper's Bazaar* who, while listening to Thompson doing Eloise on the phone one day, suggested she should write some of this material down. Ryan also introduced her to one of her neighbours, Hilary Knight, a freelance magazine illustrator who went on do all the *Eloise* books.

Knight's fine pen and ink drawings captured the grandeur of the Plaza but also gave us a wide variety of characters from patient doormen to snooty ladies taking tea. His attention to the tiny details was a big reward for me as I could spend a lot of time examining the background of each page without ever getting bored. The first *Eloise* book appeared in 1955 and I'm pretty sure we had it by that Christmas.

Keeping this six-year-old girl from being an annoying little brat was only one of the artful elements about these stories. Eloise invented her own verbs, skibbling up the stairs and skiddering down the hall. She also was resolute in always being happy with her lot. Her mother was occasionally referred to but never seen.

She was the classic poor little rich girl who Kay Thompson claimed to have created all on her own though Liza Minelli, the daughter of Thompson's good friend Judy Garland, claimed that she herself was the source material for the wealthy moppet.

There were three more of these books which all found their way into the Myers household: *Eloise in Paris, Eloise at Christmastime* and *Eloise in Moscow.*

The Moscow book was my favourite as Hilary Knight's drawings were beautifully dramatic, depicting the Moscow subway, the Bolshoi Ballet and Red Square.

Why on earth Eloise and her Nanny should be going to Moscow at the height of the cold war was a total mystery but their tours around the snowbound city were beautifully realised and in each picture, hidden in the background was a little spy-like gentleman wearing a black hat and garment who was following them. Spotting this guy became like a game on each page.

My oldest sister Nell had a complete collection of all the OZ books by L. Frank Baum which were mostly illustrated by John R. Neill. I did not read the text of these books but I loved gazing at Mr Neill's pen and ink drawings.

In *Tik-Tok of Oz* there was a little girl who traveled to a land where lunch boxes grew on trees. Being hungry she pulled one down and ate. Before long the surrounding landscape was alive with the swirling dust of the approaching Wheelers. The Wheelers were these ghastly looking creatures with wheels instead of hands and feet. Equally ghastly was the witch Mombi. I would stare into these pictures for the longest time.

Also there was Tik-Tok himself, a mechanical man whose body was a big metallic globe. He befriended the little girl and beat the Wheeler into submission. Another character was this tall stick figure whose head was a large pumpkin. The imagery in these books was stunningly beautiful and this particular one was published in 1914.

There was one occasion when three of the Hallinan boys came to sleep over on a weekend at Seymour Avenue. Tuffy, Ringo and Danny all camped out in sleeping bags and I remember Nellie reading aloud to us all from one of the OZ books.

Another story which was a Myers family favourite was *My Father's Dragon* by Ruth Stiles Gannett, who wrote the book in 1944. The illustrations were by Ruth Chrisman Gannett and it told of the adventures of 'My Father' who sailed to the faraway Island of Tangerina then made his way by jumping from rock to rock across to Wild Island where he encountered tigers, wild boars, a lion, a gorilla and crocodiles before finally finding a poor winged dragon who was being kept prisoner by all these wild beasts.

Nellie, Katie, Jimmy and I would return to all of these books again and again. They never lost their magic for us. They provided an escape from the reality of our own lives which made us aware of imaginative possibilities beyond the world we lived in. Losing ourselves within these pages was like visiting a magic friend in a faraway land and you were always welcome to visit. All you had to do was open the book.

Chapter 20

For The Love Of Harryhausen

'PEOPLE OF EARTH ATTENTION! THIS IS A VOICE SPEAKING TO YOU FROM THOUSANDS OF MILES BEYOND YOUR PLANET!'

This announcement, made by a robotic distorted human voice, certainly held my attention as I sat, wide eyed, in the darkness of a packed Sequoia Theatre.

I was watching the very first Ray Harryhausen movie I ever saw: *Earth Vs the Flying Saucers* at the Saturday matinee. It was wonderfully exciting, visually spectacular and dramatically compelling.

Shot in black and white, Harryhausen's saucers were gracefully malevolent and though they didn't actually look real, their unreal quality was a thing of great beauty to my ten-year-old sensibility.

Whether the saucers were landing in Washington D.C., at a military base or incinerating a forest at night, the sight of these whirling disks thrilled me as did the weird robot-like creatures who came out of them with dome-shaped helmets and deadly rays which shot out of the tips of their outstretched arms.

I had no idea who Ray Harryhausen was or that his work would become an obsession of mine as the years passed. I was simply transported into the thrilling world of this particular movie.

The main character was Professor Marvin played by the slightly wooden Hugh Marlowe and the story revolved around him being the scientist that the invading saucer folk chose as their contact on earth. It was through his efforts that the aliens' weaknesses were discovered and eventually the planet was saved.

This film would be beautifully spoofed many years later in Tim Burton's *Mars Attacks!* in which many of Harryhausen's animation set pieces were lovingly imitated for laughs.

The main feature at the Saturday matinee was never a new film and I'm guessing that we got a sci-fi movie about every five weeks. Among the many I saw on Saturday afternoons were *The Day the Earth Stood Still, When Worlds Collide* and *War of the Worlds*.

My next monochrome Harryhausen picture was *20 Million Miles to Earth* and again I loved it. The beautiful silver rocket ship which crashed into the sea at the beginning didn't look real but its unreality was breathtaking and the little creature which fought its way out of the gelatinous egg was such a thing of beauty to behold. It grew from a few inches tall to hundreds of feet and ended up terrorising Rome.

The art which Ray Harryhausen practised was called stop-motion animation and he was inspired as a boy to learn this craft after seeing *King Kong* at the Grauman's Chinese Theatre in Los Angeles when it came out in the 1930s.

Stop-motion was painstaking and time-consuming. After designing a flexible model with a ball and socket skeletal armature inside it, each move had to be made and photographed separately and the final result then would be superimposed onto a live action background, via a process called traveling matte. This made the lighting and miniature set construction crucially important as well.

Harryhausen's artistry was so impressive to me but back in the Saturday matinee I didn't even know his name or anything about him. I simply loved the few of his movies that I saw.

Before I ever experienced these two films at the Sequoia, I'd heard blow-by-blow descriptions from Danny Hallinan of two others: *The Beast from 20,000 Fathoms* (as described in chapter 3) and *It Came from Beneath the Sea.*

The slightly jerky unreal quality of stop-motion animation was not to everyone's taste. But I fell in love with it early when I saw a scene from *King Kong* accidentally on the television and recognized the same jerky movements I'd noticed in the trailer for *20 Million Miles to Earth.*

The film which introduced me to the man behind these monsters was *7th Voyage of Sinbad.* On the week of its opening, the Sunday Chronicle featured a big photo of the giant Cyclops bending down to pluck Sinbad from a beach and there was also a newspaper ad showing a set of Harryhausen's early drawings of the Cyclops, dragon and the dueling skeleton.

This was the first of Harryhausen's movies to be shot in colour and it seemed a step up from the black and white sci-fi monster films of his past.

My brother Jim and I went to see *7th Voyage of Sinbad* at the St Francis while on a Christmas shopping trip to the city in 1958. I fell in love with the movie and was soon back to see it again.

Kerwin Mathews was a solid hero as Captain Sinbad while Torin Thatcher was entertainingly evil as Sokura the wicked magician. It looked glorious and the musical score was one of Bernard Herrmann's best which evoked all the magic of the Arabian Nights.

For me the Cyclops was the real star of that film but none of the creatures failed to shine: the fire-breathing dragon, the two headed Roc, The dueling skeleton. They were all spectacular as far as I was concerned. Drawing the Cyclops with its angry single orb and rhinoceros-like horn became a regular feature of the top margins of my binder pages.

So it was a little disconcerting for me when I went to see it for a third time at the Sequoia and my classmate Corky Corcoran broke out in squeals of laughter on the first entrance of the Cyclops. Luckily for me he didn't repeat the performance again throughout the film but I found myself strangely, though quietly, defensive of Harryhausen's monsters.

There was an expression which the kids at school used to describe special effects that didn't convince: fakey. I guess Corky considered the Cyclops to be 'fakey.'

Goodness there were plenty of 'fakey' movie monsters around. The giant gooney bird which terrorized the skies in Sam Katzman's *The Giant Claw* was so ridiculous-looking that it completely destroyed any illusion the film had created before the hapless turkey was finally seen. The Japanese men in dinosaur suits of *Gigantis the Fire Monster* actually drove me to leave the Paramount early because it bored me so badly and the tree monster in *From Hell It Came* was excruciatingly unconvincing.

So for me Ray Harryhausen represented artistic quality in a sea of sludge.

His next film also starred Kerwin Mathews, this time as Jonathan Swift's Gulliver in *3 Worlds of Gulliver* which I dutifully went to and enjoyed. After that it was *Jason and the Argonauts* followed by *Mysterious Island*.

I kept going to see all of Harryhausen's movies right up until the last one he made: *Clash of the Titans* and continued to be beguiled by his disciples like Phil Tippet, whose stop-motion work in the 1987 film *Robocop* thrilled me every bit as much as Harryhausen's. The fact that it was a giant police robot rather than a fire-breathing dragon made no difference. It was that same slightly jerky magic and I loved it.

Looking back from a later time in life I'd say that one of the most powerful emotional responses is the joy of recognition and it is this which has made me a collector. Once I recognize an artist's style that I like, I then become interested in their history, development and body of work.

I love many beautiful paintings and enjoy visits to galleries all over the world but equally the monochrome sight of the *Beast from 20,000 Fathoms* rising up out of the Hudson River gives me a special thrill that I'll only get from the work of Ray Harryhausen.

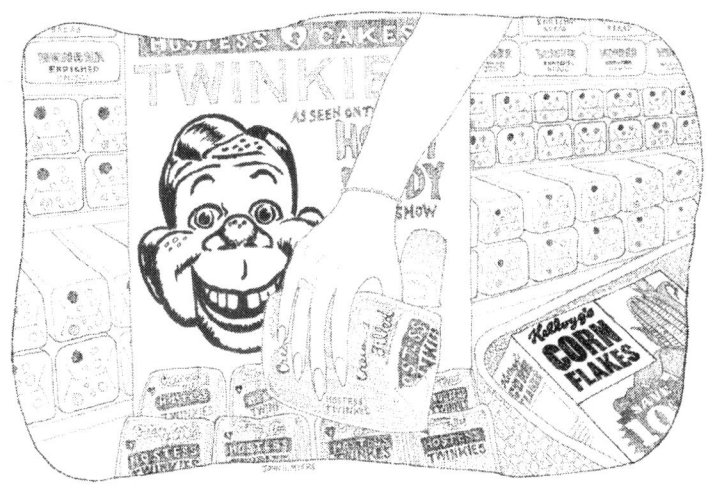

Chapter 21

So Much Better Than a Candy Bar

My mother Beth was the source of any pocket money that brother Jim and I ever had and a great percentage of it was spent on confectionery. My favourite candy bar was a *3 Musketeers* which cost a nickel. If I had a dime to spend it would go on a *Mountain* bar or a *Nestle's Crunch*. But if I had fifteen cents in my pocket, I would go into a grocery store in Mill Valley and purchase a packet of two Hostess *Twinkies*.

To eat a Hostess *Twinkie* was several notches higher than a mere candy bar and it already had celebrity status due to the endless TV commercials

I'd seen at friends' houses.

"You know, boys and girls," said Buffalo Bob in his friendly manner, "Every Hostess Twinkie is a great, great combination of golden light sponge cake on the outside and fluffy cream filling on the inside. They make really great snacks, desserts or lunch box treats. So come on, boys and girls, you ask your mom to get you a package or two of fresh Hostess Twinkies at your grocery store."

Without a pause, Buffalo Bob's pre-recorded voice for *Howdy Doody* spoke as the puppet stood by a Twinkie display case saying: "Just tell her to look for this display with the Hostess lady in the bright red heart."

I have no idea how many times I saw and heard Buffalo Bob extolling the virtues of Hostess *Twinkies* and I'm equally ignorant of just when I ate my first *Twinkie* but seeing it on television made it extra exotic when I'd see it in the store.

And it wasn't just *Twinkies*. The Hostess range included their distinctive *Cupcakes* which also got similar treatment on TV. It was a chocolate cupcake with the same cream filling inside and a curly white line across the dark icing on top.

When advertising the cupcakes on TV the host would open one up and the camera would zoom into the cream-filled centre.

The third Hostess product was the *Sno-Ball* which was basically a chocolate cupcake upside down which was then covered with a half dome of marshmallow coated with grated coconut. These would be either white or pink.

These to my young mind were special treats, much more exotic than a candy bar and while more conventional American parents would buy them for their children's lunch boxes this was not the case with Blackie and Beth.

My parents were not at all typical American consumers. They followed no trends and paid not the slightest attention to whatever the latest fads might be. The foodstuffs which entered our household were basic and not very expensive and there was no room in our budget for fluffy treats like Hostess Cupcakes. And because we had no television at home, neither of my parents was even aware of the kind of advertising Buffalo Bob was indulging in. Had they seen what he got up to on TV their contempt for the commercialism of it would have guaranteed that no such cake would ever cross our threshold.

So my enjoyment of these extravagant confections had to occur outside the boundaries of the Myers household. My brother Jim remembers: "Somehow their resemblance to baked goods gave them a bit more credibility than a shameless candy bar. I do recall that classmates who regularly had these treats in their lunch would occasionally offer them up because it was commonplace to them, and they could tell by my enthusiasm that it would be very special indeed to me."

The television advertising of sweet foodstuffs to children was and continues to be a highly questionable business as the poor little souls are new to the world and easily influenced. I doubt very much that Buffalo Bob and Clarabelle the Clown would get past the moral guardians of today as their pretence of entertaining children was a wafer thin cover for shamelessly hawking every product the network would allow.

The Howdy Doody Show did not stop at Hostess cakes. They advertised Colgate toothpaste, Wonder Bread, Halo Shampoo along with a mountain of other products.

This blatant advertising did not avoid the laser wit of MAD Magazine who featured a splendid parody: *Howdy Dooit*. Buffalo Bob became Buffalo Bill and he found himself confronted by a precocious young boy telling him that when he grew up he wanted to be a hustler like Howdy Dooit. "But child," protested Bill with seeming sincerity, "Howdy Dooit is no hustler! He needs no dollar bills to smile...no mercenary incentive to pass out happiness! Howdy Dooit is a happy wooden marionette, manipulated by strings!" Then in a wicked, grinning aside to the reader Bill confides: "I, Buffalo Bill, am the mercenary, money grubbing hustler!"

But no such candour was ever on display on *Howdy Doody*. The show itself looked relatively inexpensive. The music was provided by a single organ, in stark contrast to the programme's commercials which were pre-recorded with orchestral backing and much higher production values than the rest of the studio offering.

There is no doubting that the 1950s was the era of the television as it was the medium which caught the full attention of the American public and threw Hollywood into a panic.

In 1951 my family spent a very frozen winter in a cabin that backed onto White Bear Lake in Minnesota on our slow journey across America before arriving in Mill Valley. The first TV show I ever watched was *Howdy Doody* at a neighbour's house. After Buffalo Bob announced the opening, he went to the peanut gallery and got all the children to sing (to the tune of Ta-ra-ra boom-de-ay):

It's Howdy Doody Time, It's Howdy Doody Time,

The camera moved across the peanut gallery and then we were introduced to Clarabelle the silent clown who sprayed seltzer water at everyone and chased people around the studio.

This, almost certainly, will have been my first exposure to the high-pressured advertising of sugary foodstuffs aimed at young viewers.

Buffalo Bob's show had a long list of commercial sponsors over the years and he was adept at selling their products to children and mothers at home. He and Clarabelle were an effective double act: the clown would mime such sensations as hunger and often held the product for the camera while Bob, a middle aged man in a buckskin shirt, rhapsodised about its virtues.

At an earlier time in history he might have been a traveling salesman along the lines of Professor Harold Hill in *The Music Man* but Bob Smith was a disk jockey, singer and highly accomplished musician from Buffalo, New York, who made his name in radio during the second world war. He was clearly a talented fellow who began doing the puppet show on TV during 1947 and it caught on coast to coast.

The *Mickey Mouse Club* made its televisual debut in October 1955. This Walt Disney programme was slightly more expensive-looking than *Howdy Doody*. This is not to suggest that it was free from child-targeted advertising but the production values looked so much glossier.

My father's unyielding ban on television in the Myers household underwent a brief subversion when a cousin from my mother's side of the family came to stay with us for a time while studying. He brought with him a television set. It must have been when the

Mickey Mouse Club first came on because I soon became hooked on the show.

All the Mouseketeers were trained singers and dancers and the choreography was terrific. In the role call at the top of each program the Mouseketeers would announce themselves and I was particularly taken by pretty Annette Funicello. In true Disney fashion I was soon brainwashed with the theme song…

> *Who's the leader of the club,*
> *That's made for you and me.*
> *M-I-C….K-E-Y….M-O-U-S-E,*
> *Mickey Mouse (Donald Duck!),*
> *Mickey Mouse (Donald Duck),*
> *Forever let us hold his banner higher,*
> *Higher, Higher, Higher,*

Leading the Mouseketeers was Jimmie Dodd, a guitar-playing, singing host whose seeming sincerity was astonishing to behold. With the aid of hindsight it really wouldn't surprise me to see Buffalo Bob smoking, drinking and cavorting with wild women in a bar but not so Jimmie Dodd. He truly seemed to be the real thing and was, it seems, a born again Christian.

He was an actor, singer and songwriter and did his first work for Disney as a composer. He wrote the jingle for Ipana Toothpaste which featured Bucky Beaver and also wrote *The Pencil Song* for the *Disneyland* TV show.

Disney himself had very little to do with the making of the *Mickey Mouse Club* as he was so busy with other productions and the newly opened Disneyland.

So when the *Disneyland* TV show producer, Bill Walsh, who was very impressed with Jimmie Dodd, wanted him to host the Mouseketeer show, it was necessary to fix it so that Disney thought it was his idea. To this end he got Dodd to perform *The Pencil Song* for Walt, who immediately suggested Jimmie as host for the show.

It was no cake walk pulling that show off. The mouse ears alone were pretty ridiculous-looking, particularly on big Roy, the guy who drew all the pictures but the whole thing worked a treat thanks, in large part, to Jimmie Dodd's penetrating sincerity. Whether he was talking to camera or singing, he just came across as your best buddy in the whole world and when he'd close each show you really believed him...

> *Now it's time to say goodbye,*
> *To all our family,*
> *M-I-C....See you real soon,*
> *K-E-Y....Why? Because we like you,*
> *M-O-U-S-E*

Dodd had charm, talent, showbiz professionalism and the ability to make you believe in him. What more fertile setting could there be for advertising all those same products hawked so shamelessly over on *Howdy Doody*? Betty Crocker, Hostess *Cupcakes, Twinkies* and *Sno-Balls* coupled with the army of candy bars produced by Mars confectionery and many more lined up to be promoted on this programme.

ABC which had scored such a ratings success with *Disneyland,* started selling advertising slots before *Mickey Mouse Club* production even began. The show's huge success became a vehicle for products aimed at children but also those targeted at mothers who made up approximately a third of the viewing audience.

In addition to commercials with high production values the show's hosts also personally advertised certain products. They promoted Hostess *Cupcakes* with a particularly friendly touch.

A lot of kids turned up at Homestead School with *Twinkies, Sno-Balls* and *Cupcakes* in their lunch boxes. I do wonder, however, if these cakes would have had the same success without the assistance of this kind of advertising on television.

Another thing which kept the *Mickey Mouse Club* a must-see for me was the serial of *Spin And Marty*. This was a sure-fire formula for keeping kids watching as there was always a cliff hanger at the end of each episode just like at the Saturday matinee. Additionally the Mouseketeers were all totally professional dancers and their beautifully choreographed routines were executed with a panache which took your breath away. They were proficient in ballet, tap and ballroom dancing and the rehearsal involved cannot have left a lot of time for these children to have had much of an education to say nothing of a life.

So while Buffalo Bob and Clarabelle the Clown were busy shoveling dollar bills into their beat-up old suitcase, Jimmie Dodd and the Mouseketeers were working their socks off for scale, providing high quality old fashioned entertainment. Yet they both sold us those same cupcakes.

Thank god for MAD Magazine, the only place where I received a healthy dose of skepticism about all this carefully constructed illusion of wholesome entertainment.

In *Dizzyland,* cartoonist Wally Wood introduced us to Walt Dizzy's worlds: Tomorrowsland, Frontrearland, Adventuresland, Fantasticland and Walt's favourite: Moneyland. We saw Walt opening filing cabinet drawers to show us old animation cells but finding instead a flood of dollar bills tumbling out. He then opened a door which led to an Uncle Scrooge style money bin with big Roy, wearing his mouse ears, shoveling Walt's cash.

Jimmie Dodd came down with a voracious cancer and died at his home in Hawaii in the early 1960s. Buffalo Bob, having suffered a heart attack in the early fifties, bought himself a couple of radio stations and lived to a ripe old age.

Many years later when the world was a much

different place I was intrigued to learn of Dan White's 'Twinkie Defence' when he stood trial for murdering City Councillor Harvey Milk and Mayor George Moscone in the San Francisco of the 1970s. The claim was that eating too many Twinkies had pushed White over the edge and spurred him on to commit murder. Dan White was of the generation who would have watched Buffalo Bob proselytizing about the virtues of these lunch box treats. Perhaps the *Howdy Doody* host should have warned the children not to eat too many.

Chapter 22

Monsters On Market Street

My first three years at Homestead School I had terrifying teachers. Mrs Spaulding, Mrs Dempster and Mrs Lewis did indoctrinate me in the basics of reading, writing and arithmetic but they also scared the living daylights out of me with the regular ritualistic punishments they would inflict on those poor souls whose parents had ticked the box allowing corporal punishment.

I would grab any excuse to stay off school and, though I did learn those basic skills from these women, I didn't get any sense of how exciting or fun the business of learning could be. I came to view the classroom as some place I had to be rather than wanted to be and once the school bell rang at the end of the day I was out that door like a shot.

Of all the diversions which preoccupied my young mind at that time, The Movies was probably the strongest. Not only did I love going to see whatever was on at the Sequoia but I would also spend many hours poring over the movie ads in the Chronicle.

The styles of movie advertising fascinated me. The ads for *Rebel Without a Cause* conveyed the drama of the film with just a few photos…James Dean leaning against a wall, Sal Mineo and Natalie Wood looking anxious and another shot of Dean pulling Natalie by the arm.

I also saw stills from this movie, including pictures of the switchblade fight, in my sister Nell's copy of Screen Stories magazine. So by the time I saw it at the Sequoia I was already familiar with the images.

The average movie lasted about an hour and a half. The designers of the ad campaigns would take a visually stunning moment from that film and represent it with one still which was always gaudy and melodramatic. For *From Here to Eternity* it would be Frank Sinatra holding the barstool in his fight with Ernest Borgnine or the sight of Burt Lancaster and Deborah Kerr in swimsuits, passionately embracing each other as waves roll across them on the beach. These images which were just moments in the film, became fixed pictures in my mind.

And it wasn't just photographs. The ads for *The Man With the Golden Arm* featured a piece of modern art worthy of Pablo Picasso: a disjointed cartoon of a human arm with elbow and wrist going the wrong way.

For fourth grade at Homestead I had Mrs Blaugh, who was the first teacher that ever made me interested in the subjects we were studying. She was a handsome dark haired woman who became pregnant as the year progressed and by the end was pooching out like a toy balloon, as my father would have said.

She had a sense of humour and was gently amused by my pathetic attempts to look like Elvis Presley. Mrs Blaugh made it perfectly clear to me that she loathed Elvis Presley in every way but that didn't stop her being amused by my combed-down sideburns and greased-back hair. I began her class in September of 1956 and the main subject I recall was history: she brought it to life for me. For the first time I didn't mind coming to school.

Not that Mrs Blaugh didn't invoke the corporal punishment clause on occasions but when she did she'd drag the poor culprit out into the hall away from our field of vision. One of my good friends had a ruler broken over his backside by her and remains angry about it to this day.

Mrs Blaugh had us do projects on the Spanish missions in California and this involved us writing away for information packs which was kind of exciting in itself. I remember receiving packages with booklets from several different missions in California. We also covered the American Revolution with her.

By this time I was making regular visits to the Sequoia Theatre to see such movies as *23 Paces to Baker Street, Bohwani Junction* and *Moby Dick.*

I became particularly excited by the release of the first movie starring Elvis Presley, *Love Me Tender,* which I went to see at the Sequoia. Another film we went to see as a family was *Friendly Persuasion.*

But regardless of what was playing at the Sequoia I would always spend lots of time gazing at the movie ads in the Chronicle which were mostly for the big first run theatres on Market Street. I would only ever see a small percentage of these pictures but that didn't stop me studying them every day.

I had, by this time, become obsessed with horror movies. Having seen *Tarantula!* and *The Creature Walks Among Us* at the Sequoia, I now had acquired a hunger to see more of the same.

Monster and science fiction movies were something of a rarity in those days and I would linger longer on the ads for these than other pictures. The ads for *The Incredible Shrinking Man* gave me glimpses of the tiny human doing battle with a giant cat and a massive spider. *The Attack of the Crab Monsters* showed a giant crab holding a scantily clad young woman in its claw and *The Deadly Mantis* featured a giant insect wreaking havoc in a major city.

As summer approached there was one week in which several big movies opened: *Joe Butterfly,* a comedy starring Audie Murphy was due at the RKO Golden Gate (it looked okay but nothing special) and *Island in the Sun* with Harry Belafonte opened at the FOX with its most arresting image, the sight of a shapely, under-dressed female, doing a limbo dance. But the movie ad which really caught my eye that week was the double bill opening at the United Artists: *The Monster That Challenged the World* and *The Vampire.*

The ad for these two pictures stopped me in my tracks and kept me staring. On the left was *The Monster,* a kind of giant snail like creature with two angry bulging white eyeballs and sharp pincers who was holding a beautiful young woman in a bathing suit within its suction-like grasp. You definitely wouldn't want to bump into this bastard in a swimming pool. The other image was that of *The Vampire,* an ugly-looking man biting into the neck of a beautiful young woman.

My soul was on fire. I had to see these two movies and somehow I managed to get the money and permission from my mother to take a Greyhound bus on my own into the city. I was ten years old and my visit to the United Artists Theatre did not disappoint me. In fact these two pictures scared the hell out of me. They were every bit as terrifying as the advertising promised. I was becoming hooked on the thrill of being frightened.

But getting the money and permission to go to these movies was not always possible. When *20 Million Miles to Earth* opened at the St Francis, all I could do was stare at the ads in the Chronicle which showed this wonderful looking creature holding a small human in one hand while ripping a lamp post out of the sidewalk with its other.

I remember the drive up to Russian River that summer where we camped. As our car would move through each small town I would keep my eyes peeled to see what was on at their local theatre and at one I spied a poster for *20 Million Miles to Earth* as we drove by. Sadly we didn't stop to see it.

1957 was to prove a bumper year for scary movies and as the summer progressed the monsters seemed to come out of the woodwork all at once. My idea of a werewolf had been formed by seeing a black and white preview for Columbia's *The Werewolf* at a San Jose screening of *Forbidden Planet* and it looked wonderfully scary. But I never had the chance to see the actual movie. These experiences all occurred in a vacuum and you had to be in the right place at the right time when you were a little kid or you didn't even know they were happening.

I went into an instant trance when I saw a large ad in the Chronicle for a movie called *I Was a Teenage Werewolf*. In the foreground a beautiful brunette was screaming as a young man crouched menacingly in front of her. To the left of her was a close-up of the werewolf's terrifying visage. It had the same frightening look of the one I'd seen in San Jose but with the added notion of teenagers. Monsters with switchblade knives.

I was now aware that certain types of movies never played the Sequoia. Films had to have a minimum level of respectability to turn up at our local theatre and gazing down at the frightening, furious face of the *Teenage Werewolf,* with its fusion of lycanthropy and juvenile delinquency, I made an educated guess that this movie would never play the Sequoia in a million years.

No. I had to make a pilgrimage once more to that street of exhaust fumes and corruption in order to witness this spectacle for, witness it I must. Of that there was no doubt in my mind and, again, I'm unable to recall the machinations which brought my plottings to fruition. My mother must not have asked what movie I was going to see for I'm certain she wouldn't have approved but perhaps I'm wrong.

I arrived on the street of dreams early enough to gaze longingly at the posters and stills at the St Francis where it was showing. A pop song of the time always makes me think of this and it was Debbie Reynolds' recording of *Tammy*. I found the contrast interesting: cute Debbie Reynolds singing *Tammy* and the snarling *Teenage Werewolf* with foam drooling out of his mouth.

The other movie on the bill was *Invasion of the Saucer Men* and I had already noted from the ads that both this movie and *Teenage Werewolf* were made by a company I'd never heard of before: American-International Pictures (see chapter 27).

When the lights went down I was immediately impressed by the logo which came flying out of a cloudy sky: an illustration of the US Senate building sat above the words 'American-International Pictures' within an oval shape.

The Saucer Men was more of a comedy than it was scary as these interesting-looking aliens with huge testicular heads would inject people with their needle-like fingernails and make them drunk. The whole thing took place in a lovers lane and wasn't completely awful but it wasn't great. Frank Gorshin, later to become famous as a Hollywood impressionist, was in the cast.

Then it was time for the main feature and again the AIP logo flew out of a cloudy sky and the credits rolled to moody and unsettling music. I vowed, as the lights went down, that I wouldn't close my eyes or look away and I didn't. *Teenage Werewolf* was terrific and I found it totally terrifying.

Michael Landon played Tony, a brilliant but disturbed teenager who kept losing his temper and getting into fights. He was eventually sent to Dr Brandon, a psychiatrist played by Whit Bissell, an actor who played small parts in A pictures and starring roles in movies like this. Brandon was a very bad apple and had been waiting for someone like Tony to come along so that he could try his hypnotism on him. He would revert the troubled youth back to his primitive past which, naturally, meant making a werewolf out of the poor boy.

One trick which all the scary movies used, almost certainly to save money, was to not reveal the monster until you were alive with anticipation. The first death occurred without us seeing the werewolf at all: Tony's friend walking home through the forest alone at night, heard footsteps tramping through the leaves behind him. The last we saw of his friend was his terrified face screaming in horror.

The actual werewolf makeup was brilliant and the film was made on a very low budget and shot in a week but, by golly it was good and scary.

This was also the summer that *Loving You* starring Elvis Presley came out and played at the Paramount but the movie that really grabbed my attention that week was *Curse of Frankenstein*. The ads showed this creature's head which seemed to be disembodied and read: *The Curse of Frankenstein Will Haunt You Forever!*

This movie was in colour, which was unusual for a horror film at that time and was opening at the Fox. I had to see it and did, sitting alone in the biggest cinema on Market Street. It was British and looked fabulous. Peter Cushing played Victor Frankenstein and Christopher Lee was the creature. I had never heard of either but would soon become very familiar with them as this was the first Hammer Film I'd ever seen and many more would cross the pond over the next few years.

Again the formula of not revealing the monster was in play and in this movie we didn't see the creature's face until over half way through. When Christopher Lee, swathed in white bandages, pulled his mask off, the camera zoomed straight up to the gruesome visage, pulsing with colour. Of course I had seen the face on all the ads but this shot made me and everyone else jump. I had already drawn it several times on the top margins of my binder paper. What Mrs. Blaugh made of this I don't recall. I guess it was just one more monster along with Elvis as far as she was concerned.

But not all the horror movies I saw that summer were good. *The Cyclops* was kind of an ugly black and white picture and the dreadful *From Hell It Came* featured a supposedly scary monster: a walking tree.

I saw *The Land Unknown* at the RKO Golden Gate and it was surprisingly very good: one that actually lived up to the poster. The dinosaurs were pathetic by today's standards but I found them convincing enough and the story was exciting.

I began to become a little more discerning in my analysis of the advertising material for these movies. In the case of *20 Million Miles to Earth* and *Teenage Werewolf,* the movies were every bit as good as the poster promised, but not so with *The Cyclops* and *The Giant Claw.* This new critical discrimination on my part was born of sitting through more than a few turkeys during 1957.

The trouble with the horror movies of this era was that the advertising was the one thing that the studios spent a lot of money on and all the posters and ads looked terrific. The same could not be said for the quality of some of the movies.

Before the year was out American-International tempted me back to the United Artists Theatre with *I Was a Teenage Frankenstein* on a double bill with *Blood of Dracula* in which the vampire was a teenage girl. Neither were as good as *Teenage Werewolf* and by the following year I was avoiding any movies made by that company.

What compelled me to seek out these frightening experiences in darkened cinemas I don't know, but I think it must have had something to do with the political persecution of my parents and their close friends. There were very real monsters in our lives, raging across the country with a reckless ferocity. Senator McCarthy and his legal counsel Roy Cohn interrogated a close friend of my parents in the summer of 1953, asking him provocative questions about my father's politics. If ever there was a time to test the quality of your friendships, the witch-hunts of the early 1950s provided ample opportunity.

Perhaps sitting in a darkened cinema watching Michael Landon turn into the *Teenage Werewolf* may have been my way of psychologically arming myself against my real fears.

But even if that was the case, I was no more conscious of it then a walnut is about the weather. I'd simply see the ads in the Chronicle and become transfixed. By the time I'd arrive on Market Street, the sight of the blood red lettering on a gigantic poster display would set my heart pounding and, like the sucker at the carnival, I'd pay my money and go see the freak show.

Chapter 23

Kissing: Agonies And Some Ecstasy

Kissing, fondling and petting came under the heading of 'making out.' Making out was an activity which became important to me during junior high at Edna Maguire School though the opportunities to engage in this intimate art were few indeed.

From my earliest days my mother Beth would shower me and my siblings with kisses, so much so that I became blasé about her heart felt affection for the four of us.

It was when I began haunting the Sequoia Theatre from the age of six onwards that I became exposed to a different kind of kissing. Grace Kelly's beautiful visage descending on the disabled Jimmy Stewart in *Rear Window* was very different to my mother kissing me. Her behaviour was not earnest like my mother Beth's. It was something else. Something totally unlike motherly love. So a divide appeared within me between maternal affection and erotic love.

My first crush occurred in San Cristobal, New Mexico before we arrived in Mill Valley. I was just five years old and the girl of my dreams was Kristina Trujille, a dark haired beauty of my age but who was about an inch taller than me. It was this disparity which kept me from telling Kristina how I felt about her, though I seized every opportunity to be around her. Many a lazy afternoon was spent with Kristina, wandering among her father's crops eating raw peas and string beans.

My first actual experience of kissing someone besides my mother occurred while I was in grade school at Homestead. There was a Halloween party at Leni Schlesinger's house and, in addition to trying to bite floating apples with your hands tied behind your back, we also played 'Spin The Bottle.' Whoever your Coke bottle wound up pointed at would have to join you in another room where you would both share a kiss without witnesses.

At some point my bottle ended up pointed at Lily Burris who treated me with gentle contempt when we went in the other room. Lily probably sensed that I was hopelessly in love with her but I could no more deal with that reality than crawl to the moon. She did kiss me but there was nothing affectionate, friendly or erotic about it.

The big problem for me with women was my size. I was, by any reckoning, absolutely tiny for my age and I had no confidence with the opposite sex. Lily was taller than I was and I'm sure this informed her dismissal of me. She regarded me a bit like Lois Pain treated the wheezing asthmatic Clark Bent in MAD comic's *Superduperman*. Poor Clark spent his life savings to buy Lois a pearl necklace and once she'd accepted it without even the hint of a smile she slapped him across the room, walked over his body and called him a creep.

Clearly Lily never treated me that badly but she did keep me at arms length.

There were many occasions in school where I was the object of cuddly attention like when I played a little bear in a class show but on a day-to-day basis I simply felt awkward and out of it.

The first big change to occur was our move to Alto School for sixth grade. I now had my very first male teacher, Mr Zander. I also made some new friends like Craig Bird who was even bigger than Alex Robertson. I got to know Eddie Smith who also became friends with Alex and my new neighbour Johnny Lem. John and his family had arrived from Texas over the summer vacation and he was a fun guy to be around. We were divided up into two classes and under Mr Zander's influence, I did pretty well with my studies.

I don't think my puny physicality troubled me too much that year but when I reached junior high at Edna Maguire it became agony.

Here I was surrounded by boys who, though the same age as me, looked like young men. They were starting to shave, they were growing tall and many were going steady with girls.

I was now thirteen and looked about eight. It was handy for getting into the movies for under twelve but in every other way it depressed me.

Also the girls were growing up and it just seemed like I was in a race I could never win. Lily Burris faded from my line of vision but the young women I found most attractive were so out of my league that disappointment became my constant companion. Top of the list was Patty Burke. You couldn't really call Patty a girl for she was a beautiful young woman who was lusted after by two prominent hard guys, Jimmy Tamburini and Johnny Secrest.

These two young princes of the greaser hierarchy had a fight one day after school up on the baseball field at Edna Maguire. It was like a circus event and attracted a big crowd.

Jim Tamburini was a Mill Valley kid who had gone to Park School while John Secrest had arrived at Alto in the sixth grade from somewhere in the city.

Both were good looking in a manly sort of way and I guess this fight was for Patty's affections though, as I recall, she was nowhere to be seen. In fact I had no idea what the fight was about at the time and only learned years later from Jim through his wife Linda.

Both combatants were calm and quiet as they walked up towards the playing field. Jimmy, who belonged to a gang of sorts, was well supported while John Secrest was pretty much on his own.

When it began there were no fisticuffs and the two simply wrestled with each other. It was a grim spectacle which didn't last long as the principal was soon sighted marching towards the field and everyone dispersed quickly.

As I moved into eighth grade my brother Jim arrived at Edna Maguire for seventh. Jim was considerably taller than me, having outgrown me when I was five and he sported a serious greaser hairdo at this time complete with a can opener hook at the front. This didn't mean he was tough, he simply looked it for awhile. Jimmy had spent his sixth grade at Homestead where he became something of a rebel who actually got his mouth washed out with soap by the principal Miss Grimm.

A new boy had moved into our neighbourhood who lived in a big house up on Ethel and, for some reason, Jim and I would join this guy walking to school. It was a long walk from Seymour Avenue over to the Alto district.

This fellow was tall with the longest hair I can recall and he used to keep combing it back into a pompadour but gravity didn't agree with this design so his hair was constantly sloping down around his head like a big Cheshire cat. He had the complexion of a redhead but his hair was chestnut going on brown and he quickly established himself amongst the greaser royalty at Edna Maguire. He had the manner of a nice guy rather than a tough guy. He always seemed to have a smile on his face, in marked contrast to most greasers who seemed to swagger with an aggressive and angry visage.

Brother Jim and I would meet this fellow in the mornings and on one particular day, it being sunny and bright, we took the steps down Una Way, crossed Miller Avenue to Park and walked over towards East Blithedale.

He was, at this time, going steady with a young lady we'll call Donna and we were constantly briefed by him on the state of their relationship. In fact I don't ever recall my brother and I saying much at all as we walked to and from school. He must have considered us to be a good audience for he did all the talking and on this particular morning he was bursting to tell us something.

"If I tell you this," he began, "Do you promise you won't repeat a word to anyone?"

Jim and I swore the oath of silence. He pursed his lips and looked down at the ground for a moment. Then his head moved back up until his eyes met ours and he announced with solemnity that he'd had sex with Donna.

This was important news. I don't believe I had ever heard a young person make such a claim before this. We probably didn't utter a sound and in no time at all he was in full flight, sparing us no detail of the carnal act.

When we reached the end of Blithedale we then walked along past the Purity supermarket and onto the railroad tracks towards Edna Maguire. By now he was repeating himself and possibly even embellishing the story as we approached the school.

Jim and I were pretty reliable when it came to keeping a secret and we certainly had every intention of keeping this one. So it was bewildering to watch this fellow's performance once we arrived at school. He approached every hard guy in the playground and regaled them all with what he had confided to us. So brazen was his retelling of the tale that poor Donna retreated to the girls' bathroom in acute embarrassment. By the time we all went into our first class, the entire school knew of their exploits.

Neither Jimmy nor I were hard guys but for some reason

we seemed to be liked by enough of these characters for us to tag along with them on journeys to and from school. I remember walking home along the railroad tracks at Alto when one of them turned to the crowd and said with great enthusiasm: "Do you know what we are, man? We're rebels." As it was not too long after Fidel Castro's fighters had pulled off the Cuban revolution I remember silently thinking: "No. You're not."

Somewhere along the line I found myself at a party where I met one of a pair of twin sisters who lived near the end of East Blithedale. They were cute and both, like me, were tiny. I have no memory of how I got to know them but I definitely took up with one of these girls while I was in the eighth grade. This involved holding hands on long walks alone, often up to Old Mill Park and, most importantly, making out.

Kissing, like any other human activity, is something we learn to do through experience and how good you are at it really does depend on who taught you. In truth I didn't really learn how to kiss a woman until I was seventeen and found myself in the back seat of a friend's car with a young lady who taught me to French kiss. She probably didn't know she was teaching me but she was.

So back in Old Mill Park with one of the pretty twins, I was a slightly awkward character. In his book *Pastime,* Alex Call remembers his teeth banging into those of his girlfriend Cheryl when he first kissed her and that resonates with me. Lots of awkward and embarrassing activity in play but no way of admitting your discomfiture for, remaining cool was always important. To be uncool was not acceptable.

So gradually I managed to design an image for myself which somehow transcended my miniscule size. This was not an easy trick to pull off but somehow I made it work. I remained scorchingly self conscious, not only about my size but also about my physical immaturity. By the time we got to Tam High I still had not reached puberty and I would find excuses to avoid taking showers in gym class, so embarrassed was I about this state of affairs. The reality was that I was a late developer on practically every front but I could neither admit this to myself nor accept it.

The example of the big guy we walked to school with must have set some kind of an aspirational precedent in my mind and to 'make it' with a young woman became a sacred goal.

Of course all freshmen boys at Tam High were automatically ridiculed for their newcomer status but the impact of this ridicule was doubled in my case because of how little I was. For reasons that were so ridiculous I cannot even remember them, I went out for the wrestling team which I managed to survive for one semester. All I recall about this fiasco is that a trick photo was taken of me lifting the gigantic Elmer Collett for the school newspaper. Two big guys actually held Elmer from either end.

Those first two years at Tam were pretty hellish for me as I found myself hanging around older guys like Jared Dreyfus and always being the token little fellow who tagged along with no real reason to be there. Having a reason to be anywhere is, after all, the *raison d'être* of every poseur. Not having a reason to be somewhere left you vulnerable to ridicule and this was to be avoided with all the stealth of a vampire evading sunlight.

So I staggered forward with these contradictory aspects of my personality and, somehow, with a great deal of bluster, I managed to reinvent myself in such a way as to convince others that I was kind of cool. After all…being uncool was not acceptable.

Chapter 24
William Castle Comes To Town

My first William Castle movie was one of the most exciting cinematic events I had ever experienced. It happened in mid-January, 1959.

A small gaggle of boys from my sixth grade class at Alto School all took the Greyhound bus into the city to see *House On Haunted Hill* at the RKO Golden Gate.

Craig Bird, Jerry Boore, Alex Robertson, Johnny Lem, possibly John Secrest as well as my brother Jim and I. Eddie Smith was invited but his father wouldn't let him join us.

It was a Saturday morning and by the time we got to the theatre there was already a long line. The full colour poster showed a tall skeleton holding a hanged woman by a noose as it stood in front of a beautifully painted Victorian haunted house. In the foreground stood Vincent Price clutching a candle in one hand and the severed head of a beautiful blonde woman in the other.

When we finally paid our money and got seated we found that the place was packed with kids, mostly boys.

As the lights went out the screen turned black. The screaming began immediately. It was so loud that you couldn't hear what the disembodied heads of Vincent Price and Elisha Cook Jr. were saying.

I managed to make out enough of Price's introduction to glean that various people had been invited to spend the night in a haunted house for $10,000 each. We met each one as their limousines drove them up the hill.

I was a bit disappointed to see that the house itself bore no resemblance to the shambly Victorian mansion of the poster. It was the art deco Ennis Brown house in Los Angeles, designed by Frank Lloyd Wright. It subsequently turned up in later movies like *Day of the Locust* and *Blade Runner*.

The movie was fun in the way of a circus and the scary bits were beautifully orchestrated. The audience we saw it with were so jumpy that they were screaming at practically nothing but it did have a few genuine shocks. When Richard Long and Carolyn Craig went down to the cellar to investigate some detail, he left her in one room to bang on the wall while he knocked from the adjoining chamber. As she moved back she felt something behind her, turned and found this silver haired woman with a face contorted in a scream and whose eyes were clear white. She was pretty scary looking. As Carolyn screamed along with the entire audience, the frightful looking woman moved out of the room as if on wheels.

The whole experience was terrific fun and I enjoyed the fact that Craig Bird, a big tough guy, kept running out to the lobby each time he got scared. Craig ran out there at least five times. I was, by now, a horror movie veteran who never looked away from the screen nor screamed and it clearly made me swell with an inner pride.

There was a gimmick: 'Emergo' which turned out to be a big skeleton on a wire that came out over the audience in a glowing spotlight. This did actually correspond with the action on the screen because, as the bones returned to base, Vincent Price re-appeared in the movie wielding this absolutely preposterous looking device with which he reeled the skeleton in.

As this was the very first William Castle movie I ever went to, it set the tone for me as, for several years, I never missed one of his pictures.

If ever there was a grinning, glad handing, snake oil salesman of a movie producer it was William Castle and I was one of millions of young boys across the country who helped him make his fortune.

I came to his work well after he'd been making pictures for many years. He had spent most of the 1950s grinding out low budget westerns and crime melodramas for Columbia. He directed them and Sam Katzman produced them.

The first movie of his which I was aware of was one I never saw. It was called *Macabre* and it had the most beautifully scary looking poster art I'd ever seen. A large human skull was superimposed on the faces of three beautiful young women screaming with a graveyard as the background. It also had the most preposterous gimmick: anyone who died of fright during the film would receive $1000 from Lloyds of London.

It seems that Castle got the idea for trying to make a scary film from the French shocker *Les Diaboliques,* directed by George Henri Clouzout. What Castle was particularly impressed by was not the artistic qualities of the French movie but rather the huge lines around the block to see it. I had seen *Les Diaboliques* with my family up at the Lark and it was a genuinely terrifying movie.

I have no memory of the reasons I didn't see *Macabre* but it sounds like I didn't miss much. The important fact about it is that it was produced for under $100,000 and took many millions at the boxoffice. Naturally Allied Artists requested another and that was *House On Haunted Hill*.

Though he'd been in the business for years, Castle now became famous and from his next picture on he would appear at the beginning of his movies to explain the gimmick.

Having made a fortune for Allied Artists on these two pictures, Castle returned to Columbia for his next movie, *The Tingler,* which was presented in 'Percepto.' This involved the seats at the RKO Golden Gate being wired with a vibrator to make the audience believe that the Tingler was loose in the theater and actually crawling in their seat.

The Tingler, so the story went, was a long many legged creature which lived in the spine of every person. When you became frightened it grew dangerously within you and the only way you could diminish it was to scream.

In one scene the Tingler in the film escapes into a movie theatre and the voice of Vincent Price came over a loudspeaker telling the audience that it was loose in the theatre and to scream. Needless to say this worked a treat at the RKO Golden Gate as everybody screamed.

I'm not actually sure that I felt anything in my seat that day as the screaming was so loud and intense but, again, just going along with it was fun.

Though *The Tingler* was in black and white there was one scene where the deaf mute woman played by Judith Evelyn went into her bathroom to find the tub full of blood which was bright red and a bloody hand reached up out of it. It was all ludicrous nonsense and that was part of the joy of a William Castle movie.

His next picture, *13 Ghosts* gave us 'Illusion-O' and featured the glorious Ghost Viewer.

Again the film was black and white but when the ghosts would appear the screen turned blue and the ghosts were red. The ghost viewer was a beautifully designed cardboard device which owed everything to the heyday of 3-D movies. Castle had directed *Fort Ti* in 3-D so knew a thing or two about it.

Each patron was handed a ghost viewer as they entered the Paramount on Market Street. It had a red transparent panel for viewing the ghosts and a blue one for not seeing them.

It was utter balderdash and the actual movie was so ridiculous but again it was Bill Castle luring you in with the promise of steaming hot nothing.

Alfred Hitchcock made *Psycho* in 1960 which broke boxoffice records and threw a spanner into the workings of a producer like Castle. *Psycho* was such an enormous hit and so artfully done it showed the likes of Castle up for the lightweight that he was.

However he was not undone and came up with a *Psycho*

imitation entitled *Homicidal* and it did have certain things to recommend it. It had a tricky and complicated plotline which bamboozled you but again it was the gimmick which sold it.

I saw *Homicidal* at the Paramount and, as you entered the theater, you were given a certificate which could be handed in at the Cowards' Corner during the 'Fright Break' should you be too terrified to stay for the film's climax.

By this time I belonged to the William Castle Fan Club so I was buying into all this nonsense in a big way. To his credit Castle did not take himself seriously and there was always a big twinkle in his eye as he came out with all this baloney.

At the beginning of *Homicidal* he appeared on screen to explain all about the 'Fright Break' and when that moment arrived we saw a big clock ticking away the sixty seconds you had to get your money back.

The Cowards' Corner stood in the lobby and I have no idea if anyone ever asked for their admission back.

By this time there was a William Castle logo which was a silhouette of him sitting in a director's chair with his cigar jutting out of his mouth. His marketing, if not his movie making, was first class.

I was an avid reader of Paine Knickerbocker's film reviews in the Chronicle and loved his writing style. Knickerbocker never gave Castle's movies a good review but each time he'd turn up in San Francisco to promote his latest picture, the critic would interview him and these articles made me warm to Castle. Knickerbocker clearly liked him as a character and must have found him to be good company. I'm sure that Castle had much in common with another schlockmeister from that time, Samuel Z. Arkoff. Both were Jewish and, though Castle did not have the educational background of Arkoff, he was very well spoken.

Arkoff was the vice president of American-International Pictures and was a very good talker (see chapter 27). Both he and Castle regarded the movies they made as product, pure and simple. They had no interest in critical acclaim and were very straightforward in saying so. Making a profit was all that mattered which ran contrary to the lofty pronouncements made by the writers and directors of higher quality films of this time.

One of the reasons I became an avid reader of Variety, which I would see every week at the Bus Depot, was the contrast between the public's perceptions of movies as art and the way the business talked to itself. The film reviews in Variety would always take account of the movie's ability to turn a profit in the market place.

Variety had about three pages devoted to the weekly grosses from all the major cities including San Francisco and I was immediately fascinated by this manifestation of greedy capitalism. They would always abbreviate a film's title to one word so *What Price Glory* would become *Glory*. A typical headline was: 'Paleface' Powerful 22G, Frisco; 'McLain' Stout $18,000, 'Tomorrow' 14G.

Variety would always preface the amount taken with a positive or negative phrase. A socko $20,000! A tired $6,000. When a movie made a lot of money in its opening week the studios would run whole page ads trumpeting the amount taken and encouraging theatres to book the film. A movie with boxoffice longevity was described as "having legs."

I soon became mesmerised by this way of thinking as it clearly wasn't meant to be seen by the general public. It didn't tax my imagination to follow the financial fortunes of that week's films including those made by William Castle.

I remained a disciple of Castle's movies up to his next one which was *Mr Sardonicus* and it featured an ingenious gimmick: the Punishment Poll. Sadly this wonderful idea was not seen through the way it should have been.

I saw *Mr Sardonicus* at the Fox and as we entered we were handed a special ballot which had a sulpher imprint of a hand with an extended thumb. We had to activate our cards in a special light box and when we got to the climax, Castle invited us to vote with our cards for Mercy, thumbs up or No Mercy, thumbs down.

I guess it would have been a nightmare to have people

actually counting the votes and deciding what to do. A gaggle of ushers did come out and pretend to count them but the reality was that he only shot one verdict which was No Mercy.

His next movie was a surreal kind of comedy called *Zotz* with Tom Poston which I never even went to see and that brought the curtain down on my interest in William Castle. I continued to be aware of his movies like *The Night Walker, Straight-Jacket,* which featured an axe wielding Joan Crawford, *I Saw What You Did* and several more.

He purchased the screen rights to *Rosemary's Baby* but Robert Evans, who was head of Paramount, would not let him direct it so he produced it while Roman Polanski took the helm.

I enjoyed spotting him in a bit part as a screaming Hollywood director in John Schlesinger's *Day of the Locust* and I was entertained by his book *Step Right Up! I'm Gonna Scare the Pants Off America.*

As people of my generation of film-goers rose through the ranks of Hollywood, cinematic tributes to Castle began to appear. Joe Dante made the wonderful film *Matinee* with John Goodman playing Bernard Woolsey a character based entirely on Castle.

I was surprised to read an interview in Filmfax Magazine with Robb White who wrote his screenplays and didn't have anything nice to say about him at all. According to White, Castle was cold, ruthless, stingy and a great big phony.

I, however, didn't know the man and am not troubled by the realities of those who did. For me he was the cinematic equivalent of the carnival huckster who came to town every summer and sold you nothing dressed up as something.

To this day I consider the ghost viewer to be a thing of beauty. I also find artistic merit in the ballots for the Punishment Poll. I think Castle took a lot of trouble to make his movies a fun experience for the kids who flocked to see them.

The only one of his films which stands up at all well, in my opinion, is *House On Haunted Hill.*

The others can only be viewed as curiosities. After all…they were only product.

Chapter 25

A Hard Guy Has To Smoke

I'm not certain at what age the importance of being cool descended upon my soul but I'd hazard a guess that it was between eleven and twelve.

Being cool meant never showing the true emotion you were experiencing if it contradicted the image of casual disinterest you were determined to display.

Probably the most prominent exhibition of this phenomenon in Mill Valley during the 1950s and 60s could be found at C's Drive-In.

Mostly hard guys hung out at C's. The vast

majority of them were older than me, bigger than me and, most importantly, could almost certainly beat the living daylights out of me if given a reason to.

So for me to be cool was a difficult proposition as I was tiny, looked several years younger than whatever age I happened to be and couldn't fight my way out of a paper bag.

As early as age ten I had taken to putting brylcreem in my hair and combing little pseudo sideburns down in an attempt to look like Elvis but that was while I was at Homestead School. I didn't actually encounter hard guys until sixth grade at Alto.

That is the time, I think, when the notion of appearing to be cool became important for me. Seeing people like Johnny Secrest and, later at Edna Maguire, Jimmy Tamburini, gave me concrete examples of this style of demeanour. For either of these two to be cool was a piece of cake. They were tall, good looking and tough. They also moved around with a gang who looked up to them.

Hard guys walked with a swagger, wore white t-shirts with jeans and smoked cigarettes. The cigarettes tended to be non-filtered, though this would change over time with the growing popularity of Marlboros. I recall that most hard guys smoked Lucky Strike, Camels or Pall Mall. Their facial expression was usually bad tempered, presumably to give off the message that anyone looking for trouble could find it in them.

This very popular subculture stood in stark contrast to the stated aims of the educational institutions we were all attending.

While still in grade school there was no question about smoking cigarettes. To be found with such contraband about your person was a very serious offence which almost certainly meant expulsion.

Once we got to junior high at Edna Maguire things changed. You were allowed to have cigarettes on your person but were not allowed to produce or smoke them until school was over and you were off the premises.

When students left school at Edna Maguire and walked down Lomita Drive, a visible cloud of cigarette smoke accompanied them as they made their way onto the railroad tracks which led to East Blithedale.

From the time I first encountered media of any kind the cigarette industry had my attention. On the radio I remember Jack Webb coming out of character as scary Sergeant Friday on *Dragnet* and addressing his audience as 'Friends (see chapter 9).' Sounding like someone you could trust, he proceeded to deliver a beautifully scripted pitch about the virtues of choosing, buying and smoking Chesterfield cigarettes.

Of course listening to these anachronistic ads now is highly amusing but the reality back then was that they were terribly effective. The word 'quality' featured a lot in the copy and the obvious concerns about health issues were neatly side stepped. Jack Webb actually died of lung cancer.

Growing up in Mill Valley throughout the 1950s I always had an opinion about cigarettes because we were so exposed to the advertising material for them. Though the Myers family had no television set, we would see plenty of shows over at friends' houses and the tobacco industry utilised radio, television and print media a lot.

To this day I can sing:

Winston tastes good,
Like a (clap, clap)

Cigarette should.

In fact all the phrases and jingles that the cigarette ads used seem to linger: I'd Walk a mile for a Camel, Light Up A Lucky, No Cigarette Satisfies Like A Chesterfield.

When you think about all the time and money which was invested in selling the American public this highly poisonous product, it is more than a bit chilling and there was never any doubt that I would smoke when I grew up.

There were so many brands to choose from. Parliaments with the recessed filter, Old Gold, Phillip Morris. You simply made a choice based on all that brainwashing from Madison Avenue.

Smoking was something that grownups did and, boy, did I want to be a grownup. I was never content with being a child. All my role models were adults and that was what I aspired to be. Needless to say, I was crushed the first time I ever heard my voice played back on a tape recording. Inside my head I spoke like Gregory Peck or Jimmy Stewart but what I heard was this terrible high pitched whine which made me wince.

There were certain activities which adults engaged in as a matter of course and smoking cigarettes was one of them. Drinking coffee was another and, of course the consumption of alchoholic beverages was right up there with things which adults did and children did not.

Both my parents smoked. Blackie's brand was Chesterfield regular sized and he'd buy them by the carton at Safeways. Beth smoked Kools, a filtered menthol cigarette which came in a green pack but, unlike my father who smoked steadily throughout the day, she was an occasional smoker and tended to light up when she was writing or reading.

Neither of my parents had any illusions that cigarettes were anything other than harmful but this didn't stop them from indulging. I guess that their example served as a role model for me.

The packaging and advertising was terribly impressive. You'd pull the red plastic tape which took the clear cover off the top of the soft cigarette pack. Then you would rip and unfold the silver paper underneath, revealing the cigarettes all neatly packed inside.

In order to dislodge that first cigarette, you'd simply tap the still wrapped portion of the pack onto your other hand and about four cigarettes would slide forward. If it was an unfiltered brand you'd then tap the end you were going to put in your mouth against the back of your hand several times so it didn't all crumble on you.

The first time I ever encountered a flip top box was for Marlboro and it was a truly slick bit of design. Unlike the other kind of pack this was not soft but hard with a top which folded back to reveal the silver paper guarding the product. The packaging was so slick and psychologically you respected it because you'd seen it on television and in magazine ads. As the fifties progressed most brands adopted this polished and impressive new packaging. Winston would display a soft pack and a flip top box side by side at the bottom of their print ads.

The Chesterfields that Blackie smoked were regular sized and non-filter but filter tips soon became popular. There was a sort of macho thing about smoking non filtered cigarettes. Hard guys would never be seen smoking filter tips in the 1950s and early 60s. It had to be a pack of Luckies or Camels which they'd lay down on the counter at Pat & Joe's next to their mug of black coffee.

It all looked so utterly glamourous to us younger kids. After all, the movie stars all smoked and could be seen in whole page colour ads in magazines advertising this cigarette or that: Rock Hudson or Kirk Douglas.

At a very early age I had made my mind up that I was going to smoke L&M when I grew up. I don't believe I ever did but that doesn't matter now.

The first time I tried smoking was when I was about twelve. Johnny Lem had got his hands on a carton of Pall Mall and he, my brother Jim and I smoked a few of them while walking up shady Ethel Avenue one afternoon. Ethel was a quiet leafy street and we were careful not to be seen by any adults as none of us looked old enough to be smoking.

The taste and sensation was utterly disgusting. There was clearly a pain threshold you had to endure in order to become a proper smoker. Two problems presented themselves immediately: if you just puffed the smoke, your mouth would burn up and if you inhaled it into your lungs it was unbelievably painful.

This first test run was not a success for me and I certainly didn't return for some time. But again it was the lure of doing something perceived as grown-up which ultimately hooked me.

Like so much else in our society, the hard guys were getting their style from pop music and the movies. James Dean was a big role model as was Elvis (though, to be fair, Elvis stated publicly that he neither smoked nor drank). Marlon Brando in *The Wild One* also made a big contribution but when it came to smoking the advertising played a huge role.

Even though all schools forbid smoking and it was looked down upon, this probably had the reverse effect on most young people. Social rebellion was rife.

That's why the advertising was truly clever. They never showed underage teenagers smoking their products in the way that millions actually did but rather they'd portray young professionals out in sailboats or on the golf course.

Smoking was cool and my generation swallowed that message hook, line and sinker. Of course there were exceptions. I don't remember Tommy Harper or Mark Symmes ever smoking cigarettes but most of my classmates did because being cool was important. At least for me it was.

When I did finally succumb to the lure of the cigarette I found that I smoked exactly like my father. Blackie would take a sizeable puff then let about half the smoke out of his mouth, inhaling the rest. This meant that he only inhaled half the smoke whereas many others would suck the entire cloud down into their lungs.

The movies played a big role in making the act of smoking attractive and I always recall being particularly impressed by someone talking the smoke out of their mouth and nostrils.

There was a scene in *The Defiant Ones* (for more on this film see chapter 29) where Tony Curtis and Sidney Poitier had, as two escaped convicts cuffed to each other, caught and cooked a frog over a small fire in the woods. Watching them eat that frog was mouth watering but when it was finally finished, Tony Curtis lit the cigarette and told Sidney Poitier some aspirational yarn and if the frog looked delicious, that cigarette looked even better. It was the perfect end to the perfect meal.

When I finally got hooked on smoking the taste of that first cigarette after a good meal was a particularly satisfying sensation.

I was, throughout my teenage years and into my twenties, an on and off smoker. When my lungs would start to ache I'd think about giving up. Also I could never face smoking in the mornings so it was always from lunchtime on. This and possibly my father's style of inhaling may have spared me, so far, from the ravages of lung cancer.

But in addition to being harmful, tobacco was also highly addictive and kicking it was no cake walk. Many was the time that I would put off, for one more day, the ordeal of giving up smoking.

I was already living in England when I learned that cigarette advertising on television had been banned in the USA and I could barely believe it. All that professional persuasion which had been such a huge part of the world we grew up in was now over. The anti-smoking consciousness which seeped into the cavity left behind was a more than reasonable substitute.

So now the tobacco companies turn their attentions to the third world where the slavery of addiction is rampant. Watching the evolution of their marketing techniques after the TV ban demonstrates just how robust and aggressive they are. We're quick to criminalise common drug dealers on the street but somehow those people that market and sell cigarettes move through society with no such stigma attached to them. Tobacco executives belong to tennis and golf clubs, coach little league teams and probably go to church. I wonder how history will view them.

Chapter 26
Visiting *Vertigo* Locations

My father Blackie always made the birthdays of myself, my brother Jim and sisters Nell and Kate, a very special occasion. Whoever's birthday it was would spend a whole day in the city with him, going to Playland at the beach or possibly even Sutro's, a movie on Market Street and having it topped off in the evening with a visit to the Gold Spike restaurant on Columbus in North Beach.

I don't remember any financial restraint coming into

the experience which was truly at odds with the way we lived in the Myers family. Although the spectre of hunger never actually crossed our threshold, we always lived like we had no money. We never ate steak so it was always hamburger. And butter was a luxury we clearly could not afford so it was margerine which, in the 1950s, was far from delicious.

Blackie was very popular with all our school friends as he tended to talk to kids like people rather than children and he was very funny. He had a flare for mimicry and his imitation of Harry Bridges with his Australian accent was particularly amusing though I'm not certain Harry would have enjoyed it as much as we did.

Blackie was a physically short man and I think one reason I haven't had much of a problem about being short myself is that I was constantly seeing the respect that much taller men had for him.

Every year the Guardian, a leftwing newspaper, would hold a big fundraising picnic up at the Hallinan's mansion in Ross and hundreds of people would attend. We all did different jobs for the day. I sold tickets one year and hot dogs the next. Black would always take the job of burning the rubbish back behind the gymnasium. That's where he would stay the entire day while hoards of people milled around the lawn and pool. Gradually, all the trade union guys would arrive at the bonfire behind the gym where they'd all talk politics. Harry Bridges, Lou Goldblatt, Tommy Cox and Bob Robertson would be there along with Barney and Pete Dreyfus. These conversations were fascinating for me even though I didn't always understand what they were discussing. All these men were forever keen to hear Blackie's opinion.

So I think it was the case for my siblings and I to particularly enjoy the special adventure our father gave us on our birthdays. To have Blackie's full attention was a treat.

We all had many of these special trips to the city but the one which stays lodged in my memory was in March 1959, the year of my twelfth birthday.

In the early summer of the previous year I had seen, a few times, Alfred Hitchcock's *Vertigo,* which had been filmed almost entirely on location in San Francisco. I saw it the first time at the Sequoia but the second viewing occurred in Santa Fe, New Mexico. My mother had taken my sister Katie, brother Jim and I on a Greyhound bus journey to New Mexico to visit our good friends Jenny and Craig Vincent who lived in San Cristobal, just outside of Taos.

For some reason we had a lengthy stop over in Santa Fe and Jimmy, Katie and I went to the movies. *Vertigo* was what we saw. I have a feeling that I saw it at least one more time but I could be wrong. I did become a bit obsessed with the movie initially because of the very familiar locations of San Francisco but the various subtexts within the film soon infected my consciousness. The musical score by Bernard Herrmann also played a big part in my enjoyment of it.

When my twelfth birthday arrived and it was my turn for a day in the city with Blackie, it was a tour of the *Vertigo* locations that I wanted.

I'm not certain that we had seen this movie as a family unlike so many other Hitchcock pictures. It was probably a bit too weird for my mother.

The first stop was Fort Point under the Golden Gate Bridge. Jimmy Stewart's Scottie had followed Kim Novak's Madeline to this location. I ran over to the edge to find the steps leading down into the water. Straight away I was confused. There were no steps. In the film, Kim Novak stood by the edge tossing the petals of a bouquet into the drink when suddenly she jumped in. Jimmy Stewart leapt forward, ripping his jacket off and ran down these steps from which he dived into the soup to rescue her.

What I didn't know was that the steps existed only in a tank at Paramount where the non-location portion of the rescue was filmed. The film crew at Fort Point, however, must have built a platform with steps on it as Stewart is seen at the location carrying Kim Novak or her stunt double up out of the water. But to my twelve year old mind it was simply a mystery. What had happened to those steps?

Next stop was the Palace of the Legion of Honour where Madeline went to sit and gaze at the portrait of Carlotta Valdez. Once Jimmy Stewart had entered the museum a delicate but disturbing pulse like music began and, of course, as Blackie and I entered the same way, there was no music. Nothing at this location was perplexing except the absence of Carlotta's portrait. As I wandered around the entrance to the room some bit of Bernard Herrmann's score echoed in my mind.

One location I didn't visit was the apartment on Lombard Street where Jimmy Stewart's Scottie lived. It had a fine view of Coit Tower but for some reason I never knew where it was.

I know that I looked for the non-existent Argosy Bookshop on Powell Street where the old proprietor told Scottie and Midge (Barbara Bel Geddes) all about the legendary Carlotta. It turned out that all of this was done on a set down at Paramount using second unit footage of Powell Street as a back projection.

Another location which was beyond my experience was Ernie's restaurant. Apparently it did exist but all of the scenes shot there were also done in the studio.

Muir Woods I knew very well and didn't feel the need to visit with Black that day.

Vertigo was a film which crept up on you emotionally. It is darker and deeper than most of Hitchcock's other offerings and, in some ways, I think it was kind of a dress rehearsal for *Psycho*. The camera moves in the scene where Madeline visits the hotel are very similar to Vera Miles' approach to the gothic house behind the Bates Motel.

My father indulged me that day, patiently driving to all these places. He seemed kind of tickled by my passion. But it was not always easy to read what Blackie was actually thinking. I had seen him turn off while having his ear bent on too many occasions to really believe he was always listening to what you said.

Throughout our childhood my siblings and I would join Blackie on Saturday morning drives into the city to pick up his paycheck down on the Embarcadero. These trips usually included a visit to Foster's Cafeteria at the bottom of Market where we would feast on English Muffins.

Inevitably we would walk past a bar and some highly inebriated acquaintance of his would come running out shouting his name and the four of us kids would stand there for what seemed an eternity while this drunk talked at our father forever. I remember tugging at his trouser leg saying: "Blackie! Can we go now?" My father, however, never even acknowledged our protests and we simply had to wait until the encounter came to its natural conclusion.

Although he had never been in the public eye in my lifetime, Blackie was once a prominent left wing trade union leader in New York and you could see the residue of his faded celebrity in the eyes of those who pursued his company. Vin Hallinan and Harry Bridges were both famous in the bay area so we were well aware of the phenomenon of celebrity but we never thought of Blackie in that way except when someone brought his past to our attention. I remember being pulled aside by Dick Wertheimer up at the Hallinans one day and told what a great man my father was.

This posed a few problems for me as I felt inclined to brag about him to my school friends but, sadly, there was no evidence to back any braggadocio up. Whenever Jim and I would spend the weekend up at the Hallinans, Danny would insist on guiding us through the scrapbook of Hallinan clippings but no such thing existed in our house. There were a few faded photographs which hinted at his notoriety but, out of context, they told no story.

As for Blackie it was not something he ever even thought about. He and Beth didn't have a high opinion of people who concerned themselves with self publicity and the subject simply never came up around our dinner table.

Returning to the subject of my twelfth birthday I'm afraid I don't remember which movie we went to see on Market Street but the cherry on the cake was the meal at the Gold Spike. It was an old fashioned Italian place with candles popping out of those bulbous wine bottles encased in woven straw linings.

The first course was a delicious soup with a basket full of sliced Italian bread. Next it was an equally delectable green salad soaked in a fine dressing. The third course was pasta in a tasty tomato sauce. The reality is that what we had eaten so far would be enough, but no. The main course was yet to come. A roasted meat of your choice and mine was beef.

Blackie really got a kick out of us having a good time and the meal at the Gold Spike was always the perfect end to a perfect day.

It would be dark by the time we drove back across the Golden Gate Bridge and I probably slept soundly that night. The movies were a form of magic to me and to have visited those locations was like touching my dreams. My dreams were vague but powerful and seemed to find shape in the form of movies, comic books and low culture of all kinds. They seemed to be what I lived for.

Chapter 27
A Strange Obsession With AIP

Obsessions, I have found, are not pre-planned. Something captures your imagination then, once lodged in your consciousness, it grows with further exposure.

Throughout my childhood I became obsessed with many aspects of low culture but one peculiar obsession was with the films made by American-International Pictures. I use the word peculiar because the vast majority of the movies made by this low budget company were absolutely dreadful.

It all began for me on a hot July day in 1957 when I made a trip by myself into the city to see *I Was a Teenage Werewolf* and *Invasion of the Saucer Men* at the St Francis on

Market Street. Because *Teenage Werewolf* was actually pretty good by horror movie standards, I was tempted, later that same year to go see *I Was a Teenage Frankenstein* and *Blood of Dracula*. Both these films were okay but there was an oddly ugly quality to them and they weren't in the same league as *Teenage Werewolf.* I was now ten years old and beginning to develop some idea of what was good and what wasn't.

The key to my fascination was monsters. Any kind of monster was immediately of interest to me but I soon learned that you couldn't tell anything about the quality of the damned things from the beautifully designed posters.

To get any idea about the special effects you needed to examine the black and white stills which were usually displayed alongside the posters.

Going to see first run pictures on Market Street was a pretty big operation. I had to con the money out of my mother, often without telling her which dreadful movie I wanted to see. So I became much more cautious about those pictures I'd take a chance on.

A question mark appeared in my mind about American-International after seeing *I Was a Teenage Frankenstein* and I gave them one more chance by seeing *The Viking Women and the Sea Serpent* at the St Francis in early 1958. The ads and posters were terrific: an impressive-looking monster bearing down on a Viking vessel in a dramatic seascape. Sadly the poster was more impressive than the movie as the sea serpent turned out to be a pretty silly-looking puppet flopping around in an obviously enlarged bucket of water.

Years later I learned from a book about the movie's producer/director Roger Corman, that the special effects man had sold him something he was unable to deliver. I remember feeling cheated.

I was now eleven years old and vowed never to see another film made by American-International.

I have to admit I was tempted because the advertising for pictures like *The Amazing Colossal Man, Attack of the Puppet People, The Spider, Night of the Blood Beast* and *The Brain Eaters* all looked fabulous. But I'd made my decision and steered clear of all AIP product.

Because I was only interested in their horror movies I wasn't even aware that they also put out just as many films about teenage juvenile delinquency with titles like *Reform School Girl, Runaway Daughters* and *The Cool and the Crazy*.

I would see the ads for these pictures in the movie section of the Chronicle and not even notice that they were made by American-International. It was clearly not a brand of movie I was interested in at this time.

AIP began as the American Releasing Company in 1954

and their early movies (the very first was Roger Corman's *The Fast and the Furious*) were single films. They soon learned that, if they were booked as second features, the theatres would only pay a flat fee as it was the main film which warranted a percentage of the profits. So in order to make any money, they needed to provide a double bill: two movies with a similar theme.

The formula hit upon by AIP's James H. Nicholson, the president and Samuel Z. Arkoff, the vice president was to make two cheap movies and put them out with highly sensational advertising material.

The first of these double bills was *Day the World Ended* and *The Phantom from 10,000 Leagues*. It became a hit. They got their investment back and ploughed the profit into making more.

The double bills became highly successful, as the target audience was teenagers who were not being catered to by the major studios. Throughout the rest of the 1950s AIP ground them out and they sold.

At the time that Alfred Hitchcock was prepping *Psycho,* one of the reasons he decided to make it on a lower budget was the example of AIP. The film's screenwriter Josef Stefano had been hoping he'd be working on a big budget Hitchcock picture but when he asked why the director was paring down his costs, Hitchcock replied that American-

International made movie after movie for less than a million dollars, yet they all grossed ten or thirteen million.

The AIP advertising campaigns were so much better than most of their films. The way their creative process worked was for Jim Nicholson to come up with a catchy title. They would then get their graphics man, Albert Kallis, in to brief him on it and as soon as humanly possible he'd return with poster art. Nicholson and Arkoff would then send the poster art out to a few trusted exhibitors with the question: can you sell this? If the answer was yes, a screenplay would be commissioned and the movie would be made as quickly and cheaply as possible.

Kallis often employed illustrator Reynold Brown to do the artwork to his specifications. Brown was, during the 1950s, in great demand in Hollywood. He did practically all of Universal International's movies including the horror entries like *Creature from the Black Lagoon* and *Tarantula!*

The dynamic between Nicholson and Arkoff was a little drama in itself. Nicholson was thin, a snappy dresser with a professional grin. He was the front man who had more to do with the creative side while Arkoff, a bit portly with a cigar in his mouth, was the lawyer and heavy. Whenever a tricky problem arose on set it was always Arkoff who went in. A producer I once met said that when you had a meeting with them they would always play good cop bad cop and Arkoff was definitely the latter.

However, as an eleven-year-old, I knew nothing about any of this. All I knew was that the goddamned sea serpent was just terrible and so I boycotted their movies all the way up to late 1960. The film that broke my resolve was the very classy looking *House of Usher* based on the short story by Edgar Alan Poe.

Our friend Augie Belden had taken a trip to Nevada with his family, bringing back whatever the local newspaper up there was and in its movie section my eye immediately went to a teaser ad with a grainy photo of Vincent Price with white hair and no moustache. The copy read: "In the tradition of *Wuthering Heights* and *Les Diaboliques."* Below the title *House of Usher* I was astonished to see: an American-International picture.

I was immediately smitten. Vincent Price, with his velvet voice and sinister good looks was, without doubt, my favourite actor at this time. *House of Wax, House On Haunted Hill* and *The Fly* all thrilled me and for AIP to have got him into one of their pictures meant only one thing: they were upping the quality of their films.

Practically all their output up to now had been the black and white double bills but this was in full colour and the ads and posters were, in my opinion, impressive in the extreme.

Famous Monsters magazine ran a beautiful full colour

cover of Price as Roderick Usher, painted by Basil Gogos, another fine artist I admired.

The names down below the title impressed me too. Richard Matheson wrote the screenplay and Les Baxter did the musical score. Matheson was a very well-known author of science fiction and Baxter was a hit parade composer/arranger whose LPs of exotic music were always in the Top 40.

The name Roger Corman had never registered with me before *House of Usher* but I soon learned that he had been producing and directing movies for AIP from the beginning.

I was now thirteen and still keeping the scrapbook which I'd begun some two years earlier when *7th Voyage of Sinbad* came out. *House of Usher* opened at the Paramount on Market Street near the end of September and, as each ad, photo and article appeared in the Chronicle, I duly clipped it and slung it into the book. Laying them out, trimming them and pasting them in was a job for later.

This would be the very first American-International film I'd included in my scrapbook. I imagine it was the success of the Hammer Films *Curse of Frankenstein* and *Horror of Dracula* which inspired Corman to talk Nicholson and Arkoff into putting a bit more money into this one feature rather than continue with the cheap monochrome double bills which were not making as much money as they had.

According to Corman, Sam Arkoff wanted to know where the monster was and the director spontaneously said: "It's the house." Jim and Sam obviously bought that one.

It was a gamble which paid huge dividends. Just as *I Was a Teenage Werewolf* had put them on the map in 1957, *House of Usher* carved out a whole new place in the business for AIP in 1960.

I was there the first Saturday after it opened. The second feature (In those days every movie had a second feature) was *How to Make a Monster* which had already made the rounds on a double bill with *Teenage Caveman*.

There was something charming about the second feature's premise that American-International was a big studio with busloads of tourists coming to see the making of yet another teenage monster movie. It was all hokum as AIP leased an old television studio and were as low rent as you could get.

How to Make a Monster wasn't bad and it made a nice contrast to see an old style AIP feature just before watching the brand new full colour *House of Usher* with which I was not disappointed. Everything about it looked terrific and Vincent Price, furniture-eating ham that he was, gave a beautiful performance as Roderick Usher, whose senses were so acute that he could even hear the rats in the walls.

The thing about AIP is that whenever they had a hit they immediately set up a sausage factory to reproduce it as many times as possible. As soon as the grosses on *Usher* became impressive, Roger Corman was immediately prepping the next Poe pic: *Pit and the Pendulum.*

So this film company I had discovered at age ten, boycotted at eleven then re-discovered at thirteen was about to hold my attention for the better part of my teenage years.

I began following their progress more closely. My scrapbook now had to make space for AIP as well as Columbia, Allied Artists and all the other companies.

By now I was reading weekly Variety up at the Bus Depot and was aware of all the movies in production as well as seeing the weekly grosses for those already in release.

I knew that *Pit and the Pendulum* was their next Poe outing but I was still wary of AIP who, after the huge success of *Usher,* began putting out more movies in colour. So I waited until *Pit and the Pendulum* opened and it was, by my standards, very good indeed. Richard Matheson had taken one of the shortest short stories ever and spun it into a full length plot with plenty of twists and turns but which also clung to the theme of the first movie: the horror of being buried alive.

Although I wasn't conscious of it at the time, my preoccupation with these movies was very much a private concern which I didn't share with anyone else. Not by choice, it was simply that nobody else was interested. My brother Jim's indifference to anything I felt passionate about was quietly aggressive and though our friend Augie Belden was curious, he sort of came and went in his enthusiasm.

I saw *Pit and the Pendulum* in the summer vacation before starting my Freshman year at Tam. Poe's short story had been set in the Spanish Inquisition but really the only thing that happened in it was that this razor sharp pendulum descended from the ceiling to begin slicing this poor devil's chest open.

From my earliest visits to the Sequoia I was always fascinated by the movie posters and the idea of actually owning one was a dream of mine but they were always on the inside of the locked glass cases in which they were displayed.

The closest I ever got was when I was in Mr. Zander's 6th grade class at Alto. Americ Higashi was my best friend and his dad was an officer in the army. His family was stationed at Fort Cronkhite. I remember they lived in a beautiful, somewhat old wooden house surrounded by several identical houses in a leafy, almost New England-like part of the military base. There was an unglamorous movie theatre which showed films before they were actually released. The posters would end up in the garbage can from which Americ took one and gave it to me. It was for a terrible Japanese monster movie called *Gigantis: Fire Monster* which Warners released.

I probably would have got more posters from Americ but he and I had a fairly tempestuous friendship which meant we kept falling out with each other. I don't think he was on board when we moved across to Edna Maguire school.

My weekly reading of Variety was now exposing me to the cruder capitalistic side of the movie business which came as a shock to me, growing up in a socialist family. Seeing whole page ads whose total thrust was: "Make More Money with our Movie!" gave me pause for thought. It certainly wasn't noble or artistic.

Maggie Grant, the woman who ran the Bus Depot kept a marvellous selection of reading material in stock. In addition to Variety she also had the New York Times and when *Pit and the Pendulum* opened in Manhattan I was able to see the ads for it.

Another occurrence brought me closer to the movie business. On a brave day during a summer vacation in the early 1960s, I ventured inside the office of Columbia Pictures on Golden Gate Avenue and asked the young lady at reception if I could get a poster for the Ray Harryhausen film *Mysterious Island*. She told me I should speak to Walt and directed me down to the basement where I entered the world of the real movie business.

As my feet landed on an edgy concrete floor, I saw that the

walls were lined with shelves of large film cases. A balding man with glasses, stacking some of the cases onto a hand truck, asked if he could help me so I said I wanted to see Walt. He beckoned me past him towards a long section of the cellar with a counter, behind which were more shelves stacked with promotional material. Each shelf had a different title. *Experiment in Terror* here, *Lawrence of Arabia* there and on another was *Guns of Navarone.*

A tall good looking young man with blond hair identified himself as Walt and asked me what I wanted. I explained.

"These posters are not available to the general public," he said. "They're only for theatre managers."

His name was Walt Von Hauff and I would guess he was in his early twenties. It was probably his youth which made him sympathise with my request. Warning me I must not tell anyone, Walt sold me a poster and, more importantly, gave me a pressbook. I had never seen such a thing nor even knew they existed. It was a glossy catalogue of all the press ads a theatre manager could order to promote the movie. The smallest was a single column by one inch and the largest four columns by ten inches.

The ads were sold as mats, a kind of hardened cardboard, the texture of an egg box. The mats had been molded against the actual metal plate of the ad then dried. They would be sent to the newspaper's print shop and placed in a frame where hot lead would be poured into the spaces, recreating the metal plate. This was then used to print the newspaper ad.

The pressbook encompassed all the promotional items a manager could purchase to promote *Mysterious Island*. In addition to mats, there were posters, lobby cards and no end of press copy and ideas for selling the picture.

As the Greyhound bus hummed back across the Golden Gate Bridge, I pored over every detail of the pressbook. The sight of all those ads together on a glossy sheet excited me tremendously.

Over that vacation, I haunted the cave of treasures that was the basement at Columbia Pictures. Walt made me welcome as did the others and by summer's end I had become something of a fixture. "Junior" was the name I answered to and I could be counted on to run any errand or carry out any job. I got to know the folks up on the street level as well as below stairs and used to get a lift back over to Marin County with Mel, who was in charge of bookings upstairs. Mel lived in Terra Linda and would drop me off at the Strawberry junction on Highway 101. He was a very nice guy and would tell me that movies were doomed, dying out in the face of television's ever growing popularity.

So I began collecting not only posters but pressbooks, radio ads which came on LPs, open-end interviews and anything associated with movie promotion (more on this subject can be found in chapter 31). Walt, like all the other guys in the basement, managed his own theatre out in the avenues. They all lived and breathed movies.

But getting back to AIP, they continued grinding out the Poe pictures, expanding their cast of older stars to include Ray Milland, Basil Rathbone, Peter Lorre and Boris Karloff. They also went in a completely new direction with a teen oriented movie called *Beach Party*.

In addition to Frankie Avalon they were able to hire Annette Funicello, who had been one of Walt Disney's most popular Mouseketeers but was now a well endowed and attractive young woman.

When Disney discovered that AIP had signed his "little girl" he was enraged and telephoned Arkoff, badgering him with an insistence that his mouseketeer should not appear in a bikini.

Beach Party, another gamble for Nicholson and Arkoff, paid off impressively at the boxoffice and a string of beach-related pictures hit the assembly line.

Both Arkoff and Nicholson were, by this time, very wealthy men, having built AIP from practically nothing to the only Hollywood studio that wasn't losing money but actually making it. They were equal partners but something happened to change that.

Jim Nicholson fell in love with Susan Hart, a beautiful young actress in one of the Beach movies. When his wife sued him for divorce part of the settlement was that he had to surrender 50% of his stock in AIP to his wife which tilted the balance of power between him and Arkoff.

In a peculiar way I had become, without noticing it, an apologist for AIP. I was not without an inner filter for quality and knew that much of their output was decidedly inferior but chose to ignore it. I remember our school friend Mark Symmes looking at my growing collection of AIP pressbooks and saying: "Come on Myers, Admit it. They make junky movies." However true his words were, I was oblivious.

In the summer between my junior and senior year at Tam I took a Greyhound bus to Los Angeles where I stayed with a good friend of my parents. I arranged to have a meeting with Milton I. Moritz, who was the head of publicity at American-International and through other contacts managed to see a guy out at Universal Studios. The guy at Universal was horrible to me, castigating me for bringing my somewhat crude pen and ink sketches of ads in and basically told me to go home and forget it. Moritz on the other hand was a very nice guy and advised me that I should finish my education then come back and see them. If, however, college wasn't for me, he said, he was sure they could find me a job to do at the studio when I finished high school.

My senior year, however, was a peculiar time, as the slithering mist of the coming hippy era crept subversively through the halls of Tamalpais High School.

By the time I graduated, the thoughts of going to Hollywood to work as a messenger boy at AIP had been forgotten entirely.

I did continue to see their somewhat ridiculous films that cashed in on the new youth culture. *The Wild Angels,* starring Peter Fonda and Nancy Sinatra was followed by *The Trip* and poor old Vincent Price was cast in the *Dr Goldfoot* movies while Ray Milland wound up in *X-The Man with the X-Ray Eyes.*

When I began living in London I never lost my interest in AIP and caught such delights as *The Abominable Dr Phibes, Count Yorga-Vampire, The Wild Party, Food of the Gods* and the perfectly ghastly *Frogs* starring Ray Milland which had amongst its cast, a young man from Mill Valley named David Gilliam. I didn't know David at this time but met him years later when I began working as an actor. In the film, David's character wound up being killed by tarantula spiders in a Florida swampland.

By the time that AIP brought out *Dillinger* the name of James H. Nicholson had vanished from the credits. It was some time later that I learned what had happened. After

Nicholson's power within the company diminished due to his divorce settlement, Arkoff began calling the shots. One decision he made that his partner didn't like was to hire Larry Gordon to head up production and, eventually Jim Nicholson left AIP in 1972. He took with him two film properties which he put into production at Fox but before the first movie was even released he suffered a seizure in a restaurant and tests revealed that he had brain cancer. In December of that same year he died.

The film credits had always read: Produced by James H. Nicholson and Samuel Z. Arkoff. These two names together meant AIP but now only the latter appeared.

A book I came across on Columbia's Harry Cohn began with a description of the author having a meeting with Arkoff and comparing him to Cohn as an exact opposite. Cohn he described as practically illiterate but someone who had an instinct for making great movies. Arkoff, he said, talked like a merchant prince but made movies like a mug.

My friend the late Jim Clark whose book, *Dream Repairman,* I helped him write, directed Vincent Price in the last film he ever made for AIP, *Madhouse.* He described meeting Arkoff in his sumptuous suite at the Savoy before filming began. As Jim was about to leave, Sam Arkoff, with an enormous cigar in his mouth, told him: "Hey Jim, remember. No Fellini shit!"

This fast-growing film company had, in the course of its meteoric rise, given first opportunities to many of the biggest names in Hollywood and yet, as Mark Symmes so accurately surmised: they made junky movies.

Obsessions, such as the one I had developed with AIP, are indiscriminate. They make no distinction between that which is good and that which is downright dreadful. It is all "of interest."

Some record collectors value the flawed out-takes of famous discs by the likes of Duke Ellington or Bing Crosby as much as those which were released. In this spirit, I went to see *The Beast with 1,000,000 Eyes* at a vintage sci-fi film festival at the Barbican here in London. I had known about this film from several different sources on AIP but was not prepared for the numbing tedium of actually sitting through this ghastly movie.

If there is medication one can take for obsessions, perhaps I ought to try some.

Chapter 28

Of Pantsing and Presidents

At what point does a noun become a verb? The plural noun in question is the word 'pants,' meaning trousers and the verb is the very same, meaning to pull someone's trousers down.

I'm sure that the ritual of 'pantsing' was not unique to Mill Valley in the late 1950s and early 60s but a ritual it was indeed. The victim of a 'pantsing' was never a six foot Clark Kent lookalike. No. It was invariably someone a bit weedy, small and physically immature. During 1960 that someone was me. This would be my thirteenth year alive but I probably looked about eight.

Young men of this age were beginning to shave, their voices deepening and, terribly important to their status in a locker room, they had pubic hair. On all three of these fronts, I was a serious latecomer, a fact which made me burn with self consciousness.

In my mind I was not a microscopic wimp but rather a dashing and attractive sort of person who had beautiful women fawning over him. The gap between these two realities was the size of an ocean but one should never underestimate the human mind's ability to kid itself.

There were a fair few young men at school who did fall into the he-man category and they tended to hold court so in this arena I became kind of a court jester. I was always an entertaining character to have around. A little guy with a loudspeaker voice and sometimes witty banter.

I was in eighth grade and my main teacher was Miss Huguet who I liked. I was no longer a record collector, at least not of pop music, but I did hear all the Top 40 hits on the radio and through the repetition that this kind of brainwashing brings, knew them all by heart. While Elvis had been in the army it didn't stop his recording career at all but the records he was putting out didn't excite me the way his early material had. *Are You Lonesome Tonight?* just didn't have the raw fire of *All Shook Up* or *Hound Dog*.

In fact most of the popular music at this time was banal. A few numbers like *Save The Last Dance For Me* and *Poetry In Motion* were okay but the majority of the hit records did not thrill me.

This was also the time of the presidential election between John Kennedy and Richard Nixon. Kennedy's nomination at the Democratic Convention in July had caught my attention from a couple of angles. One was the daily Chronicle which I was in the habit of reading when the news interested me. The other was what I heard from my parents, Blackie and Beth. Through these two sources I gleaned that John Kennedy's father had bought him the Democratic nomination.

My father did not hate many people but prominent amongst that small group he did actually despise was Joseph Kennedy. I never interrogated Black about this but have since learned that Joe Kennedy had been appointed to head Roosevelt's Maritime Commission in 1937 which was a time that my father was a prominent and active vice president of the radical National Maritime Union.

I can only guess at what specifically made Blackie hate this man but hate him he did.

So it was natural enough that Black would be more than a bit sceptical about young Jack Kennedy and as for Nixon, he had utter contempt for him. Nixon had made his name politically as part of J. Parnell Thomas's House Un-American Activities Committee.

The sight of young Dick Nixon and Robert Stripling earnestly examining microfilm allegedly found inside a pumpkin on Whitaker Chambers' farm was ridiculous but in those dark days of the witch hunt, most Americans took this amateur dramatic performance seriously. They also fell for Nixon's 'Checkers' speech in which he skillfully sidestepped all the accusations which had been made against him and concentrated on irrelevant details of his personal finances building to the emotive climax of insisting that they would keep Checkers the dog.

The film in which he made this speech went down so

well with the American public that he was cleared to remain on the ticket as Eisenhower's candidate for the vice presidency.

Nixon had been christened 'Tricky Dick' by Helen Gahagen Douglas who ran against him for the California senate seat in 1950 after Nixon had consistently smeared her as "The Pink Lady." His campaign posters all said "The man who broke the Hiss Case!" Nixon's campaign strategy worked and he won the contest.

Interestingly Jack Kennedy and Nixon both entered national politics at the same time as junior congressmen and they also both ran for the senate in 1950.

I remember Blackie saying that there were a few good things about these two. They were both young which he said was a good thing and Kennedy, if elected, would be the first Catholic president which he also seemed to consider a good thing.

I never saw the television debates as we were still living up on Seymour Avenue and didn't have a set but I did read all about them. I took an active interest in the election probably because of my parents whose close friends all constantly talked politics.

The hand of Joe Kennedy was all over young Jack's campaign. Joe had had presidential ambitions of his own until FDR had fired him and from that point on his political focus shifted to his sons. He marketed young Jack like a packet of cornflakes and selling was something old man Kennedy knew everything about.

The formula for JFK's campaign was built around image. Jack Kennedy was a good-looking guy who spoke well and was the product of the best education that money could buy. In the debates he looked good while Nixon came across as sweaty and unshaven. JFK was also skilled at sounding confident while promising nothing and his example has been replicated ever since by politicians all over the world. In fact when Nixon ran successfully for president in 1968 he had learned all of his old rival's tricks.

Perhaps it was the dishonesty in the political arena which fascinated me so but my interest in politics was not something I shared with my friends at school. At Edna Maguire my over riding ambition was to be liked.

There were a few exceptions such as the time that I was part of the school team debating Red China's admission to the UN. John Elder, David Einstein and I won this debate on the side of China's admission even though one of the judges, Miss Huguet, disagreed with practically every political position I ever took, but had to concede that we put our case more effectively.

I had Miss Huguet for social studies and liked her enormously but we used to have very colourful arguments. She was an unquestioning conservative politically. I remember taking exception to her telling the class that Castro was "just a jerk." One time I arrived late in the morning for some reason to find her prattling on and as I entered, the entire class groaned because they knew I'd argue with what she was saying.

The reality was that nobody was interested in politics which, I have found, is a pretty universal state of affairs. What my friends were interested in was sex, smoking cigarettes, rock and roll records and cars.

I longed to be cool but being thirteen and looking eight was a considerable handicap. I was friendly with several of the hard guys at Edna Maguire. Jimmy Tamburini seemed to be top banana amongst them. Jim was tall, very good looking and tough. He and his colleagues all wore a kind of uniform which consisted of jeans, black shoes, a black collarless sweater which was worn over a white tab-collared shirt. The shirt was buttoned up and snapped. The crowning effect was the pompador hairstyle kept aloft by much Brylcreem.

Jimmy Tamburini's uniform was worn by a gaggle of guys: Mike Chirco, Wayne and Mike Cleland, Garret Testes and Johnny Lem. Whether they were a gang or not I didn't know but they could always be found in a group and usually walked home from school along the railroad tracks at Alto.

My brother Jim and I usually found ourselves tagging along as we had to go the same way. There was never any doubt that we were separate from these guys but for some reason our presence always seemed welcome. My guess is that we were a good audience for the stories these characters would tell, the veracity of which was always questionable.

One lazy afternoon brother Jim and I walked down Lomita Drive from the school along with Garret Testes and a few other hard guys. I would have pulled my pack of Chesterfields out of my shirt pocket and lit a cigarette. Brother Jim never smoked. Down where

Lomita turned left, we joined the railroad track and carried on towards the Purity supermarket at the junction of Camino Alto and East Blithedale.

The hard guys were rather thick on the ground this day. Among their number was Craig Bird, Jim Tamburini and probably about another seven or so, all dressed in the uniform collarless black sweaters.

I have no memory of who was boasting but there had to be an entertaining yarn or two being spun to keep this crowd entertained as it moved up Blithedale turning left on Locust and down to Sycamore where another left was taken.

There was a small wooden house on Sycamore Street which must have belonged to one of these guys and the crowd, including my brother Jim and I, ascended the steps and entered. As we walked into the living room somebody shouted: "Get Myers!" I was grabbed from behind while someone else pulled my trousers and underpants down.

As I lay, partially naked, on this living room floor I could see the faces of all these guys staring quietly down at me. It didn't last long but long enough. I guess they wanted to satisfy their curiosity that I hadn't yet reached puberty.

As they turned away I pulled my trousers back up and Jim and I left. I never heard a single word about this incident from any of the participants. It hadn't happened in a public place so if it became general knowledge I certainly didn't know of it.

One of the reasons that I was of interest at school was that I had a talent for drawing. I was also a confident performer of sorts in spite of my size but all of this counted for nothing when it came time to 'pants' me in that little house on Sycamore.

I was little and they were big and the law of the jungle prevailed. I suspect, though, that their pantsing of me was not something which made them feel proud.

Chapter 29
Political Films in Marin County

You will have gathered by now that I loved going to the movies and that I grew up in a very left wing family during the McCarthy years. There were certain advantages to this, most of them political. For example: I was spared the ordeal of figuring out the idiocy of racism for myself.

I remember the first time I heard a friend's father use the N word. I was absolutely shocked. I kept it to myself but it shook me to think that an adult could use such a word as it was never uttered or tolerated in our household or amongst our close friends.

I took many opinions from my parents including a wish for nuclear disarmament. Every time I'd hear a jet break the sound barrier in the skies above Homestead School I would think the worst. It didn't take much imagination to contemplate the kind of destruction a nuclear war would inflict upon our world and how ridiculous getting under your desk would be in the event.

The disadvantages of such an upbringing were that all the political opinions I considered to be correct ran totally counter to the status quo. This was the era of the anti-Communist witch-hunts and even being liberal in those days was seen as suspicious. And my folks were far left of liberal.

So when I would go to the movies it was always with a big bag of attitudes and by my ninth year I was at the Sequoia Theatre three times each weekend. Because we had no television we went to the movies a lot. I'd be there Friday night, Saturday for the matinee and usually with my sisters on Sunday afternoon when the theatre changed features.

I saw westerns, comedies, action and adventure films by the barrel. Not everything I saw was good, in fact most of it was rubbish but during the 1950s and 60s a small number of bold and thought-provoking movies made their way to the general public.

Hollywood rarely touched on serious subjects in those days but a few film makers were able to get their pictures made which invited the audience to think about serious things.

One such movie was *12 Angry Men* which I saw when I was ten. Several themes percolated up through this drama of a courtroom jury who retired to decide the fate of a young Puerto Rican boy accused of a knife murder in New York City.

One of the twelve, played by Henry Fonda, was unsure about convicting the boy. To the annoyance of the other jurors, he insisted they re-examine the evidence over and over, something they were all reluctant to do. One had tickets for the ball game and was anxious to get away. But, little by little, Fonda sowed the seeds of doubt in their minds.

Directed by Sidney Lumet, *12 Angry Men* was not only gripping and entertaining but it made you think about the importance of the jury system and the responsibility that citizens have in a democratic society.

Racism was another issue as the boy on trial was not a Caucasian and the jurors all were. My mother Beth instructed all four Myers kids from an early age about the evils of racial prejudice. She had seen ample evidence first hand as a reporter in the deep south during the 1930s where she witnessed lynchings and had a terrifying run-in with the Ku Klux Klan in which a close friend had one of his eyes burned out.

Mill Valley was a town populated predominantly by white people. Practically all the black people in our county lived in Marin City which was between Mill Valley and Sausalito just off Highway 101. The housing in Marin City had been put up for maritime workers in Sausalito during World War II.

There was one exception to the Caucasian demographic of Mill Valley and that was the Collins family who lived high up on Summit. Doctor Collins was a dentist and managed to buy his house direct from the owner rather than through a real estate agent. His sons, the only black kids in an all-white town, went to Old Mill School.

One film to grapple with race prejudice was *The Defiant Ones* which came to the Sequoia in 1958.

It starred Sidney Poitier and Tony Curtis as two southern convicts, one black, one white, who were chained together and escaped when the prison van crashed.

The movie was gripping and dramatic. Stanley Kramer directed this picture in a very realistic way. One thing I noticed, because I saw it more than once, was that there was no musical soundtrack. There was music which one of the posse kept playing on his transistor radio but no lush score to emphasise the dramatic or heartfelt moments. We were left to make up our own minds as to how we felt about what we saw.

The physical journey which both men went on was harrowing enough, thrashing through treacherous swamps with a pack of hounds on their trail but they also took an emotional journey in which they discovered that they'd become, without noticing it, close friends.

Another movie which dealt less directly with the subject of prejudice was *Compulsion*, a story which was based on a real murder trial which had happened in Chicago in the 1920s: the Loeb and Leopold case.

One advantage of my family was that my parents knew all these bits of relatively recent American history so I would hear about them around the dinner table. Nathan Leopold and Albert Loeb were two very rich and highly educated Jewish students who meticulously planned and carried out the fiendish murder of a schoolboy in Chicago and when they were caught the fires of anti-semitism were ignited. They were saved from the gallows by the impassioned defence of legendary lawyer Clarence Darrow.

The movie *Compulsion* was directed by Richard Fleischer and the young men were played by Bradford Dillman and Dean Stockwell. Orson Welles put in a weighty performance as the Darrow character.

This was not the only film inspired by the case. Alfred Hitchcock's *Rope* in 1948 based its two young murderers on Loeb and Leopold.

Another subject which preoccupied me was the risk of atomic warfare. The sonic booms which regularly made me think that World War III had begun, kept me in a near state of terror throughout my childhood and that terror found expression in Stanley Kramer's next movie, based on Nevil Shute's novel *On The Beach*.

Set mostly in Melbourne, Australia, it told the story of an American submarine captain played by Gregory Peck who guided his vessel to the one place in the world which hadn't yet been poisoned by the radiation of World War III. Melbourne looked wonderful with traffic that mingled cars with horses and buggies.

An excellent cast and fine photography made this a moving but melancholy experience. Ava Gardner was Peck's love interest and Anthony Perkins played a young naval officer with a wife and child. As Perkins was, at this time, a young leading man, this would probably be one of the last normal roles he would play before taking on the mantle of Norman Bates in Hitchcock's *Psycho.*

A good surprise was Fred Astaire's turn as a nuclear scientist playboy who raced his Ferarri and drank too much.

All the characters made an honest attempt to live a normal life but the knowledge of their imminent doom hung over them like a cloud.

Peck's submarine was ordered across the Pacific to check out an indecipherable morse code signal coming from San Diego but they stopped first at San Francisco.

As all of us in Mill Valley grew up fifteen miles north, it was particularly shocking to see the submarine cruise through the Golden Gate with no cars on the bridge. Equally unsettling were the sights through Peck's periscope of nothing moving on the streets crossing Russian Hill in North Beach.

When the sub reached San Diego the search party discovered that someone had left a coke bottle tied to a morse code device which sent out the ghostly signal which had brought the sub all the way from Australia.

Back in Melbourne a banner was erected reading: 'There's Still Time, Brother' and the Salvation Army made music and tried to save souls. When the film's end came and we saw barren shots of Melbourne's empty streets, the final image was of this banner with no people, only bits of paper blowing in the wind.

I saw this movie at the Marin Theatre in Sausalito on a Sunday matinee and as I came out I was handed a leaflet which featured an illustration of the banner from the film and an invitation to become active in the Marin County anti-nuclear campaign.

Of course I was not one of those who needed to be convinced by this movie and from what I understand the biggest concern of United Artists was that nobody would turn out for Kramer's film but it didn't do too badly at the boxoffice and Kramer was allowed to ride again.

He was ultimately a political film-maker as his next movie, *Inherit The Wind,* would tackle another controversial topic: Darwin's theory of evolution being taught in southern schools which was based on another true life event.

In 1925 John Scopes, a teacher in Dayton, Tennessee, was arrested and put on trial for explaining Darwin's theories to his students. William Jennings Bryan, an old politician who had found god, came south to prosecute this agent of the devil and, once again, it was Clarence Darrow who stepped forward to offer Scopes a defence.

Kramer cast his picture with big name star talent and a fabulous parade of solid character actors. Spencer Tracy played Henry Drummond based on Darrow. Frederic March was Matthew Harrison Brady inspired by Jennings Bryan.

Kramer must have had a thing about casting song and dance men in serious roles for this time he had Gene

Kelly playing E.K. Hornbeck, a journalist based on E.L. Mencken.

The musical soundtrack by Ernest Gold was spare and made lots of room for the song *Give Me That Old Time Religion* to be sung acoustically throughout.

Set in the fictitious town of Hillsboro, *Inherit The Wind* played its politics in an even-handed way giving us access to the inner workings of the town council and its serious concerns at the national headlines their town was receiving and how the northern press was making a laughing stock out of the case they'd brought against the teacher. The movie was a rich and satisfying yarn based largely on the truth.

All of these films were shot in black and white. Somehow monochrome seemed more in keeping with the seriousness of the various subject matters. It wouldn't be until the late 1960s that such movies would be made in colour. Also they seemed to arrive at the Sequoia on a Sunday rather than a Friday or Saturday.

Downtown Mill Valley was a very different place on a Sunday afternoon as most of the stores were closed. I regularly attended the Sequoia's Sunday matinee with my sisters during the 1950s.

It was late 1961 that my brother Jim and I went to a Sunday matinee of Stanley Kramer's *Judgment at Nuremberg*. It was a gripping and important film.

My father Blackie was not a bitter man even though his livelihood had been taken by the blacklist but there were certain subjects which brought forth an unforgiving side of him. One of these was what he perceived to be the hasty rehabilitation of the German nation after World War II and one person personified that rehabilitation: Werhner Von Braun.

As far as Black was concerned, Von Braun was a Nazi war criminal, responsible for designing the rockets, produced with slave labour, which had rained down on Great Britain, killing and maiming countless human beings and yet, he was now an American hero, heading up the US space programme.

A good looking man with a healthy tan, Von Braun was often photographed with well known faces like President Kennedy and Walt Disney. His respectability angered my father.

Blackie also felt that Hollywood played down the crimes the Nazis had committed and instead made new demons of the Russians.

This rewriting of recent history suffered a setback in 1960 when the Israelis captured Adolf Eichmann in Argentina and put him on trial for war crimes. It brought to the world's attention unavoidably gruesome details of the final solution which Eichmann had been instrumental in carrying out. Those forces within the US government who wished to downplay Nazi war crimes were severely undermined by these revelations which were not widely known about by the general public in the United States.

So *Judgment at Nuremberg* marked a change for Hollywood's portrayal of the Nazis.

It featured an all-star cast: Spencer Tracy played the presiding judge, Richard Widmark was the prosecuter and the German defence lawyer was Maximilian Schell. It was a courtroom drama and inventive camera work kept things interesting.

Tracy presided over the trial of four German judges, the most senior of which was played by Burt Lancaster. These men were responsible for sending many people to fates so terrible they were difficult to contemplate.

Montgomery Clift gave a heartbreaking performance as a simple-minded fellow who had been sterilised because his father was a Communist. Judy Garland was equally effective as a woman who had been accused of sleeping with a Jew. The Jewish man had been hanged for the offence.

Like Kramer's previous films, *Judgment at Nuremberg* was scrupulously even handed in its politics and gave expression to all points of view regarding postwar Germany.

It was a sombre and thought-provoking movie and after it was over my brother Jim and I walked down to the recently opened Le Cirque, a small soda fountain which nestled in amongst the shops on the north side of Litton Square right near the Bank Of America. It was run by two neighbours of ours, Mr and Mrs Sukey whose son Nelson was known to us.

It was clear from their accents that the Sukeys were either German or Austrian. They greeted us in a very friendly manner and Mr Sukey took our order for two banana splits. He then asked what we had been doing and we said we'd been to the movies. But when we told him which movie we had just seen, Mr Sukey became immediately cross. "The past is the past," he said angrily. "They should not make such a movie."

I was fourteen years old and even though we came from a family where being young did not disqualify you from arguing a point with an adult I found myself tongue tied by Mr Sukey's anger. We ate our banana splits in silence sitting on the stools at the small counter.

This exchange raised questions in my mind but it was never mentioned again. Mill Valley was a small town and these people lived on Janes Street in the house just below our property. We hardly ever encountered them though we'd occasionally see their son Nelson, who had a club foot and walked with a limp, but we didn't really know him.

I don't recall ever going into the Sukey's soda fountain again after that day and I don't remember it as ever really taking off like Meyer's Bakery or Esposti's.

The movies the Sequoia showed from Sunday to Tuesday seemed to be the more serious kind like *The Children's Hour* while the lighter films like *Lover Come Back* or *Blue Hawaii* filled the Friday and Saturday night slots.

Birdman of Alcatraz starred Burt Lancaster as Robert Stroud, the convicted murderer who became a renowned expert on birds while serving his lifetime in prison. Moody, tough and not very likeable, Stroud became tender and sensitive towards a baby sparrow he found in the exercise yard. The movie should, however, have been called *Birdman of Leavenworth* as Stroud never took his birds with him when he transferred to Alcatraz.

I had been very gripped while at Edna Maguire by the execution of Caryl Chessman in the gas chamber at San Quentin. I remember Marlon Brando leading a parade of protesters up to the prison. Stroud's story was slightly different from Chessman's but there were similarities. I participated in a school debate on capital punishment and, though we won the debate, in real life, Chessman died in the gas chamber.

The prison on Alcatraz was a grim landmark for all who lived in the bay area. The searchlight revolving steadily at night mingled with the fog horns to give a darker image to San Francisco bay. I always took Alcatraz for granted and never thought for a moment it would ever be a tourist attraction one could visit. In years to come, however, I too would make the trip with the tourists.

Birdman of Alcatraz was not really a very pleasant film to sit through though it did highlight just how destructive the penal system could be. Burt Lancaster was one of those Hollywood stars with politically liberal instincts and in addition to many swashbuckling pictures he also co-starred with Tony Curtis in the excellent *Sweet Smell of Success* all about a powerful gossip columnist and a sycophantic press agent. Lancaster's role was based on Walter Winchell who was, at this time, a syndicated columnist. Winchell wielded his immense power in much the same way as Lancaster's J.J. Hunsecker.

Another film, *To Kill a Mockingbird,* came to the Sequoia. Set in a small southern town during the depression, it was adapted from the bestselling novel by Harper Lee.

Gregory Peck played Atticus Finch, a liberal white lawyer in a deeply racist southern town, who was called upon to defend Tom Robinson, a black man accused of raping a young white woman.

It was a gentle film involving the lawyer and his two children, Scout and Jem. Scout was the little girl who kept getting in fights whenever kids used racial taunts to insult her father and when a lynch mob arrived at the jail to find Atticus keeping a vigil to protect Tom Robinson it was Scout saying hello to one of the men which made them ashamed of themselves.

This movie came out at a time when George Wallace, the governor of Alabama, made headlines proselytizing about racial segregation while federal laws had been passed to de-segregate schools. A terrible battle was happening down south where Medgar Evers, a black civil rights activist was assassinated.

Martin Luther King had become an international figurehead for the fight against segregation and the press ran daily stories of southern police attacking crowds of black protesters with dogs, water cannon and truncheons. The brutality of these clashes were shocking.

I always found the news in the paper to be fascinating though at school none of my friends were interested in racial segregation or the possibility of nuclear war.

By the time *Fail-Safe* came out in 1964, America had already experienced the Cuban Missile Crisis so the film's subject matter was timely in the extreme.

Ironically *Doctor Strangelove* came out first and it took

the same situation as *Fail-Safe* but made a very funny comedy of it.

I saw *Dr Strangelove,* not at the Sequoia, but in a screening room in San Francisco before it opened. This was a perk of my hanging around Columbia Pictures in the early 1960s.

In addition to Peter Sellers playing three different roles, the film also marked the return to screen acting for Sterling Hayden, who put in a very funny performance as Jack D. Ripper, the deranged general who triggered the nuclear conflict.

Sterling Hayden had recently moved to Sausalito and had gone to great lengths to recant his damaging testimony before HUAC when he named names in the early 1950s.

I had, by this time, inherited the job at the Bus Depot from Jared Dreyfus and was sitting up behind the counter one day when the phone rang and it was Sterling Hayden wanting to know if a particular book he'd ordered had arrived. I went to check and it had so Hayden said he'd be in to collect it within the hour.

I had only seen one movie he'd made which was terrible. Somehow I seemed to have missed his very good performances in other films. But the bearded giant who walked into the bus depot that day was a very impressive person. Friendly and polite, he collected his book and left me with a slightly altered opinion of him.

At this time I was in Miss Rogers' journalism class at Tam High and, in addition to drawing cartoons, I also wrote regularly for the school paper. When I saw *Dr Strangelove* and thoroughly enjoyed it, I decided to ask Sterling Hayden for an interview. I don't remember how I got in touch with him but I soon found myself sitting opposite him on board his houseboat in Sausalito.

The first thing I said was that my mother Beth could never forgive him for naming names. He told me that he couldn't forgive himself either and from that point on we got on very well indeed.

Another movie which opened not long after The Beatles invaded our shores was *Seven Days in May,* one of the best political thrillers ever. With a screenplay by Rod Serling and directed by John Frankenheimer, this movie crackled with tension.

Frederic March played the president who had

negotiated a disarmament treaty with the Russians and Burt Lancaster was a general who was organising a military coup to unseat him. This highly secret plot was uncovered by the general's assistant played by Kirk Douglas and a marvellous yarn it was to behold.

The supporting cast was also excellent with standout performances by Edmond O'Brien and Ava Gardner. The musical score by Jerry Goldsmith supported the story's tension admirably.

All of these movies were important as they made people think. The actors who played in them were mostly politically liberal. We got all our Hollywood gossip from the Hallinans who regularly reported to us who in tinsel town was politically left and who was right.

These movies should be required viewing in schools along with those which followed in the 1970s, 80s and right up until now: *Medium Cool, Coal Miner's Daughter, Missing, Silkwood, Under Fire, The China Syndrome, Matewan, Executive Action, Platoon, Bridge of Spies* and *The Post*. I believe that they will come to be viewed in the same way as classic literature.

Chapter 30

Days At The Bus Depot

My two sisters probably spent most of their free time at the library up on Lovell Street but for me the three locations which I returned to with all the regularity of a devoted churchgoer were Village Music, the Sequoia Theatre and the Bus Depot.

It is interesting to me to see how little is known by the younger residents of today's Mill Valley about the Bus Depot. I suppose my generation of Mill Valley kids were equally ignorant about the trains which originally ran in and out of town. That's the problem with progress. The old gets torn down, built on, and a way of life is forgotten forever.

The main reason I was in the Bus Depot so much was the comic book rack which sat opposite the main counter as you entered from the Thockmorton side. I bought and collected a lot of comic books but they were only a small percentage of the ones I read for free. I never purchased *Archie, Little Lulu, Casper* and countless other titles, but I read them all.

From a very early age I was also on a first name basis with the ladies who worked there. I knew Margo and Brun pretty well and they tended to give me special dispensation with regards to comic book reading, whereas most boys were told to put the comics back.

Over the years I spent a lot of time in the Bus Depot. Whenever my brother Jim and I found ourselves downtown that's the place we'd hang around.

Sometime in the very early 1960s Jimmy and I became friendly with one of the Greyhound bus drivers. We got to know him through Margo who Jim thinks had a crush on him. He was a very good looking guy of about thirty five and he was always a happy sort. His name was Arleigh. We took to spending Sunday afternoons down around the Depot and Arleigh would let us sit in his parked bus while he awaited his next departure.

Over time when we were off school Arleigh would let us ride into the city and back on his bus but we had to be careful not to get caught because the Greyhound Company hired spotters to ride the buses checking up on the drivers. Arleigh always gave us tickets and we had to pretend we didn't know him on these journeys.

The usual route was out through Tam Valley, making a stop at Marin City, which was where you would change to go north to San Rafael or Novato. The bus would then continue on through Sausalito and across the Golden Gate Bridge. Once we were through the tollgate, we'd take the second exit off the freeway by the Palace of Fine Arts then on up Lombard Street with its endless parade of motels, until the bus would hang a right on Van Ness. We would then motor over the hill until we turned left on Golden Gate. The final leg of this journey was to cross Market at 6th, go around the corner to 7th and into the depot where there was a special angled parking space for the Mill Valley buses.

Amongst our toys from very early on was a fleet of tiny Greyhound buses and I remember running one of these in and out of Bearville, the imaginary town which my brother and I constructed for our sizeable teddy bear collection.

I had a medium sized Greyhound Silverside which would come along the top of a concrete wall just below our front lawn and stop for a gaggle of imaginary bears on their way somewhere important.

Apart from pretty regular car journeys with my father to the San Francisco waterfront on Saturdays, the usual form of transport to the city for us was the Greyhound bus which ran on the hour out of the Depot. Most of our early trips were with my mother Beth who would buy the tickets across the counter. There was a huge stamp that Margo or Brun would bang with their fist once the tickets were within its jaws.

The drivers all wore a pretty smart military-looking uniform: grey shirt with a tie, matching grey trousers and each man, for I rarely saw a woman driver, had a military-style hat which he would or would not wear. Attached to their belt was a leather holster which held the driver's individual ticket punch. The mark that was made by the punch was never the same and, thus, later identification of the driver could be made.

Great play was made in Greyhound advertising copy about leaving the driving to them and, doubtless, the daily commute in and out of Mill Valley must have been a relatively painless business. Longer journeys, however, were a different story. I remember becoming impossibly bored and constrained on long Greyhound journeys like one we took to New Mexico in 1958 .

It was while sitting in his bus one day that we met one of Arleigh's colleagues, Ernst Heinemann. Ernst was very tall, dark haired and German. We learned that Ernst had been in the Hitler Youth as a kid and told us, quite calmly in his excellent English that Hitler had his good points as well as his bad.

Ernst didn't feel the persecution of the Jews was a good thing but the concept of full employment and sense of purpose he saw as positive.

Now my father Blackie had a very strong prejudice against Germans in general which was interesting because it was the only nationality he seemed to hold a grudge against. It was clearly to do with the Nazis for he didn't feel that way about the Italians or Japanese. He always told me that the Italians made 'lousy fascists' as their hearts weren't in it, whereas the Germanic character fitted the mould perfectly in his opinion.

One restaurant our family never went to was the Mountain Home Inn with its Germanic décor and draft beer served in big metallic mugs. I can only guess that Blackie hated the huge success that Volkswagen Beetles and camper vans had in America during the sixties.

I don't believe that either Jim or I ever mentioned our friend Ernst to Beth or Blackie but, I suspect, that if Blackie had met him he probably would have liked him as we did.

One of the anomalies of growing up in a family where politics played such a strong role was the fact that most people we knew hardly ever thought about politics. It just never came up with my friends at school. So, for me, all these political opinions that followed me around, were hardly ever used at all, but they were always there.

It was hardly twenty years since that war had ended and so much had changed for my parents during that time and here we were, no longer in Greenwich Village but in beautiful Mill Valley.

Mount Tamalpais in all its glory attracted hikers from all around the world. Most would arrive by Greyhound bus on the weekends and head up Throckmorton to climb up any of the wooden steps which ascended towards the mountain. Quite a few of these hikers were German and Austrian.

That downtown junction where Miller ran into Throckmorton always was a nice part of town and on the weekends it was busy but not unpleasantly so. Directly opposite the depot on Miller stood Women's Mayers, a sizeable clothing store while the Men's Mayers was about a third of the way down the block near where Sunnyside joined in. Also along this strip was Meyer's Bakery where I used to enjoy a cherry Coke at their soda fountain.

This was a time when the stores in Mill Valley had a practicality about them. Lockwood's the Drugstore, Strawbridge's cards and stationery, The Redwood Book Store, Ben Franklin five and dime, Esposti's ice cream parlour and many more.

Sy Weill, a very tall bald man could usually be seen, immaculately attired, standing in front of his store,

Redhill Liquors, smoking and watching the world walk by. His shop was on Throckmorton next door to the diner which had been known as Stuyvesant's but by the early 60s had become Pat & Joe's.

I used to hang out around the Depot, sometimes sitting on the bench with a clear view of the taxi cabs which parked there. One late afternoon while I sat on that bench I saw Ernst Heinemann wearing his full Greyhound uniform with military-looking hat talking to this much shorter German man who was dressed entirely in Lederhosen complete with a little cap that had a large feather in it. Naturally they were conversing in their native tongue and they made quite a picture standing by the clock tower with the Old Mill Tavern in the background and pine trees ascending in the distance. It looked to me like a Nazi officer conversing with a German civilian during the war in some Bavarian village. I sat and watched them chatting away for some time. The fellow in Lederhosen was much older than Ernst and almost certainly would have been active during the great fracas.

It must have been at least two years later when I read a story in the Chronicle all about our friend Ernst. He'd been arrested and taken off to the psychiatric hospital at Napa and the story in the paper involved Patty Burke's father Bill. Bill Burke was a Greyhound driver who seemed to be kind of a shop steward. He enjoyed the sorts of privileges which come with seniority.

Heinemann turned up on Bill Burke's doorstep one evening carrying a copy of William L. Shirer's *Rise and Fall of the Third Reich* and telling Bill: "We must get the men together. We're all meeting up on the mountain."

Presumably Bill humoured him and, once he'd gone, called the police.

The next incident reported in the story was up in the parking lot at Bootjack Camp where the Marin Sheriff's deputy, John Goff, who regularly patrolled Stinson and the mountain, confronted Heinemann near his car.

When the officer became convinced that Ernst should be taken into custody, the big German jumped in his vehicle and raced down the mountain. A high speed chase then occurred and the deputy managed to shoot one of Ernst's tires out, after which poor old Heinemann was, indeed, taken into custody and shipped off to Napa.

It's rather difficult to find a moral to this sad story. I can only guess that the Nazis had more of an impact on poor Ernst's consciousness than he cared to admit and that, just as I had noticed the similarity between a Greyhound uniform and that of a Nazi officer's, something must have snapped in his mind convincing him he was back in the fatherland in 1942.

By the time of this incident, we hadn't seen Arleigh in quite awhile and I don't think I ever saw him again so we never had a chance to find out what became of Ernst.

It's strange to sit outside what's now called the Book Depot amongst all the flamboyant new citizens of our home town and remember what it was like when big Greyhound buses would come through on the hour.

Mill Valley is so different these days. I remember my brother Jim lamenting the fact that there was only one real café left where you could get bacon and eggs with a short stack without any garnish.

Change is an essential component of life but I can't help missing Pat and Joe's, all the stores which used to light up downtown Mill Valley and the wonderful old Bus Depot, comic books and all.

Chapter 31

The Raven at the Fox

The plan had its good points. I was going to attend the premiere of *The Raven,* the very last movie to ever be shown at the Fox Theatre on Market Street and then to interview Peter Lorre as he came out.

Peter Lorre, for those too young to know, was one of the most famous character actors in Hollywood during my childhood. He had bug eyes, spoke with an eastern European accent and had a voice like a snake.

I had mentioned this idea to my Drama and English teacher Dan Caldwell and he asked me to bring the tape of the interview into class so that everyone could listen.

For reasons I cannot recall Jared Dreyfus sat next to

me in Mr Caldwell's class. It was the spring of 1963 and the only time we were ever classmates. Jar was a senior and I was a sophomore.

Jar and I were very good friends because our parents were terribly close but in the generational hierarchy of Tam High School I occupied a socially inferior position and would go to great lengths to hang out with him. He drove an Austin Healey and my abiding memory of riding in that car was him pulling up at whatever the agreed destination was and saying: "Okay Myers. Out!"

So here we were, colleagues in Mr Caldwell's class. Dan Caldwell was a wonderful teacher. He really brought things to life for me and I cannot say that for many of the teachers I had. I was a terrible dreamer at school and getting my attention was no easy thing.

I remember Mr Caldwell getting up on the small stage which ran across the far end of his classroom in Wood Hall and demonstrating how he, a tall man over six foot, could convey the illusion that he was a small child. He achieved this by bending his knees and stretching his right arm up as if it were being held by a giant adult, then walking with a goofy bounce across the stage as the entire class collapsed in helpless laughter.

He also involved us in reading aloud which I loved. The first time I ever encountered Richard Connell's short story *The Most Dangerous Game* was in Dan Caldwell's class and it was very exciting. In fact, there was a whole collection of short stories which Mr Caldwell had us read and they were all highly melodramatic adventure yarns. Nothing dull ever happened in his class.

So I made my preparations for attending the premiere of *The Raven* which was actually a historic event and a lucky one for American-International Pictures as the biggest and grandest of the Market Street movie palaces, the Fox, was going to be torn down and this was to be its final show.

The Raven starred Vincent Price, Boris Karloff and Peter Lorre, the latter of whom was to be presented on stage after the screening. This was the fourth of the Poe pictures which Roger Corman had directed for AIP and they'd been a huge success which, along with the *Beach Party* films, had lifted the company up the ladder in Hollywood from their low budget beginnings. Practically all their output was now shot in colour and they were, unlike the major Hollywood studios, making a mountain of money.

My hobby at this time was collecting pressbooks and posters for many movies but particularly the product of AIP which, for some reason, held an absolute fascination for me. In addition to the drama class, I also wrote movie reviews for the high school newspaper so I was hoping I could get a good interview with Peter Lorre for my article in the paper.

By this time my collection of pressbooks was sizeable and I had taken to writing off for all the free things I could get my hands on, pretending to be a theatre manager. I would type: 'John H. Myers, Manager' at the bottom of the letter and it seemed to work.

In this way I collected many radio ad spots and open-end interviews. These were interviews with the film's stars which came on a vinyl disc along with a script, including the questions you could ask in the allotted silent space on the record. It took a little practice but after a few times through, it sounded like you were interviewing the person. It was for small radio stations across the country to have their local personalities in conversation with the actors when, in fact, they never even met them. Ad mats cost money as did posters and I did acquire a fair few of them but the radio spots and interviews were free.

I knew all the movie theatres on Market and the street itself was throbbing with a cloud of contamination. I always returned on the Greyhound after a day on Market Street with a headache, caused, I guess, by exhaust fumes. It was a pretty seedy place. There was a joke shop on the corner of Market and Golden Gate where they sold things like magnetic mummies inside plastic coffins. They had this sign for sale which featured a cartoon of an ugly man's head coming up out of some water. It read: *We don't swim in your toilet. Please don't pee in our pool.*

The Fox, by contrast to the ghastly side of Market Street, was a truly spectacular place. The theatre's forecourt was tiled in swirling shapes and bright colours, a bit like Dorothy's yellow brick road.

Once you'd purchased your ticket and it had been taken by a uniformed usher, you entered the lobby through one of four double doors. What a fabulous sight that lobby was: huge gilded pillars stretched forever up past gaudy displays of winged angels and flaming cups to a ceiling every bit ornate as a museum.

The candy counter was large and the selection of pogey bait diverse but the next thing to catch your eye was that staircase. Situated directly back from the entrance it was what every small movie theater aspired to but never quite achieved. The Sequoia in Mill Valley, built in the same year as the Fox, had a mere five or six red carpeted steps up into its auditorium but here, before me stood a sweeping massive staircase with red carpet climbing up it. The banisters on the sides descended to ornate pillars each with a massive candelabra perched on top like a flaming head dress. In a few months this whole place would be knocked to the ground.

Its demise was sad indeed, however, the business of America was business and the movies were, at this time in steep decline. This was 1963 and television had become the dominant medium. Only AIP was winning the war against the small screen while the big studios were all slipping regularly and pulling down The Fox was symbolic of this decline.

Part of the problem with The Fox was that it was much larger than the other Market Street theaters. It held four and a half thousand people while the Paramount and Golden Gate could only accommodate two thousand, six hundred or so. Also it was quite a distance away. All the movie theatres on Market were within close proximity of each other but the Fox was a good ten-minute walk away, far enough away to make a difference.

So come the big day and I was on the Greyhound bus into the city with my portable cassette tape recorder. In all honesty I had spent many more hours in those other Market Street theatres than I ever had at the Fox, probably because they showed fewer of the horror films which were the magnets that got me all the way from Mill Valley.

But I do remember coming to the Fox to see Vincent Price in *The Fly* as well as AIP's biggest budget film, Jules Verne's *Master of the World*.

So I arrived there for this big World Premiere and they had the most appalling picture as a second feature which was a British film called *Peeping Tom* which should not have been seen by my young self at all. It was about this maniac photographer in London who attached a knife onto a film camera and recorded his murders of young women. I have since heard people like Martin Scorcese describe this movie as some kind of a masterpiece but I'm afraid I have to disagree in the strongest possible terms. I watched it again as an adult and found it just as sick as when I first saw it.

So when the grainy agonies of Michael Powell's *Peeping Tom* had passed, we moved onto Roger Corman's latest Poe picture which was really a comedy.

His previous Poe movie, *Tales of Terror,* had featured a comic version of *Cask of Amontillado* blended with *The Black Cat.* There was a very funny wine tasting scene between Price's foppish grape expert and Lorre's drunken oaf. As Lorre got soused, the camera angles became more extreme. I guess Corman and screenwriter Richard Matheson were getting bored with the formula and decided to play all of *The Raven* for laughs.

This film was the first time I ever saw Jack Nicholson who played Lorre's son. I have to confess that I didn't "get" Jack Nicholson on this first outing and thought that he must be related to James H. Nicholson, the president of AIP. I was amused years later to read that Vincent Price thought the same thing. It wasn't until I saw his performance in *Easy Rider* that I finally "got" Nicholson's acting style.

I was such a fan of AIP at this time that I wasn't capable of being critical about the film. I loved it and as soon as it was over, some local smoothie was up on stage warming the audience up for Lorre's appearance.

These were tense moments for me as I had my cassette recorder and was roughly rehearsing questions I could ask. Peter Lorre came out on stage wearing a dark suit and was interviewed about the film and he seemed to be very friendly and charming talking in that utterly recognizable serpent voice of his. As soon as he said his goodbyes to the crowd I dashed up the aisle, out across the massive lobby, through the main doors and onto the sidewalk where a big limousine stood waiting for him.

It was only a few minutes before I saw Peter Lorre walking briskly through the ornate doors towards the car. Turning my tape machine on and holding the microphone up I managed to say: "Mister Lorre could you..."

As his not-very-tall body came close to mine I was overwhelmed by the smell of red wine and he had a burning cigarette in one hand. With the other hand he slapped at my chest and pushed me back shouting: "Get out of my way! Leave me alone!" He then jumped into the limousine.

I stood on the pavement in front of the Fox, somewhat shell-shocked as the limousine pulled away into the night. Feeling dejected, I took the long walk down Market to the

Greyhound station on 7th where I caught the next bus back to Mill Valley.

I was shocked by a few things: how drunk he was surprised me, particularly as he hadn't appeared so from the stalls of the Fox. I was also taken aback by how seriously unpleasant he was.

My father Blackie knew a lot of actors, mostly from New York and if you prodded him he'd express personal opinions about them. It usually took something serious for him to dislike someone and Peter Lorre was on his list of people he didn't care for. It seems Peter Lorre didn't adhere to Blackie's somewhat strict moral code. George Raft was another, but most of the actors he met in his trade union days he found charming.

I returned home to our house on Catalpa feeling morose about the whole experience. After all I had bragged to Mr Caldwell that I was going to interview Peter Lorre. I simply was not able to report the truth of what had happened to me.

Then it struck me. I got out the open-end interview which I had received in the post from AIP. After a few run-throughs with the script, I recorded my voice in pseudo-conversation with the drunken bad tempered Austro-Hungarian. I then took this tape recording to Mr Caldwell's class.

Dreyfus was the only person who knew that my interview was a fraud and I think he was rather impressed by my chutzpah in passing this piece of flimflammery off as authentic. I'm ashamed to say that Dan Caldwell fell for it as did everyone else.

I guess I simply couldn't bear the truth about it all and could not face telling the class of the humiliating experience I'd had at the hands of Mr Moto.* Truth and I were not well acquainted at this time and it would be many years before we became cautious friends.

*Peter Lorre starred as *Mr Moto* in a series of eight movies for 20th Century Fox between 1937 and 1939.

Chapter 32

A Shocking Day In November

By 1963 the Myers family had moved from Seymour Avenue down to a small wooden house at 48 Catalpa Street. No more high hills to climb coming home from school, as we now resided in the relative flatlands where many of the streets were named after trees like Sycamore and Willow.

One change my father Blackie made in our new house was to buy us a television set. Why he did this after refusing to do so for ten years, I don't know, but all that time of going to friends' houses to watch programmes must have taken a toll on my enthusiasm for the medium as I don't recall watching very much TV in our new house.

Most people who were alive and of an age to

comprehend, know exactly where they were on November 22nd, 1963. For readers too young to recognise this date, it was the day John F. Kennedy was assassinated in Dallas, Texas.

I was sixteen and in the early stages of my junior year and it was a very normal day at Tam High. The weather was clear and bright and I had to visit the office before my second class in the morning which was history with Mr. Pohlmann.

I took a note from my parents into the office and I remember standing at the long counter on the ground floor in Wood Hall while one of the secretaries was either dealing with my note or just making me wait.

A loud male voice suddenly blared through the room: "The president has been shot!" All eyes turned to the source of the noise which was the principal's office. Mr. Prather, our principal, stood, grim faced, at his door as the news broadcast he had turned up continued, telling us that Kennedy had been shot in Dallas and was on his way to the hospital. At this stage they seemed to think he was not dead.

I headed out into the hall and up the stairs towards Mr Pohlmann's class. As it was going to be me who would deliver this utterly shocking news I was pretty certain that I knew what would happen. And it did.

I entered the classroom and loudly announced that Kennedy had been shot in Dallas. In an instant Mr Pohlmann left the class, presumably heading for the office.

I had known of Mr Pohlmann from my sister Nell who had him years before me. Any day I hadn't done my homework, which was often, I only had to formulate an articulate and politically astute question and he would lapse into a lengthy and long- winded answer which would take up the remaining time of the class. The ringing of the bell was usually a rude interruption to his monologue followed by the hasty exit of his pupils. The fact I hadn't done my homework, which was the purpose of my question, was glossed over and forgotten.

Nellie had a reasonable regard for him though she did disagree with a few of his political pronouncements. She told me that he dismissed the Spanish Civil War as not important enough to be included in their textbook. I remember him denouncing Senator McCarthy but by 1963 this was a fairly safe position to take. Whether he denounced him in 1953 would be a more interesting question. I liked him but I suspect he had decided to coast by the time I got to him.

As we would enter his class on a normal day he would be standing at a kind of podium on which he had a list of the students and he would silently check each name off as we took our seats without looking up more than was absolutely necessary. When he had finished this ritual he would then shut the door, purse his lips, look out the window and then begin rubbing the hair on the top of his head for a surprisingly long time.

All of this performance art was actually pretty compelling and I don't think he was at all boring, just a bit long-winded and maybe a little self-important. I'm sure it was this last quality which caused him to leave the room so immediately on the news that Kennedy had been shot and doubtless he felt the need to be somewhere closer to the importance of the moment rather than stuck in a room with high school students.

So we were left without a teacher. This was a Friday morning and there was a rally scheduled for the afternoon in the Boys' gym. Jeff Mayer, a jocular and fairly rotund student in the class was also, at this time, the Rally Commissioner. "Does this mean that my rally is going to be cancelled?" he asked. Most of the students took this remark badly as the shock of the news was pretty severe. We didn't yet know that Kennedy was dead and I believe we all just sat there, unsupervised, and talked about the little we knew had happened until the bell rang.

The regime at Tam High School at this time was pretty rigid. The bell denoted the beginning and ending of each class and students found loitering in the halls during class time had to account to any passing teacher for their presence.

When the bell rang at the end of Mr. Pohlmann's class the students poured out onto the campus and by this time the word had spread that President Kennedy was dead. I don't remember going on to another class at all. I believe that school just kind of dissolved and everyone wandered away.

I spent the afternoon with Creighton Wyatt. Creighton was a senior and his brother Randy was in my year.

It might well be that Creighton had a car or perhaps we hitch-hiked to his home in Sausalito. Randy and Creighton lived with their mother in a very modern house just below Highway 101 on Waldo Grade. It had a spectacular view of the bay.

I remember playing chess with Creighton and the television was on the whole time. We saw Lee Harvey Oswald being brought through the hallways of the Dallas Police Department protesting that he had no idea why he was there. When asked by a reporter how he got the wound near his eye he said a policeman had hit him.

The next morning I hitch-hiked back to our house on Catalpa Street. My brother Jim was there as well as my sister Kate and both my parents. The TV was on constantly. It was lucky that Blackie had finally bought us a television set which on this occasion was pretty dramatic as all other programming was cancelled for the live coverage of events in Dallas and Washington.

So here we were at the Catalpa house on the Saturday after the assassination and that day's Chronicle had big blank spaces where the department store ads would normally be. All that appeared were the tiny logos of the various stores like Penney's, Macy's and City of Paris.

It was a terrible shock. We were very familiar with the look and sound of all the Kennedys with their strong Boston accents and for this to happen, regardless of one's opinions of their politics, was dreadfully upsetting.

By the time I had returned home, Oswald had been charged with shooting Kennedy as well as Police Officer Tippett. The televised journeys up and down the Dallas Police corridors continued throughout the Saturday and we saw the photos in the Chronicle of LBJ being sworn in on the airplane as it flew back to Washington with an ashen-faced Jackie Kennedy standing next to him with blood stains on her dress.

On Sunday morning something happened which has stuck in my memory all these years. It was announced that Lee Harvey Oswald was going to be transferred from the Dallas Police Headquarters to the county jail. Blackie then said: "They're not gonna let this guy live." Within minutes of my father's prediction, Jack Ruby stepped forward and shot Oswald dead on television for all the world to see.

Blackie clearly understood how power manifested itself

in the world and recognised the entire assassination as a professional job. With no hesitation he used the word 'they.'

Those four days were strangely dreamlike. It was as if the entire society we lived in melted away somewhat. Of course the public services kept operating. Street lights came on and water and electricity flowed but the vast majority of people seemed in a state of suspended animation.

The analysis of the evidence and how the Warren Commission had concluded that Lee Harvey Oswald was the lone assassin came to be challenged most effectively by Mark Lane in his book *Rush to Judgement* and since that time the conspiracy theories have abounded.

It was by no means a certainty that JFK would have won the 1964 election had he lived but it was known that he planned to pull out of Vietnam, a military adventure which was in its early stages in 1963. It must also have been a concern to his enemies that a lengthy succession of Kennedys was lined up to run for the presidency and there is no doubting the fact that the campaign old Joe Kennedy ran for his son has become the model for political candidates the world over. A combination of good looks, confident swagger and ambiguous political claims have since become the accepted way to get elected.

The expression "Regime Change" had not been coined back in those days but it many ways that was what we got on that

Friday in November, 1963.

It was all the more shocking because it happened in the television era and for four days nothing else seemed to matter as much.

It was not until after we were back in school the following Tuesday that I heard the first joke about the whole thing. 'What happened when the elephant walked into the Dallas Police Department?' somebody asked. 'Nothing. Nobody noticed.'*

- *The second joke I heard from Jared Dreyfus was: "Get in the unemployment line with Vaughan Meader." Vaughan Meader had made a career out of Kennedy family sketches with a best-selling LP entitled *The First Family*.

Chapter 33
The Week The Beatles Arrived

By the beginning of 1964 I had stopped buying singles altogether but this didn't keep me from dropping into Village Music for a regular chat with Sara Wilcox. I bought records at this time but they tended to be film soundtracks or comedy albums.

The shop had moved from the Sequoia Theatre building up to one of the new units on Blithedale just about where it made the transition from East to West.

Sara was the nicest person that I ever encountered in any of the stores in downtown Mill Valley. She was smart, funny, attractive, impeccably dressed and it didn't matter to her whether I bought anything or not. Though I had been going to her shop from age six, she had never ever treated me like a child unlike the adults in Bennett's or Ben Franklin.

Sara enjoyed telling me all about the record company parties she regularly attended and her yarns were never dull. She spoke the jargon of professional sales and of the business she was in but her syntax was original and her stories were very funny.

John Goddard, who I didn't know at this time but who worked for her and subsequently bought the business, tells me that she was a reliable and entertaining source of dirty jokes and I certainly would have been open to hearing them. Maybe I did but it isn't a detail which sticks in my memory. What I do remember was that she was constantly amused by the ludicrous lengths the record companies went to in promoting their products and, as she regularly attended these shindigs, she always had a new tale to tell.

I think my singles buying fizzled out throughout the year of 1958. I know I bought *Tequila* by the Champs and loved its infectious rhythm. I also had a few discs by Chuck Berry, the Everly Brothers and Jerry Lee Lewis but by 1959 I think I simply heard the records on the radio rather than buying and collecting them. This didn't prevent me being brainwashed with all the new releases, some of which I liked and many which I didn't. It is with a profound sense of irritation that I know many of these songs by heart to this day. Top of my 'Most Hated' list would have to be *Tell Laura I Love Her* by Ray Peterson. I despised everything about this song: The shameless melodrama, the whining crybaby voice and the ghastly use of sentiment combined to make it totally loathsome. It was, however, a well-crafted song which got into your head and wouldn't go away.

The early sixties played host to a mix of popular musical styles. Folk was represented by the Kingston Trio as well as Peter, Paul & Mary. Surf music came in the form of the Beach Boys and Jan & Dean and there were dance-crazes like The Twist and Mashed Potatoes. Though I heard all this music on the radio I had become a passive listener.

I remember being surprised by the film *Bye Bye Birdie* which came out in early 1963 as its story was based on the hysteria which had surrounded Elvis Presley up until the time he got drafted. Conrad Birdie was going into the army and his fans, who swooned and screamed, were clearly distraught. Screaming girls were not something which accompanied any of the popular music of the early 1960s and *Bye Bye Birdie* reminded me that such a phenomenon had once existed with Elvis.

So I popped into Village Music one day after school in early February, 1964 and what should Sara be telling me about but this new British band on Capitol called The Beatles. She'd been to a reception and was given this roll of stickers with four mop topped hairdos and the slogan: The Beatles Are Coming!

I had a look at the album cover and was immediately struck by the fact that the four Beatles all had haircuts like Moe Howard in the Three Stooges. That took a bit of getting used to as Moe was my least favourite Stooge and I actually hated all three. He was the bully amongst them who was constantly dishing out hideous punishments like hitting them over the head with a hammer or jabbing them in the eyes with two fingers.

The photo on the back had their names and I saw that Paul McCartney looked very much like my school friend Johnny Lem. Also the drummer was named Ringo like Ringo Hallinan. In fact another Ringo had been in the charts recently which was a single by Lorne Greene the star of television's *Bonanza*.

I don't think Sara played the album for me but I soon heard *I Want to Hold Your Hand* on the radio and was very taken by it. I'd never come across a song about holding hands before and it seemed to speak to me about being a teenager. I was, at this time, sixteen.

I wasn't overly fascinated about The Beatles until the Friday night of this particular week. I was at our house on Catalpa getting ready to go out to a dance in Sausalito. I'd shaved what little beard I had and doused my face in English

Leather. The television sat right next to our front door and Walter Cronkite was reading the news as I was about to leave. He reported the arrival of The Beatles at JFK Airport. I paused to watch and was stunned to see massive crowds of screaming girls. This was the same phenomenon that *Bye Bye Birdie* had reminded me of with Elvis. These four skinny guys with pudding bowl hairdos came running down the steps from their plane and jumped in a limousine. They were all laughing.

I delayed my departure long enough to watch all of the report and when it was finished, Walter Cronkite gave a caustic glance to the camera and said: "And *that* is what some people consider to be news. Good night."

I thought about what I had seen on the news as I walked over to the 2am Club on Miller and stuck my thumb out to hitch a ride to Sausalito.

The dance I attended was in a hall up on the hill above Bridgeway and the band was The Jesters which my friend Mark Symmes played drums for. Their repertoire would have included such numbers as *What'd I Say* by Ray Charles along with other staples like *Louie, Louie*. Within a few weeks that would change as all the musical combos in Marin County would race to learn every number the Beatles recorded. This, however, was Friday night and the true conversion for millions of American teenagers would not come until Sunday when the Beatles made their appearance on the Ed Sullivan Show.

The Jesters were a fine group. Dave Shallock played lead guitar, Gary Fay rhythm and Jim Michaelson was on bass. In addition to playing the drums my friend Mark also sang as did all of them. They looked good and were always highly professional. Another classmate of mine who was a musician and always had a band working the dance halls was Bill Champlin. Bill and Mark Symmes were both students of Mister Greenwood who ran the music department at Tam High. They were both in Mr Greenwood's marching band. Another disciple of Mister Greenwood's was George Duke whose jazz trio was working professionally throughout his years as a student at Tam.

One more schoolmate of mine was part of this musical club and that was Billie Bowen who I'd known well when we were in grade school at Homestead. I remember seeing Bill walking home from Village Music in the late 1950s carrying a Chuck Berry album and when I asked him why he had a whole album he told me it was to practice his drums to.

The thing which makes this particular dance at Sausalito something of a mystery to me is the fact that I'm pretty certain I went alone and without alcoholic enhancement. The usual routine for the weekend was to find a way to secure enough booze to become inebriated, then stagger onto the dance in Mill Valley in the hope that your drunkenness would give you the courage to successfully pick up a young lady. The fact that this scenario never seemed to work out in no way discouraged me from trying again and again.

One of the most stunningly beautiful young women in my year at Tam High was Hollis Hite, someone I had an agonizing crush on ever since I had first met her. As I looked much younger than my sixteen years, I'd become accustomed to the dreadful syndrome of unrequited love. I was constantly falling in love with unattainable women. I was so far from cool it made me ache.

However, I was pretty good friends with Hollis Hite and simply had to keep my feelings secret. She was, at this time, going out with another good friend of mine, Bruce Crawford. Bruce, unlike me, was tall, blond, extremely handsome and easy going in a way that I was not.

By the time Sunday came around I found myself up at Hollis's house to watch the Ed Sullivan Show. Bruce was there along with Christy Flagg and Chuck Collins.

Ed Sullivan's show was one of those American institutions in the 1950s and 60s. He had a face like a pickle and the weirdest speaking voice. He always pronounced the word 'show' like 'shoe' and seemed to be the most unlikely fellow to be in the entertainment business at all but in it he was. He and Steve Allen had a deadly rivalry for ratings being on opposite networks.

There was nothing remarkable about The Beatles' first appearance on the Sullivan show except the screaming was pretty loud. As the camera did close-ups, the name of each Beatle would appear and I think by the end of the evening I knew John, Paul, George and Ringo by sight.

They were something totally different. Their press conferences were very funny and they took delight in making fun of their inquisitors. In spite of the Moe Howard hairdos they seemed to have much more in common with the Marx Brothers than the 3 Stooges.

Their witty replies to the asinine questions of the American press were made all the more colourful by their thick Liverpool accents.

The Beatles seemed to take America in one week and by the end of that week I was, like everybody else, a Beatlemaniac. I bought the LP *Meet The Beatles* and loved all the songs. Paul McCartney had the most amazing rock and roll voice as demonstrated on *I Saw Her Standing There* and John Lennon's vocals had such a lyrical quality. Their songs were all about the agonies of teenage love but in a new and original way and their use of vocal harmony was inventive.

Coming, as I did, from a highly non-conformist family, I did not often find myself going with the flow when it came to popular culture so it was a strange kind of liberation to be swept along with everybody else in total admiration of the Fab Four.

I Want to Hold Your Hand went to number one which was soon followed by *She Loves You* and *Please Please Me.*

Before long the other British bands began landing on our shores. The Kinks were great even though all their songs seemed to have the same riff. Much publicity was made of The Dave Clark Five but they were so mediocre that they faded fast. The Animals, Gerry And The Pacemakers, Herman's Hermits, Billy J. Kramer & The Dakotas, Peter And Gordon, The Zombies and Donovan all came across in what soon was referred to as the British Invasion. I remember a photo of The Rolling Stones was published in the Chronicle under the headline 'Here come five more!' They looked so ugly I couldn't imagine ever liking them.

It is difficult to under-estimate the cultural impact which The Beatles had on the United States at this time and their huge success was to change show business and the media in fundamental ways.

Probably the most impressive thing about The Beatles was the fact that they kept coming out with amazingly fresh and memorable new music for several years to come and, together with Bob Dylan, The Rolling Stones, The Byrds and countless other sixties groups, provided the soundtrack for the teenage years of my generation.

Of course there was more to come. The Vietnam War and the emergence of drugs within the white middle class of America stirred up a complex brew which gave that era a unique place in American history.

But The Beatles came along before the confusions of the drug culture wrought such carnage and the horrors of Vietnam got out of control. For that brief moment in time these four giggling Liverpudlians led us, like the children of Hamlin, away from our otherwise undiluted Americanism. We would never be the same again.

Chapter 34

The Mountain That Follows you Round the Town

The sight of Mount Tamalpais as you drive down Waldo Grade past Marin City is what those who grew up in Mill Valley think of as the shape of that mountain. Seen from Corte Madera or Larkspur, however, it could be a different mountain altogether.

It looks like Mother Nature took a giant saw horse, put a wooden A-frame in front of it then covered the whole thing over with a huge green carpet. The folds fall away with a quiet kind of majesty a bit like theatre curtains.

There are so many natural wonders in this world but the Mill Valley view of Mount Tam is, for me, one of them. I didn't really discover a true appreciation for the mountain until I'd been away from the bay area for ten years and I can still recall my first sighting, on returning, as a startling, almost religious experience.

Growing up in Mill Valley during the 1950s and 60s, I took the mountain for granted. It was simply there and sometimes you could see it and sometimes not at all. I don't believe I ever even had an opinion about it.

We had no view of Mount Tam from our house on Seymour Avenue but that mountain was a bit like the eyes of a painting which follows you around the room. I was constantly surprised by new and impressive sightings.

Most summers when I was very young my sisters Nell and Kate would take Jim and I on a hike up to Bootjack Camp. This was something of an operation which required an early start. Sandwiches were packed and canteens filled.

As the Pixie Trail began just outside our house we'd set off on it and follow its course all the way up past Mister Krag's red brick house to Edgewood where we would then join the road. Walking on the road was slightly perilous as the cars sped up and down at quite a clip. We walked up to the horseshoe bend where car drivers would continue on up to Four Corners. We, however, walked up the road through the farm on that hill until we reached the Panoramic Highway. More risky road walking followed until we finally arrived at Mountain Home Inn.

The beginning of our trek on the Matt Davis trail was fairly steep and much like being in the desert. Even if it was foggy down where we lived it was always sunny up here with a steady patrol of turkey vultures circling in the clear blue sky above us.

When we finally got onto relatively horizontal trail it remained desert-like for some time before dipping into shaded corners where streams would cross the path and rocks of all sizes mingled with the trees. Lizards darting across the trail were a constant sight.

Our little foursome was pretty quiet while making our way along the Matt Davis and its twists and turns always brought unexpected and beautiful sights.

Occasionally we'd pass hikers going the other way and we always said hello. There's something about being out in the glories of nature which makes casual contact with other people a friendlier business than encountering them in Safeway.

I don't remember how long the hike to Bootjack took but it was quite a distance and we always knew when we were almost there because of that enormous boulder the path curled around. It sat just above the road and from it you'd get a glorious view of all that was below.

Whenever we went with our family for a picnic at Bootjack we would always play games of make believe battles on that big rock. On one picnic with the Dreyfus family I remember Jared on that rock wielding a big stick as a Robin Hood sword and addressing both my sisters as 'fair damsels.'

The hike back always went quicker and the whole experience put you in touch with the adventurer within you. After all you weren't just around the corner at the playground or out on the Pixie Trail. You were miles up on that huge mountain which dominated the landscape of all Marin County.

The Pixie Trail also had a remote and wild quality to it but if you ran you could always be home in a few minutes. During the summer months we would lug big cardboard boxes up to the enormous hill we called 'Windy Corners' and slide down to the bottom at tremendous speed stopping just short of the barbed wire fence which kept you from flying onto Montford as it snaked its way around Homestead Valley. I remember clutching the edges of the cardboard and pulling it in, making it more like a boat. Of course the long grass turned practically white during July and August and the speed we'd fly down on that cardboard was every bit as exciting as the big slide in the Funhouse over at Playland at the beach.

The grass we had in Mill Valley used to produce these little pods which looked a bit like tiny ears of corn. If you squeezed one, a milky white liquid would come squirting out.

I would often pinch the bottom of several grass stems between my thumb and first finger then run my hand up, pulling the pods off at the same time leaving me with a small bouquet of them.

The mountain stood tall above the valleys below and trees of all kinds carpeted the hills which sloped down into them. My sisters Nell and Kate both went to Old Mill School which was in one valley while Jimmy and I went to Homestead School over in a different valley. And when we got to sixth grade we moved over to Alto which was almost a world away from the lush greenery of Old Mill and Homestead Valley where fresh water cascaded over boulders and filled the creeks. Alto was out in the flatlands and was more desert-like.

While on a recess at Alto School one day I walked out amongst the rocks which lined the base of the hill that ascended behind the playing field. Kicking away one of the big stones, I found a sizeable black widow spider, not scuttling away but standing still in its web with a fearsome confidence. Its bright orange hourglass glowed against its bulbous shiny black abdomen.

The land around Alto was definitely more barren than Old Mill. All the freshness of that waterfall behind Old Mill Park seemed to keep that part of town cool, fresh and green. By the time you walked all the way out to Alto, the creek had run a little bit dry and the lizards scampered across the sun-baked rocks.

My teacher in sixth grade, Mr Zander, was charming, thoughtful and engaging and I remember responding to him with enthusiasm. We learnt all about Canada and did projects in which my artistic skills came into play.

During this term a huge collection of paintings by Vincent Van Gogh came to the De Young Museum in San Francisco and our class took a field trip to see them. I collected colour postcards of the paintings and drew imitations of them.

When we moved across to Edna Maguire for seventh grade I had another fine teacher in Mr Healy who taught English and History. He was a wonderful showman who kept me engaged for the whole year.

He had a punishment for pupils who fooled around which was called 'Vulture Watch.' The idea was that you spent your recess up on the walkway opposite the class making sure that the vultures didn't come down and carry any kids off.

Mr Healy had a huge impact on me. I copied his style of writing which was printing in capital letters. He also liberated the word 'system' for me. My parents were always saying: "the system's rotten," or "you can't beat the system," and I naturally had a negative interpretation of the word. Mr Healy, however, said: "You've got to have a system. If you don't have a system you can't do the work." He was talking about how you organized your binder, your thoughts and the way you tackled problems. For those two years with Mr Zander and Mr Healy, I was, temporarily, a good student but it soon faded when I moved onto less inspired and inspiring teachers.

One teacher I never had at Edna Maguire was Mr Peterson, a tall imposing man with a bald head, a military style about him and a voice like a foghorn. He always wore a short-sleeved white shirt and a tie and I don't remember him ever smiling.

One day he addressed the male student body out on the playground. "On the other side of those mountains," he said in his gruff menacing voice, "Is San Quentin Prison." He paused, surveying his audience for a long moment. "One day some of you may be there." I'm unable to recall the exact purpose of this speech but it did have a chilling effect.

There was a graduation ceremony when we left Edna Maguire and went onto our freshman year at Tam and it was actually held in the girls' gym at Tam itself. Mr Peterson was the man in charge of the ceremony.

We had several rehearsals for it and there was a woman who played piano competently but for some reason she would always play a bum note. It was in a riff with five chords, the fifth one of which was different to its predecessors and this was the one which went wrong every time she played it.

We were graduated by size which meant that I was the first one to go and it also meant that I was sitting out in the front row next to a boy with blond hair who was maybe a half an inch taller than me. Mr Peterson drilled us all in how to behave and he tolerated no fooling around.

When the evening of our graduation arrived we were all excited. We had to march up onto the stage to the lady's piano music and take our places.

So there I was, sitting in the front row under strong lights so that we couldn't actually see individual audience members in the packed auditorium.

The proceedings commenced and soon the lady on the piano had to play that riff again. Without thinking about it I had subconsciously imagined that she would sort the bum note out in her spare time but come the moment and the five chords were played exactly as they had been in rehearsal with that dreadful clam in the fifth chord. I was so surprised that I started to giggle. My laughter soon infected the boy next to me and, within moments we were both chortling helplessly while at the same time, trying to pretend that we weren't. But our trembling shoulders and the exposed position we had out front soon brought the ominous presence of Mr Peterson into the wings. In my peripheral vision I could see his short-sleeved white shirt and bald head. His stage whisper was slow and penetrating: "You two idiots shut up!"

I'm unable to remember the outcome of this incident. The two forces at work: our helpless giggling and our fear of Mr Peterson were at complete odds with each other. It's always difficult to recapture your composure once it runs away like that but I guess we must have.

And so my three years in the desert climate of those two schools came to an end in an awkwardly memorable moment of helpless mirth.

* * *

I probably spent as much time alone out on the Pixie Trail as I ever did with friends. Certain pop records would go through my head at such times because I always think of those locations when I hear *Searchin'* by the Coasters or *Old Shep* by Elvis Presley.

A lot of the lyrics to *Searchin'* were unintelligible to me but I loved the sound of it and played the 45 over and over at home. I got "I been searchin' every we-ee-ee-ee-eek away, yea, yea," but the rest of it wasn't so clear. It was, I learned later, a list of movie detectives who would never be as good at tracking down their quarry as the particular Coaster who sang lead would be at hunting down his lover.

Not understanding lyrics posed no problem as I was used to skating past mysteries without explanation. I regularly hallucinated the words to pop songs. I had no difficulty with Doris Day or Frank Sinatra whose diction was perfect but on the wilder rock and roll records the pronunciations were not always that clear.

As much as I loved my Elvis Presley records I simply couldn't make out all of the words. I could always understand enough of *Don't Be Cruel* to get the idea but it never bothered me sufficiently to find out what they actually were.

Little Richard was another one I had trouble getting all the words to but again his records were just so exciting that it didn't matter. And then there was Jerry Lee Lewis who didn't slur his words like Elvis so I always understood what he was singing about.

It's odd but all these records remind me of the Pixie Trail where I'd just be hanging out by myself. I know that most composers have particular themes and ideas which their music is supposed to be about but I think we humans paint our own pictures to music and it's almost always to do with the location in which we first hear it.

My mother used to play her classical recordings while cleaning the house and when I hear them now they always conjure up images of reading comic books in our front yard. Schubert's *The Trout* and Beethoven's *5th Symphony* both bring back that memory.

When something touches your soul in a profound way it becomes a part of you forever. So the Coasters singing

Searchin' will always take me back to the Pixie Trail, covered in a rich carpet of eucalyptus bark and pixie cap acorns and the Miller Avenue view of Mount Tamalpais will always remind me of growing up in such a special place as Mill Valley.

About John H. Myers

On the left is a recent picture of the author while on the right is a school photo from 1956. *(photo on left by Christopher Baines)*

The author was born in New York City, the third of four children to parents Blackie and Beth Myers in March, 1947. Due to political blacklisting the family moved west in 1952 where the author and his siblings grew up in Mill Valley. His first professional involvement with media occurred at age 19 when he was hired by the late Bill Graham to paint signs at the Fillmore Auditorium in 1966. He subsequently designed a mere four of the legendary Fillmore posters, the bulk of which were crafted by friends Wes Wilson and Bonnie MacLean.

The author moved to London at the beginning of the 1970s and worked first as a graphic designer then later as a singer in the jazz field. His singing work eventually led him into the world of acting, a craft he still practices to this day. He began his writing career by conceiving and performing a critically acclaimed one-man show at the Edinburgh Festival entitled *Invasion Werewolf,* a piece done in the style of a 1950s sci-fi/horror movie which was directed by his wife Clare Bradley.

He later interviewed the Oscar-winning film editor Jim Clark for Filmfax magazine. Subsequent articles featured interviews with Ned Sherrin, Carol Cleveland and Ed Bishop. When Jim Clark decided to publish his memoirs, *Dream Repairman,* he asked the author to co-write it which he did.

He began his online column, *Miller Avenue Musings* in 2011 and this collection is distilled from that output.

The author describes himself as a semi-retired actor and writer. He and his wife live in Stoke Newington, London with their dog while receiving occasional visits from their two grown-up children.

Bibliography

Alvarez, Eugene, *Just the Facts, Ma'am - The Authorized Biography of Jack Webb* Seven Locks Press 2001

Arkoff, Sam, *Flying Through Hollywood by the Seat of my Pants* Birch Lane Press 1992

Auiler, Dan, *Vertigo – The Making of a Hitchcock Classic* Titan Books 1999

Barson, Michael, *Red Scared - The Commie Menace in Propaganda and Popular Culture* Chronicle Books 2001

Beauchamp, Cari, *Joseph P. Kennedy's Hollywood Years* Faber and Faber 2009

Bessie, Alvah, *Inquisition in Eden,* Macmillan 1965

Bessie, Alvah, *The UnAmericans,* John Calder 1957

Betrock, Alan, *The I Was A Teenage Juvenile Delinquent Rock 'n' Roll Horror Beach Party Movie Book* Plexus 1986

Biskind, Peter, *Seeing is Believing - How Hollywood Taught Us to Stop Worrying and Love the Fifties* Pluto Press 1983

Bryson, Bill, *The Life and Times of The Thunderbolt Kid - Travels Through My Childhood* Transworld Publishers 2007

Buhle, Paul, *Tender Comrades - A Backstory of the Hollywood Blacklist* St Martin's Griffin 1997

Call, Alex *Pastime: A Baseball Story* 2012

Chalmers, Claudine, *Images Of America - Early Mill Valley* Arcadia 2005

Chapman, Peter, *Bananas – How the United Fruit Company Shaped the World* Canongate 2007

Clark, Jim, *Dream Repairman – Adventures in Film Editing* LandMarc Press 2010

Cocchi, John, *Second Feature - The Best of the 'B' Films* Citadel Press 1991

Coffey, Thomas M., *A Mad, Mad, Mad, Mad World* Aurum Press 1997

Collins, Charles, *How The Collins Family Came to Mill Valley* the Mill Valley Historical Society Review Spring 2015

Collins, Dr. Daniel A., *How The Collins Family Came to Mill Valley* the Mill Valley Historical Society Review Spring 2015

Collins, Edward, *How The Collins Family Came to Mill Valley* the Mill Valley Historical Society Review Spring 2015

Collins, Max Allan, *Men's Adventure Magazines in Postwar America* Taschen 2008

Cook, Bruce, *Trumbo* Scribner's Sons 1977

Corman, Roger, *How I Made a Hundred Movies in Hollywood and Never Lost a Dime* Random House 1990

Dalton, Tony, *An Animated Life* Aurum Press 2003

Dawson, Jim, *Rock Around The Clock - The Record that Started the Rock Revolution!* Backbeat Books 2005

Dick, Bernard F., *The Merchant Prince of Poverty Row-Harry Cohn of Columbia Pictures* University Press of Kentucky

Diehl, Digby, *Tales From The Crypt - The Official Archives* St Martin's Press 1996

Dunleavy, Steve, *Elvis: What Happened?* Ballantine Books, 1977

Eliot, Marc *Walt Disney, Hollywood's Dark Prince,* Harper Collins 1993
Field, Frederick Vanderbilt, *From Right to Left - An Autobiography*
     Lawrence Hill & Co. 1983
Finney, Jack, *The Body Snatchers* Dell Publishing 1954
Freberg, Stan, *It Only Hurts When I Laugh,* Times Books 1988
Geissman, Grant, *Foul Play! The Art and Artists of the Notorious 1950s E.C. Comics!* Harper Design 2005
Geissman, Grant, *Tales Of Terror/The E.C. Companion*
     Gemstone Publishing 2000
Goldman, Albert, *Elvis* Allen Lane 1981
Gorman, Ed (editor), *"They're Here…"Invasion of the Body Snatchers - A Tribute* Berkley Boulevard Books 1999
Guralnick, Peter, *Last Train to Memphis - The Rise of Elvis Presley*
     Abacus 1994
Hagenauer, George, *Men's Adventure Magazines in Postwar America*
     Taschen 2008
Hajdu, David, *The Ten Cent Plague,* Picador 2008
Hallinan, Vincent, *A Lion in Court,* Putnam 1963
Hallinan, Vivian, *My Wild Irish Rogues,* Doubleday 1952
Harmetz, Aljean, *The Making of the Wizard of Oz*
     Limelight Editions 1984
Harryhausen, Ray, *An Animated Life* Aurum Press 2003
Harryhausen, Ray, *Film Fantasy Scrapbook* A.S. Barnes & Co. 1972
Hebler, Dave, *Elvis: What Happened?* Ballantine Books, 1977
Heimann, Jim (editor), *All-American Ads - 50s* Taschen 2001
Heller, Steven, *Men's Adventure Magazines in Postwar America*
     Taschen 2008
Heller, Steven, *Red Scared - The Commie Menace in Propaganda and Popular Culture* Chronicle Books 2001
Hellman, Lillian, *Scoundrel Time* Quartet Books 1978
Hersh, Seymour, *The Dark Side of Camelot* Harper Collins 1997
Hopkins, Jerry, *Elvis, the Biography* Plexus 2007
Jacobs, Frank, *The MAD World of William M. Gaines,* Bantam 1973
Jerome, Jim, *How I Made a Hundred Movies in Hollywood and Never Lost a Dime* Random House 1990
Johnson, Diane, *The Life of Dashiell Hammett* Chatto & Windus 1983
Jones Jr., William B., *Classics Illustrated, a Cultural History,*
     MacFarland 2002
Kahn, Albert E., *The Game of Death - Effects of the Cold war on Our Children* Cameron & Kahn 1953
Kahn, Albert E., *High Treason - The Plot Against the People*
     The Hour Publishers 1950
Kazan, Elia, *A Life,* Andre Deutsch 1988
Kinnard, Roy, *Beasts And Behemoths - Prehistoric Creatures in the Movies* Scarecrow Press 1988
Kinzer, Stephen, *The Brothers – John Foster Dulles, Allen Dulles and their Secret World War* St Martin's Griffin 2013

Kraft, Jeff, *Footsteps in the Fog – Alfred Hitchcock's San Francisco*
    Santa Monica Press 2002
Kramer, Stanley, *A Mad, Mad, Mad, Mad World* Aurum Press 1997
La Valley, Al (editor), *Invasion of the Body Snatchers - Don Siegel, Director*
    Rutgers University Press 1989
Lax, Eric, *Bogart* Weidenfeld & Nicholson 1997
Leventhal, Aaron, *Footsteps in the Fog – Alfred Hitchcock's San Francisco*
    Santa Monica Press 2002
Lumet, Sidney, *Making Movies* Bloomsbury 1995
Manfull, Helen (editor), *Additional Dialogue - Letters of Dalton Trumbo,*
    1942 -1962 M. Evans & Co. 1970
Marsh, Graham, *Film Posters of the 50s* Aurum Press 2000
McAleer, Dave, *The Warner Guide to UK & US Hit Singles*
    Little Brown 1994
McCarthy, Kevin (editor) *"They're Here..."Invasion of the Body Snatchers*
    -A Tribute Berkley Boulevard Books 1999
McElwee, John, *Showmen, Sell it Hot!* GoodKnight Books 2013
McFadden, Cyra, *The Serial - A Year in the Life of Marin County*
    Alfred A. Knopf 1976
McGarry, Annie, *The Wacky World of the 3 Stooges* Bison Group 1992
McGee, Mark Thomas, *Invasion of the Body Snatchers: The Making of a*
    Classic Bear Manor Media 2012
McGee, Mark Thomas, *Beyond Ballyhoo - Motion Picture Promotion and*
    Gimmicks McFarland 1989
McGee, Mark Thomas, *Roger Corman - The Best of the Cheap Acts*
    McFarland 1988
McGee, Mark Thomas, *Fast and Furious - The Story of American*
    International Pictures McFarland 1984
McGee, Mark Thomas, *The J.D. Films - Juvenile Delinquency in the Movies*
    McFarland 1982
McGilligan, Patrick, *Jack's Life - A Biography of Jack Nicholson*
    Hutchinson 1994
McGilligan, Patrick, *Tender Comrades - A Backstory of the Hollywood*
    Blacklist St Martin's Griffin 1997
McGilligan, Patrick, *Alfred Hitchcock – A Life in Darkness and Light*
    John Wiley & Sons 2003
McHenry, Beth, *Home is the Sailor,* International Publishers 1948
McHenry, Beth, *I Had Illusions* The Henkle Company 1935
Meikle, Denis, *Vincent Price - The Art of Fear* Reynolds & Hearn Ltd. 2003
Miller, Arthur, *Timebends, A Life,* Methuen 1987
Milton, David, *The Politics of U.S. Labor - From the Great Depression to the*
    New Deal Monthly Review Press 1982
Minear, Richard H., *Dr Seuss Goes to War - The World War II Editorial*
    Cartoons of Theodor Seuss Geisel The New Press 1999
Moyer, Daniel, *Just the Facts, Ma'am - The Authorized Biography of Jack*
    Webb Seven Locks Press 2001
Myers, Beth, *The Doctor Is A Lady,* Corgi 1954

Myers, Beth, *The Enchanted Land* Avalon Books 1953
Myers, Beth, *The Steady Flame* Avalon Books 1952
Myers, Frederick N., *Home Is The Sailor,* International Publishers 1948
Myers, John H., *Dream Repairman – Adventures in Film Editing*
 LandMarc Press 2010
Naha, Ed, *The Films of Roger Corman: Brilliance on a Budget*
 Arco Publishing 1982
Nelson, Bruce, *Workers on the Waterfront - Seamen, Longshoremen and*
 Unionism in the 1930s University of Illinois Press 1990
Price, Victoria, *Vincent Price - A Daughter's Biography* St. Martin's Press 1999
Nourmand, Tony, *Film Posters of the 50s* Aurum Press 2000
Rebello, Stephen, *Alfred Hitchcock and the Making of Psycho*
 Marion Boyars 1990
Reemes, Dana M., *Directed By Jack Arnold* McFarland 1988
Reeves, Thomas C., *The Life and Times of Joe McCarthy* Stein & Day 1982
Riley, Philip J. (editor), *This Island Earth, the Original Shooting Script*
 MagicImage Filmbooks 1990
Schickel, Richard, *The Disney Version,* Avon Books 1968
Schulberg, Budd, *On the Waterfront - The Final Shooting Script*
 Samuel French 1980
Schwartz, Nancy Lynn, *The Hollywood Writers' Wars* McGraw-Hill 1982
Smith, Steven C., *A Heart at Fire's Center - The Life and Music of Bernard*
 Herrmann University of California Press 1991
Sperber, Ann M., *Bogart* Weidenfeld & Nicholson 1997
Stock, Stuart H., *Twenty All-Time Great Science Fiction Films*
 Arlington House 1982
Summers, Anthony, *The Secret Life of J. Edgar Hoover* Ebury Press 1993
Talbot, David, *The Devil's Chessboard – Allen Dulles, the CIA, and the Rise of*
 America's Secret Government William Collins 2015
Thomas, Bob, *Walt Disney, a Biography,* Simon & Schuster 1976
Trubo, Richard *Flying Through Hollywood by the Seat of my Pants*
 Birch Lane Press 1992
Trumbo, Dalton, *Additional Dialogue - Letters of Dalton Trumbo, 1942 -1962*
 M. Evans & Co. 1970
Von Gunden, Kenneth, *Twenty All-Time Great Science Fiction Films*
 Arlington House 1982
Walsh, James P., *San Francisco's Hallinan* Presidio Press 1982
Wasserman, Abby, *How The Collins Family Came to Mill Valley* the Mill
 Valley Historical Society Review Spring 2015
Weaver, Tom, *Attack of the Monster Movie Makers* McFarland 1994
Weaver, Tom, *Science Fiction Stars and Horror Heroes* McFarland 1991
Weaver, Tom, *They Fought in the Creature Features* McFarland 1995
Weldon, Michael, *The Psychotronic Encyclopedia of Film* Plexus 1983
West, Red, *Elvis: What Happened?* Ballantine Books, 1977
West, Sonny, *Elvis: What Happened?* Ballantine Books, 1977
Williams, Lucy Chase, *The Complete Films of Vincent Price*
 Citadel Press 1995

Printed in Poland
by Amazon Fulfillment
Poland Sp. z o.o., Wrocław